Reading and Writing the Latin American Landscape

Previous Publications

Jerry Hoeg

Science, Literature, and Film in the Hispanic World. Ed. Jerry Hoeg and Kevin S. Larsen. New York: Palgrave Macmillan, 2006.

Science, Technology, and Latin American Narrative in the 20th Century and Beyond. Bethlehem, PA: Lehigh University Press, 2000.

Beatriz Rivera-Barnes

Midnight Sandwiches at the Mariposa Express. Houston: Arte Público, 1997.

Playing with Light. Houston: Arte Público, 2000.

Do Not Pass Go. Houston: Arte Público, 2006.

African Passions and Other Stories. Houston: Arte Público, 1995.

When a tree Falls. Houston: Arte Público, forthcoming.

Reading and Writing the Latin American Landscape

Beatriz Rivera-Barnes and Jerry Hoeg

READING AND WRITING THE LATIN AMERICAN LANDSCAPE
Copyright © Beatriz Rivera-Barnes and Jerry Hoeg, 2009.

All rights reserved.

First published in 2009 by PALGRAVE MACMILLAN®
in the United States—a division of St. Martin's Press LLC,
175 Fifth Avenue, New York, NY 10010.

Where this book is distributed in the UK, Europe and the rest of
the world, this is by Palgrave Macmillan, a division of Macmillan
Publishers Limited, registered in England, company number 785998,
of Houndmills, Basingstoke, Hampshire RG21 6XS.

Palgrave Macmillan is the global academic imprint of the above
companies and has companies and representatives throughout the
world.

Palgrave® and Macmillan® are registered trademarks in the United
States, the United Kingdom, Europe and other countries.

ISBN: 978-0-230-61519-9

Library of Congress Cataloging-in-Publication Data

Rivera-Barnes, Beatriz.
  Reading and writing the Latin American landscape/Beatriz Rivera-Barnes and Jerry Hoeg.
      p. cm.
  Includes bibliographical references and index.
  ISBN 978-0-230-61519-9
  1. Latin American literature—History and criticism. 2. Nature in literature. 3. Ecology in literature. 4. Conservation of natural resources in literature. 5. Philosophy of nature in literature. 6. Ecocriticism. 7. Literature and society—Latin America. I. Hoeg, Jerry, 1951– II. Title.

PQ7081.R5345 2009
860.9'98—dc22   2009034601

A catalogue record of the book is available from the British Library.

Design by Scribe Inc.

First edition: November 2009

10 9 8 7 6 5 4 3 2 1

Printed in the United States of America

Contents

	Introduction	1
1	To Discover, an Intransitive Verb: Christopher Columbus's First Encounter with the American Landscape *Beatriz Rivera-Barnes*	9
2	Is There Such a Thing as Too Much Water? The Hurricanes that Foundered and the Swamps that Hindered Alvar Núñez Cabeza de Vaca *Beatriz Rivera-Barnes*	25
3	Picaresque Nature: Conquistadors, Parrots, Parasites, Mimics *Beatriz Rivera-Barnes*	39
4	Andrés Bello's "Ode to Tropical Agriculture": The Landscape of Independence *Jerry Hoeg*	53
5	"I Do Not Weep for Camaguey": Gertrudis Gómez de Avellaneda's Nineteenth-Century Cuban Landscape *Beatriz Rivera-Barnes*	67
6	Rebellion in the Backlands (*Os Sertões*): The Darwinian Landscape *Jerry Hoeg*	83
7	Yuyos Are Not Weeds: An Ecocritical Approach to Horacio Quiroga *Beatriz Rivera-Barnes*	101
8	The Landscapes of Venezuela: *Doña Bárbara* *Jerry Hoeg*	117

9 "It didn't work, Mother. You should have let me stay here."
   Alegría's and Flakoll's *Ashes of Izalco*   131
   Beatriz Rivera-Barnes

10 Pablo Neruda's Latin American Landscape:
   Nations, Economy, Nature   145
   Beatriz Rivera-Barnes

11 Love in the Time of Somoza: Gioconda Belli's
   Ambivalent Ecofeminism   159
   Beatriz Rivera-Barnes

12 The Landscape of the Consumer Society:
   Fernando Contreras Castro's *Unica mirando al mar*   177
   Jerry Hoeg

Works Cited   187

Index   199

Introduction

Reading and Writing the Latin American Landscape is an interdisciplinary research project involving the study of the relationship between Latin American literatures and ecology. The rubric "Latin American" includes any country or area that was once a colony of Spain (including the southern United States). With a nod to equal time, we have also included one chapter on what many consider Brazil's foundational text, one that certainly is a pioneering work in the scientific study of nature, especially human nature, namely Euclides da Cunha's *Os Sertões* (*Rebellion in the Backlands*, 1902). The research treats Latin America from its beginnings in 1492 up to the present time, and consists of analyzing both literary and testimonial texts through an ecocritical approach. The testimonial texts include the writings of Christopher Columbus, Alvar Núñez Cabeza de Vaca, and Euclides da Cunha, while the literary texts analyzed are those of Gertrudis Gómez de Avellaneda, Horacio Quiroga, Pablo Neruda, Andrés Bello, Rómulo Gallegos, Gioconda Belli, Claribel Alegría, and Fernando Contreras Castro. It should be noted that earlier versions of the chapters on Columbus and Quiroga were published previously in the journals *Ometeca* (12:1) and *ISLE* (16:1), respectively.

As to our methodology, let us begin by observing that, basically, ecocriticism is the study of the relationship between literature and the environment. But above and beyond that, it is also a way of scrutinizing the ecological implications and relationships between man and nature, or nature and culture, in both the aforementioned texts and in the Latin American reality that inspired them. Some of the questions involved in this approach are How does a text represent the physical world? What moral questions are raised relative to man's interaction with nature? How does a text direct the reader's awareness to a specific ecosystem?

It was in the late 1980s that the scholar Cheryll Burgess Glotfelty first considered organizing a field called ecocriticism, and so set about compiling a bibliography of nature writers and scholars who wrote about the environment. In 1992, a group of likeminded scholars founded the Association for the Study of Literature and the Environment and began publishing the journal *Interdisciplinary Studies in Literature and the Environment*. It was not long before environmental studies began to include the humanities. Literature, in turn, began to tap into ecological aspects of nature and, in doing so, gained a new dimension that focuses on place-connectedness.

There is a great diversity in ecocriticism. It is also known as Environmental Literature, Green Literature, and Literature of Place, depending on the focus. For example, Lawrence Buell, at Harvard University, focuses on the idea of place. Other scholars who have greatly contributed to the immense literature on ecocriticism produced in the past twenty years include the abovementioned Cheryll Glotfelty, presently teaching Ecocriticism at the University of Nevada, John Elder at Middlebury College, and David Orr, who is at Oberlin College.

In the present study, we have attempted to widen our approach to include studies from both the natural sciences and the social sciences. Thus we look at Charles Darwin's influence on Euclides da Cunha and that of Alexander von Humboldt and Aimé Bonpland on Andrés Bello. We also look at scientific data in order to evaluate the goals espoused in Latin American literature, and so we view Bello's call for a return to the land through the lens of global climate change and Contreras Castro's critique of consumerism in light of the history of human exchange, dating back some 1.5 to 2 million years.

Specifically, the focus of this particular research project is the Latin American landscape. Therefore the hope is that such an approach will prove that deforestation and pollution are tangible and measurable realities, shed light on how to preserve the remaining forests, control or curb pollution, promote conservation, and also contribute to a dialogue between the arts and the sciences. Throughout, we are constantly aware that nature includes human nature.

By way of example, let us consider the short stories of the Uruguayan writer Horacio Quiroga. These are set in the Argentine tropical frontier and were instrumental in awakening an ecological awareness of this fragile ecosystem in the Argentine public at the beginning of the twentieth century. In these works, we initially see Quiroga's relationship with nature, an intense and obsessive one, and the stories that are the result of this relationship. These stories, in turn, portray not only the conflicts and dynamics between man and the physical environment, and how nature responds to man's presence in the jungle, but also convey relationships among land, labor, and capital in the colonial jungle. This is evident in the story "The Return of Anaconda" (1925), in which it is not so much the local farmer, but rather the logging company that represents the power of capital. But in this intriguing tale, the spirit of the place is not always aware of this imbalance of power, so the animals quickly come to see one dying laborer as representative of all the exploiters. Politically speaking, all the animals except Anaconda end up confusing labor and capital. But in spite of the animals' confusion and the need to separate labor from capital, it is important to keep in mind that the local farmer cannot help but do his share of cutting and burning, thus making a fragile environment all the more fragile. In fact, the tourist who is merely there to see and the preservationist who is there to protect also have their impact on the environment, and so we see that early on, Quiroga laid out many of the same issues we face today.

The impacts these issues have on both nature and humanity can be measured either with scientific rigor or with tropes. Nature can respond in any number of ways: with erosion, with storms, with floods, with droughts, with deluges. Quiroga conveys this by having the animals of the tropical zone plotting against man and planning to blockade the upper Paraná River.

Regardless of whether or not Quiroga's stories have a moral, a green, or a political agenda, call it what you will, they undoubtedly deserve consideration in modern day attempts to study the relationships between literature and ecology. The reason for this is that by virtue of both their contents and their artistic value, these stories created awareness of the nature of the South American tropical jungle long before it came to resemble a square fragment of rain forest left standing on land cleared for pasture. An analysis of these stories can subsequently indicate that it is necessary to preserve the remaining forests and contain the crisis of deforestation. Furthermore, it may very well be that well-crafted stories such as these awaken the reader's awareness more effectively than a pamphlet or hard scientific fact. And speaking of scientific facts, let us note here that we have endeavored not to lose sight of empirical data, lest we be swept away by a romantic vision, the pursuit of which actually serves precisely those ends we seek to thwart.

Christopher Columbus's *Journal of the First Voyage* is another text examined through an ecocritical lens. Christopher Columbus is, in fact, the first American landscape writer. The irony is that the first words describing the American landscape were written by someone desperately trying to convince himself he was somewhere else. There was an impossibility of writing about the Americas when Columbus first set foot on the Caribbean islands, simply because the Americas did not yet exist and consequently there were no old words to describe the New World, the Americas. A close reading of the letter of the *Journal* shows the beginnings of the fabrication of the American landscape. We can see in Columbus the same underlying traits that still drive exploitation of the region today. But at the same time, Columbus is an excellent reminder of that great constant of human nature: making the impossible possible. Just like Columbus, we too can forge a new American landscape through the power of science and literature.

In the chapter "Is There Such a Thing as Too Much Water? The Hurricanes that Foundered and the Swamps that Hindered Alvar Núñez Cabeza de Vaca," the question is, does biophobia have a place in environmental writing or in a corpus of ecocriticism? For Cabeza de Vaca and the other expeditioners, there seemed to be no going forward and no going back. Cabeza de Vaca describes the ailing explorers' desperate attempts to leave this bad place where their sins had taken them. Instead of reifying or mystifying the explorers, the horses soon began to serve other purposes. In their desperate attempt to leave this bad place, the horses' hides were cured in order to make vessels for water, and by September 22, 1528, all the horses had been eaten. In what the critic Beatriz Pastor describes as a narrative discourse of failure, the American natural environment is always hostile and threatening. It is the most formidable enemy. Nature becomes extreme and excessive, and the European explorer feels alienated in this destructive place that he knew nothing about.

In the chapter "Picaresque Nature: Conquistadors, Parrots, Parasites, Mimics," the initial thesis is that if nature writing is what ecocriticism likes best, then ecocriticism will frown upon Hernán Cortés's *Letters from Mexico* (1519–26) and José Joaquín Fernández de Lizardi's 1816 picaresque novel *El Periquillo Sarniento* (translated either as *The Mangy Parrot* or *The Itching Parrot*). While Cortés, a top carnivore, a mimic's model, pays no respect to ecological values, Lizardi's *pícaro*, a member of a lower trophic level than Cortés but a predator and parasite all the same, is always at odds with nature. Mindless of the natural world, caught in the city-jungle, well aware that no two species can occupy the same niche indefinitely, both characters—Cortés and Pedro Sarmiento, nicknamed *El Periquillo*—struggle to adapt, to survive, and ultimately to eliminate their competition. The struggle is so intense that it leaves no room for reflection, doubt, awe, or contemplation. In other words, the urgency of the moment eliminates all possibility of respect or care for the environment. Three centuries may separate those two *pícaros*, but their actions and reactions, their improvisations, and their treatment of society as wilderness—and of wilderness as society—are quasi identical. This is the picaresque; it wants to take over nature.

Andrés Bello's "Ode to Tropical Agriculture" ("Silva a la Agricultura de la Zona Tórrida"; 1826), is a foundational narrative for the newly independent republics of Spanish America. At the same time, it is perhaps ironic that this blueprint for life after the revolution contains a fundamental contradiction. Bello, a là Virgil in book 3 of the *Georgics*, attributes the woes of civilization to the seductions of the city, and so advocates a return to the simple but honest values of rural life. But the problem with the idea of abandoning the evil of the cities for the healthy joys of farm life is that cities themselves are a product of agriculture by virtue of the necessities of economic exchange systems. The contradictions inherent in the relationship between urban and rural life have remained part of the foundation of the Latin American landscape—political, economic, social, and literary—up to the present day.

Indeed, one hundred years later we see the same themes in Venezuelan author, and later president, Rómulo Gallegos's novel *Doña Bárbara* (1929). As with Bello earlier, this novel can be read as an effort on the part of Gallegos to orchestrate a new solution to the problems engendered by the barbarous behavior he sees as ubiquitous in Latin America, namely the anarchy, civil war, and despotism that had followed close on the heels of political independence. In line with much of the thinking of the period, he sees the origins of these troublesome conditions as rooted in race, and the final line in the novel prophesizes a new utopian mix as the final solution, "*una raza buena*" (a good race). The issue here is that of the nature of human nature, and so too the limits of social engineering, issues still very much a part of current ecological debates.

In "I Do Not Weep for Camaguey: Gertrudis Gómez de Avellaneda's Nineteenth Century Cuban Landscape," we propose that the idea of endless fertility, of the impossibility of future scarcity, that later morphed into a romantic, anthropocentric vision of the American natural world is at the root of a colonial myth of Eden that has not only silenced and damaged the Caribbean landscape but also interred a violent and unjust history that equally contributed to the degradation of this landscape. This is a vicious circle of greed and destruction taken to the twenty-first century. The idea of fertility itself leads to forgetfulness and inattention, in the sense that there was little or no environmental concern for anything that produced huge heaps and ceaseless income. It would be there forever, for the giving, and for the taking. The result is a landscape that has been permanently altered, therefore *unhomed*, or alienated, and also degraded. In "'It didn't work, Mother. You should have let me stay here.' Alegría's and Flakoll's *Ashes of Izalco*," the objective was not to victimize women and nature or to demonstrate that Alegría and Flakoll are ecofeminist theorists. Nonetheless, certain ecofeminist precepts were kept in mind. These involved the connection between women and nature, nature not only being the Central American ecosystem, but also the nations, cities, towns, and finally the house. It would be easy to oppose nature and nation. Perhaps nature could be to women what nation is to men, but that is too simplistic an analogy. The truth of the matter is that nation has much to do with the birth cycle. As the etymon implies, in the *nat*ion there is the *nat*al. Alegría's birthplace inhabits her just as Gioconda Belli is also inhabited by her birthplace, and it should be quite clear why Belli's testimonies always refer to this lack of boundaries between her body and her country.

In "Love in the Time of Somoza," the focus is on how the Nicaraguan landscape is portrayed in Gioconda Belli's novel, *La mujer habitada* (*The Inhabited Woman*), a fictional, sort of mirror version of her memoir, *El país bajo mi piel* (*The Country Under My Skin*). The purpose is not so much to identify women with nature, and much less to show that in Nicaragua women are treated or mistreated like nature is treated and mistreated. Woman is not necessarily a victim here, only a potential victim in that she is a daughter of history. Woman may be likened to the landscape and be as untouchable as the volcanoes that cannot be moved, but unlike volcanoes she is confronted with a choice, a weighing in. Because there is either a delicate, or at times a brutal balance of forces, the question arises of how to react when confronted with Central American reality and all its consequences. Should one accept, protest, resist, or give in to whatever is the most appropriate and opportune term for violence, be it armed struggle, terrorism, revolution, or war. In this sense, and by virtue of the choices to be made, woman, instead of embodying nature, transcends it.

In "Pablo Neruda's Latin American Landscape: Nations, Economy, Nature," the point of departure is Pablo Neruda's *Oda a la Madera* (*Ode to Wood*) where the future had the smell of trees falling because fresh lumber was the promise of a building. "Mi pecho, mis sentido / se impregnaron/en mi infancia / de árboles que caían / de grandes bosques llenos/de construcción futura" (*Obras Completas* 1035). [My childhood heart and my senses were filled with falling trees, with great forests full of future buildings.] Now that there are no more great forests, simply endangered forests, the future has changed, and the utilitarian approach to nature is no longer as acceptable. There is a marked effort to become more environmentally conservative, regardless of the outcome, and whether or not there is any hope. So the poet was wrong, and nature is something other than a raw material out there, waiting to be written, consumed, experienced, or used.

The ultimate goal of this project is to awaken a latent biophilia and a conservation ethic through an ecocritical reading of both artistic and testimonial texts. Its significance will be scholarly in that it approaches texts with the aforementioned ecocritical methodology and considers how they can be tied to social change. The hope, however, is that this project will also motivate the reader to turn to these engaging texts and appreciate them for their artistic value, while at the same time considering their messages in the light of scientific knowledge. The result is a symbiotic relationship between the arts and the sciences, as well as a different approach to Latin American culture. We hope that the power of both art and science, working in concert, can produce a new appreciation for, and understanding of, the nature that both surrounds us and imbues us with our humanity.

Chapter 1

To Discover, an Intransitive Verb

Christopher Columbus's First Encounter with the American Landscape

Beatriz Rivera-Barnes

Although the admiral's main objective was not to write, and certainly not to write literature, it is with the verb *to write* that Columbus refers in the journal to his expedition. "I thought of writing on this whole voyage, all that I would do and see and experience" (Dunn and Kelley 19–21). The admiral needs to write this journey, for the journey cannot be justified without the writing. And the writing is there to make up for the absence of the sovereigns of Spain who have funded the journey. Isabella and Fernando need to be convinced that their money was well spent. The act of writing in the journal is therefore tied to an effort to gain and also share knowledge and understanding of what lay beyond the rim of the horizon, to unveil the ocean's secret, ultimately an unrecognizable object, the American natural environment.

And the effort was double. On the one hand, there were the trees so *very* green, there were the plants, and there was the vegetation that the admiral did not recognize; on the other, there was the task of communicating the scenery to the Spanish sovereigns, who had not yet seen the object. This attempt *to write* the American landscape makes Columbus one of the earliest, if not the earliest American naturalist. Now the question is, with what cognitive baggage did Columbus interpret this very green world? He had read Pliny, as well as Marco Polo, but the conceivability of scarcity and the notions of change, fragility, first growth, erosion, and pollution did not yet belong to his world. Should it therefore be taken for granted that for Columbus this abundance before him would always be there, that the water would always be clean and clear and the trees so very green? Antonello Gerbi believes that the historians of antiquity and the early naturalists of America had no concept of evolution. "They believed in the fixity of the species, nature as immobility, or as variety fully unfolded in space, unmarked by the silent and unending march of time" (3).

If there is no concept of evolution, then there is no notion of an endangered world. It is with this conditional phrase in mind that I choose to approach the journal of the first voyage.

Time and circumstance have given many dimensions to this text that can be approached as a diary, as a letter or the rough draft to a letter, as a journal, and also as a diary, a letter, and a journal in different persons. In the beginning, the text is in the first person but soon the *I* becomes *he* and remains that way until October 13. Moreover, this *he*—which alternates with the *I*—is not only attempting to put words to the landscape, but also talking to *them* (the sovereigns) and trying to justify this landscape. Granted, this text is not literature, but it can be approached as a literary text, not so much because of its intention to be literary, but for the epistemological change that it originated by its gaze, for its effort to find words for an unknown and incomprehensible world, and even for the liberty that this gaze takes with the first, second, and third person singular, regardless of the fact that this liberty is accidental. In other words, initially this text written by Columbus had no literary intentions, neither did the text written by Las Casas, but the literary happened, and at times the *I* and the *he* are so intertwined that they share one and the same sentence (December 21, 1492).

So Columbus proceeded, from Friday, August 3, 1492, "writing down each night whatever I experience during the day and each day what I sail during the night" (ibid.). The act of writing (much like the act of naming) also has everything to do with taking possession. From day one, the day they made landfall, this unknown world, so full of water and so *very* green, was there for the naming, the writing, and the taking. Therefore, from the moment the admiral and his crew spotted the first signs of land, there was need for a new language. But to invent a new language means running a risk, "siendo que el destinatario del mensaje no ha visto el objecto es, simplemente, producir un discurso ininteligible" (Mignolo 61). [To invent a new language when the recipient of the message has not seen the object amounts to producing an unintelligible discourse (my translation).] This haste to name and to take possession, in turn, will be instrumental in this effort to determine whether or not Columbus interpreted this landscape with no notion of the concept of evolution.

It was on Thursday, October 11, that *they* saw sandpipers, a green branch, a cane, a stick, another small stick, a small branch, vegetation that grows on land, and a small branch covered with vegetation. Even at this early juncture there is certain monotony in the discourse, mostly due to the repetitive use of nouns and adjectives such as stick, small stick, branch, small branch, green reed, brown cane. It would appear that the admiral is already at a loss for words. These remain, however, the first words used to announce what lay ahead, the American landscape.

Obviously, the Americas did not yet exist. Although Las Casas transcribes the lost journal with hindsight, on October 11, 1492, the objective was to discover a new route to the Indies, certainly not a New World. At that point, the brown sticks and the green reeds were merely harbingers of Cipangu. Oddly enough, Columbus had no qualms about renaming these islands that *had* to be of the Indies because they were exactly where the Indies should be. Tzvetan Todorov believes that this approach gives insight into the admiral's character and manner of knowing and gazing at the world. According to Todorov, Columbus has none of the qualities of a modern empiricist, for the decisive argument is not one that comes from experience. Columbus knows beforehand what he will find and real-life experience is not to be questioned; it serves only to illustrate the truth (25).

At 2 AM on October 12, Rodrigo de Triana, who was on the lookout on the Pinta's forecastle, saw something that resembled a dark line of land in the moonlight and shouted, "*¡Tierra! ¡Tierra!*" Early that same morning, the famous landing that is often depicted by artists without much respect for the actual topography took place (Samuel Eliot Morison 228). The admiral and his crew set foot on a small island of the Lucayos that the natives referred to as Guanahaní, what is present day San Salvador or Watling's Island. Morison believes that there can no longer be any doubt that it was indeed Guanahaní, as opposed to Grand Turk, Rum Cay, Samana Cay, or Cat Island because if it is worked backward from Cuba, the position of San Salvador alone fits the course laid down in the admiral's journal (ibid.).

When they set foot on Guanahaní, they saw naked people living in a state of nature. According to Morison, the virtuous savage myth began precisely with the Taínos on Guanahaní, which means iguana, a reptile now extinct on Guanahaní (ibid., 233). May I add that the Tainos, as a people, are also now extinct on Guanahaní.

"Thus put ashore they saw very green trees and many ponds and fruits of various kinds" (Dunn and Kelley 63). Those are the first words used to describe the American landscape. They are few words and they are simple words, nothing but *very green* to describe the trees. It is in this sense that Columbus *writes* or attempts to write a silent landscape. At this point in time, nature is silent not because it has been poisoned or silenced—although that will occur soon enough—it is silent because it is unknown. The words needed to describe the American landscape do not yet exist. Certainly, these islands were inhabited by natives who had words for their fauna and their flora, but Columbus and his crew do not yet have access to this language.

The critic Anderson Imbert writes that Columbus did not have "una visión directa de América, sino el reflejo, como de nubes en un lago quieto, de figuras literarias tradicionales" (21). In other words, for most of the first voyage the gaze is not yet turned toward the American landscape; it is either turned inward (toward the conviction that these are the outer islands of Cipangu) or it is turned back, toward Europe and it is using the words or elements from medieval literary tradition to describe the landscape. These elements are few and invariable: trees, water, air, birds. They are used time and again to describe a pastoral scene, or the Garden of Eden. Mignolo explains that knowledge is not only extracted from an object, but it is also the result of what we know before taking the object into consideration (61). The admiral and his men landed with all their cognitive baggage; they saw, they interpreted, they named, and they took possession of the very green world before them.

The first voyage is *a first* and therefore an ideal place to begin reading the American landscape. For the first time ever, the European mind is attempting to decipher this new geographic dimension, an unknown natural world. It is so new that the cognitive abilities cannot yet recognize it as new; they are quite literally stunted. The place that they are beholding for the first time has to be given either old names such as the Indies, Cipangu, the land of the Great Khan, or new names such as Isabella, San Salvador, and Fernandina. As to the available adjectives to describe this world, they are scarce, and they lack *local color.*

This first encounter with the American landscape will therefore serve as an epistemology, an epistemology of environmental science, botany, anthropology, ecology, and knowledge itself. How indeed does knowledge happen? How is it possible? What can be known of the natural world? Was there an inkling of the fragility of the natural world? Where and when to start naming and classifying? The Admiral of the Ocean Sea had the answer: immediately. The minute he sets foot on an island, he names it and takes possession of it. He came, he saw, he took: a strange foreshadowing of the tourist from a cruise ship buying a little bottle that contains sand and seashells from the

Caribbean beaches, a symbolic way of reenacting the first landfall and of taking possession of each and every island. Columbus's haste also suggests a certain fear of *losing the place*. Now there are different ways of losing a place: it can be destroyed or taken away. It is important to remember that in Columbus's time there was hardly any pristine nature left in Europe and that Columbus took this vision of Europe with him to describe this unknown place.

The October 13 journal entry describes the island renamed San Salvador as, "quite big and very flat and with very green trees and much water and a very large lake in the middle and without any mountains; and all of it so green that it is a pleasure to look at it" (Dunn and Kelley 71).

Again, Columbus and Las Casas are working with the traditional elements: trees, water, air, birds. The trees continue to be *very* green; there do not seem to be other words to describe them. And although the word *so* does not appear in the original Spanish version, it is nonetheless implied. "y toda ella verde, es plazer de mirarla" (ibid., 70). It could be argued that the Spanish sovereigns were always in the admiral's mind and that he was addressing them in this journal. Moreover, this journal can very well be and is a "dress rehearsal" for the letter that the admiral will write to the Spanish Crown on his way back from this first voyage in an effort to convince them that the expedition they had funded had been a total success, and that they had not wasted their money. Indeed, he will seek to convince them that they should fund a second voyage because there was no time to waste in this harried search for an alternate route to the Indies, and also for gold and alternate sources of wealth. It could therefore be argued that by simply stating that is was a pleasure to gaze upon the greenness of the island, the admiral was already trying to "sell" the place to Ferdinand and Isabella.

The economist Joseph Vogel and the literary critic Camilo Gomides write that, "From the lens of economic theory, the Journal would seem to be the Fifteenth Century version of a modern business plan. The entrepreneurial Columbus had to persuade the venture capitalists of his day (The Spanish Crown) that the benefits of his future voyages would outweigh the costs" (210). They then point out that critics such as Beatriz Pastor do not consider adjectives such as *green* and *beautiful* on their face value, but rather as synonymous of abundance and fertility.

In this first instance, however, there seems to be no linkage to a use value as there will later be, because Columbus is simply deriving pleasure from the color green. Indeed, green does suggest fertility and abundance, but Columbus is not yet suggesting, as in the October 15 entry, that there is profit to be made from these islands. "These islands are very green and fertile and with sweet-smelling breezes; and there may be many things that I do not know about because I do not want to stop, so I can investigate and go to many islands to find gold" (Dunn and Kelley 83). On October 13, he was merely trying to make sense and draw conclusions from his observations of the landscape. In this effort to express the environment in the Castilian language, his expression does indeed become monotonous and he has no choice but to compare what he is seeing to what he has already seen before. Finally, the admiral could also be emulating Marco Polo, who was in turn following the distant footsteps of Herodotus, who introduced the categorical distinction between plants and animals *like* ours and *other than* ours (Gerbi 5).

The use of similes will also allow the admiral's target audience (the Spanish Crown) to make sense of the landscape. In the October 14 entry, immediately after naming the second island Santa María de la Concepción, Columbus compares the greenness and the fullness of leaf of the loveliest group of trees he has ever seen to the greenness of the trees of Castile in the months of April and May. For the time being, he has left the word *very* behind and he is trying harder to describe what he sees before his eyes, and this simile is as close as he can come to describing the color and the beauty before him. Furthermore, the Spanish crown can fully understand the beauty of the trees of Castile and may even be flattered by reading that the beauty before the admiral's eyes is only comparable to the beauty of their kingdom. What Gerbi sees here is an implicit and categorical Europeocentrism that is of crucial importance because it means accepting the unknown landscape, "within one's own mental horizon, appropriating it to the known and familiar world, recognizing that it possesses the normality, traditionality, and rationality of the animals and plants of our own climes. It means, therefore, automatically extending the knowledge that we have of the nature of our own world to the nature of every part of the world . . . The exotic becomes familiar" (6). But if the exotic wilderness becomes familiar, then the exotic wilderness could easily be lost to farmland or pasture.

On October 16, Columbus makes further attempts to describe the vegetation of the island he has named Fernandina, presently known as Long Island, in the Bahamas. After having repeated that the island is very green and flat and very fertile, he adds,

> I saw many trees very different from ours, and among them many which had branches of many kinds, and all on one trunk. And one little

branch is of one kind, and another of another, and so different that it is the greatest wonder in the world how much diversity there is between one kind and another; that is to say one branch has leaves like those of a cane and another leaves like those of a mastic, and thus on a single tree [there are] five or six of these kinds and all very different. Nor are they grafted . . . Rather, these trees are wild, nor do these people take care of them. (in Dunn and Kelley 89)

Although the island is again described as being very green and very fertile, in this particular entry Columbus makes further attempts to write the landscape. This time around, however, he is describing the landscape in a negative way, negative in the sense that he is writing what the landscape is *not* like. It is as if he were describing what is not in a place instead of what is in it, and as if this were the only possible way he could speak about it. What are the trees like? They are very unlike ours. "Muy disformes de los nuestros" (ibid., 88). In that same sentence, he adds, "y tan disforme" (so unlike). It is by means of a differential comparison that he is attempting to make this landscape come to life.

In the October 16 entry, Columbus is also making every effort to say something besides *very green* and *very fertile*. Before his eyes he has a tree he has never seen, a tree he cannot name. All he knows is that while some leaves resemble those of a cane and others those of a mastic, this tree has not been grafted. This could be the first instance of New World botany. Morison, however, believes that no plant even approaches this polymorphy and that Columbus must have observed a tree full of the different parasites that are common in the West Indies (243). Vogel and Gomides, in turn, would argue that such a description captures the essence of biophilia, "the notion that sheer diversity of life generates wonder" (214).

After having described this odd tree, Columbus quickly mentions that the people of the island could easily be converted to Christianity, then immediately proceeds to describe the fish "so different from ours that it is a marvel . . . of the finest colors in the world" (Dunn and Kelley 89). According to Vogel and Gomides there are sixty-five references in the journal to the root of *marvel* or its synonym *wonder* in the English translation and that twenty-four of these references can be classified as environmental (213). Such a description of Fernandina makes Morison interject, "Poor Long Island! Nobody has praised you like that since 1492; most of your visitors nowadays are glad to leave your shallow harbors, arid soil, impoverished pastures and scrubby vegetation" (Morison 246).

From October 16 on, Columbus alternates between comparing the vegetation to that of Castile in the months of April and May and expressing how unlike it is anything he has ever seen. As Mignolo observes, island after island, the descriptions will take very few lines and seem to be a repetition of the previous descriptions (62). The October 19 entry describes a passage that, according to Morison, is presently one of the world's most frequented waterways, through which steamers from North Atlantic ports of the United States pass on their way to eastern Cuba, Hispaniola, Jamaica, Costa Rica, and Venezuela (247). Morison's "presently," however, is 1940. Columbus writes, "We saw an island to the east which we bore down upon . . . at the north point where it forms an isleo and a reef of stone outside of it to the north, and another between the isleo and the big island, which these men from San Salvador that I bring with me, call the island of Saomet; to which I gave the name *Isabella*" (Dunn and Kelley 97).

Again, there is reference to beauty and marvel in this journal entry. "The island is the most beautiful thing that I have ever seen. For if the others are very beautiful this one is more so" (ibid 99). Columbus then proceeds to describe the trees, very green and tall, and an elevation that beautifies the island. Columbus is so taken by the beauty of the place that he decided to name a point Cabo Hermoso. There are numerous repetitions of the words "fermosura" in this entry: "ver tanta fermosura" (98) [to see such beauty]; "este cabo the allá tan verde y tan fermoso" (98) [such a green and beautiful point]; "ni me se cansan los ojos de ver tan fermosas verduras y tan diversas de las nuestras" (98) [my eyes do not tire of beholding such beautiful verdure that is so different from ours].

In total, Vogel and Gomides counted ninety-two references to the word *beauty* in the journal, twenty-two of which have nothing to do with the environment (houses, people, canoes, etc.), fifty-five of which are environmental in the context of a use value, and fifteen of which have no reference to any use value (214). Link after link, the repetition of the word "fermosura" in the October 19 entry does certainly lead to a use value. Although gold has not yet been found, perhaps many of these herbs and trees could be valuable in Europe for dyes and medicines and spices, "but I am not acquainted with them, which gives me much sorrow" (101). Critics such as Vogel, Gomides, and Pastor can readily use this as an example of Columbus's business plan. Morison, in turn, seems to believe in Columbus's delight when he recalls sailing those same waters on the night of June 10–11, 1940. However, Morison observes that no one would call that Cape Hermoso today. "Low cliffs of dark, weathered Aeolian limestone, which is far from a beautiful rock, interspersed with a few small sand beaches, support a plateau that is covered with scrubby trees and bushes" (248). Morison adds that the island must have been covered with an exceptional growth of tropical hardwood to have aroused such enthusiasm in Columbus and that Columbus was right about the use value of the dye wood. "The Bahamas were once rich in logwood; a shipload of it from Eleuthera in 1641 paid for a house and a lot in the Harvard College Yard" (ibid.).

Day 9, Sunday, October 21, no gold, and perhaps this has something to do with the absence of gold: Columbus writes that the island he has named Cabo del Isleo (present-day Crooked Island) is lovelier, greener, and more fertile than all the other islands. "With large and very green groves of trees. Here there are some big lakes and around them the groves are marvelous. And here and in all of the island the groves are all green and the verdure like that in April in Andalusia" (Dunn and Kelley 105). Reading that entry arouses a definite feeling of *déjà vu* or *déjà lu*. Critics such as Pastor argue that Columbus is deliberately exaggerating in order to link the beauty of the environment to a use value (51). Pastor's argument is sustainable. At times Columbus gives himself away, it is obvious that he is often engaging in hyperbole and at other times comparing the natural beauty to the beauty of Andalusia because he has nothing better to say. Moreover, he is in a hurry to find gold and he needs to justify his expedition every day. The return voyage is lurking: Columbus alludes to it in the October 19 entry.

Pastor's thesis, however, often fails to take Columbus's dilemmas and complexity into consideration. After having written that the vegetation is as green as the vegetation of Andalusia in April, Columbus adds, "And the singing of the small birds is so marvelous that it seems that a man could never want to leave this place" (Dunn and Kelley 105). Upon reading this part of the journal entry, critics such as E. B. Palm would point to the birds, one of the four elements of the Italianate lyrics and novellas, in other words, of the landscape that continues to be the ideal landscape of that epoch and that suggests paradise. But it is the second part of that sentence that points to Columbus's dilemma, a desire to stay there, in spite of being in such a hurry to find gold and to justify himself. On the other hand, it could very well be that the thought of not finding gold makes him want to stay there instead of having to face Queen Isabella.

Regardless of the admiral's intentions and apprehensions, at this point the discourse on the American natural environment is gaining layers. There seems to be a pattern. First there is allusion to the marvel and the beauty, then there is the simile (Andalusia in April), the use of at least two of the four elements in the similes, followed by differential comparisons (so unlike ours), and finally hints of truth, conflict, and dilemma such as sadness or a vague desire to stay. Immediately, Columbus seems to brush that desire away to marvel at the different kinds of trees and birds and fruit. But then he is back to hinting at his own internal psychological truth, "I am the most sorrowful man in the world, not being acquainted with them" (Dunn and Kelley 105). Obviously, not being able to tie the birds and the trees to an immediate use value make Columbus sad, but not knowing itself, not being able to name what he is beholding also makes him, as he says, the saddest man in the world.

In the October 21 entry, there is also mention of a large snake (seven palms in length), which Morison believes to be an iguana (251). The minute it saw Columbus and several men from his fleet, the snake or iguana tried to flee (much like the natives did) by throwing itself into the lagoon, but to no avail because Columbus and his men immediately went after it and killed it with their spears (Dunn and Kelley 107). Obviously, the creature presented no immediate danger so there was no need to kill it, but it was collateral damage. Not having found gold, not yet having any proof of value to give the sovereigns, Columbus was amassing everything he could in hopes that it could be worth something. The snake or iguana was skinned and the skin was added to the collection, as were the ten quintals of what Columbus believed to be valuable lignum aloes and that Morison described as "useless agave" (251).

Still, on Sunday, October 21, Columbus goes in search of good water and encounters natives who gave him water quite willingly. After having secured the water, Columbus writes that he will go round the island until he has had "speech with this king and see if I can get from him the gold that I hear that he wears" (Dunn and Kelley 107–9).

Progressively, the language of the natives is making its way into Columbus's ears and psyche. There is mention of an island called Bohío near Colba, or at least Columbus believes that Bohío is in fact the name of an island. *Bohío* in fact means *house* in the Taíno language. Palm-thatched huts are still called *bohíos* throughout the Spanish speaking Caribbean islands. Unfortunately, no one will ever know what the natives were trying to convey to Columbus.

On October 23, Columbus expresses, once again, how he is chagrined because he has no knowledge of spices and herbs and cannot recognize the trees. This could have something to do with the fact that not much botanical literature was available to the earliest explorers of the New World and that they were therefore not culturally equipped to discover and name the flora of the Americas. "The botanical corpus literati for the Portuguese and Spanish explorers was ridiculously small, and predominantly useless. It was as though the explorers could start with a clean slate to discover the world far away" (Petersen 35). This clean slate much troubled Columbus. Now the question is whether the admiral is sorrowful because he does not know or because he cannot determine the value of what he is beholding. It all depends on the chosen perspective. Readers can approach the journal as economists, psychologists, psychoanalysts, epistemologists, ecologists, and the list goes on. There is an argument for either side. According to Petersen, the Spanish were not interested in things natural, but only in the plunder they could gather. There was therefore no effort at recognition of plants for the sake of knowledge, but only for the possible exploitation (36). On the other hand, the landscape remains very silent, so there must some frustration at not being able to describe or to recognize. The landscape is also affecting Columbus who is trying to convince himself, as well as the absent sovereigns, that he is where he thinks he is and also to come up with arguments as to why this journey is a success. And of course there is no gold.

So very eager to recognize, to name, and to find intrinsic value, Columbus mentions aloe, but Morison observes that aloe was not introduced to the Americas until the following century and that Columbus must have come across an agave such as the Bahama century plant (249).

Morison adds that almost every town in eastern Cuba claims to be the San Salvador that Columbus entered on October 28, but that from the admiral's description of the harbor there is no doubt that this was Bahía Bariay. Again, little does it matter if Columbus believes he is approaching the city of the Grand Khan; he has no qualms about renaming the rivers and the peaks before him. In the October 29 entry, Las Casas mentions that one river was christened Río de la Luna, and another Río de Mares. To name is to possess, indeed, but seventeen days into the journey, Columbus is taking possession in a different way. Instead of naming rivers and mountains after the Spanish sovereigns, he is naming them in an effort to describe them and also communicate his enthusiasm.

Las Casas's rendering of Columbus's description of Cuba repeats most of what has been said before: the trees were lovely and green, and different from ours, there were many birds that sang sweetly, the island was the most beautiful he had ever seen, there were good harbors, deep rivers, beautiful mountains. A river is described as "very deep; and in the mouth, ships can be laid alongside the shore. Fresh water is short a league of reaching the mouth, and it is very fresh" (Dunn and Kelley 129). Beatriz Pastor considers water to be the third element in Columbus's fabrication of the American landscape (34). (The word Pastor uses in Spanish is *ficcionalización*, which I have chosen to translate as *fabrication*. Also, the other elements are nature in general, the air, the fauna, and the verdure.) This third element, according to Pastor, suggests abundance, fertility, and exuberance. Pastor believes that this process of fabrication is tied to yet another process that deforms reality whose origin is not literary but economic and that this process transforms each unknown tree into a source of rare spices and each river into a deep harbor (49–51). In this sense, Columbus is already transforming the American landscape into the European landscape and initiating the process of destruction. In spite of the not being a concept of evolution per se, nature is certainly being considered usable and transformable, therefore fluid. In other words, there is no fixity in this nature.

After having anchored and gone ashore, the admiral again describes a river mouth that forms a large lake, a very deep and excellent harbor, and a very good beach "for careening ships and much firewood" (Dunn and Kelley 131). Having climbed up a hill to get a better view of the island, nothing can be seen because of the big groves of fresh and fragrant trees that make Columbus come to the conclusion that these must be aromatic plants. Columbus also mentions palms "different from those of Guinea and from ours, of moderate height, and at their feet had no bark, and the leaves were very large; with them they cover their houses" (ibid.). Again, Columbus seems to be at a loss for words. The fact that the palms are different from those of Guinea and from ours says nothing about the palms, nor does *moderate height*, nor does *very large*, for these adjectives could mean one thing to Columbus and another to a twenty-first-century reader of the journal. The only descriptions that are close to precise are those that state there is no bark at the feet of these palms, the land was flat, some plants are recognized (purslane, periwinkles, and wild amaranth), and there were dogs that never barked. "These small dumb dogs which the Spaniards observed throughout the Antilles, were not a special breed of canine, but common yellow hound dogs that the Taínos domesticated largely for eating purposes. They gave a sort of grunt instead of a proper bark" (Morison 255). As to the plants, they are a constant reminder that no gold has yet been found.

With five hundred years of hindsight, Petersen writes that some twenty years later Portugal was reaping the profit from spices (by having been granted the eastern route to the Indies by Papal bull), and that Spain had not only failed to find the Spice Islands by sailing west but was yet to exploit the fabled gold (47). But that is jumping ahead and away from the contents of the journal.

If I alternated between quoting Columbus and Las Casas, it is because the journal jumps from the first person to the third person indiscriminately. However, from October 25 to March 14, 1493 which marks the end of the first voyage, all the entries are in the third person with two exceptions: the December 21 entry where Las Casas alternates between the first person and the third, so much so that at a given moment both the first and third person appear in one sentence, and the March 15 entry where Las Casas again quotes the admiral.

From this point on in the journal, namely October 29, I will no longer focus on the repetitious aspects of the journal. In other words, I will no longer be pointing out that the verdure was very green and that the landscape was a pleasure to behold. Instead, I will be concentrating on what is added to the landscape, now that the admiral has had a chance to explore and that he is certainly better acquainted with the lush green and water world surrounding him. On October 29, "He says that he found trees and fruits of wonderful flavor and he says that there must be cows on it and other livestock because he saw skulls that appeared to him those of cows. [There were] birds of different sizes, and the singing of the grasshoppers all night delighted everyone. The breezes were pleasant and sweet all night long, neither cold nor hot" (Dunn and Kelley 121–23).

This is the first time that there is any reference to taste and also to the possibility of livestock on the island. By mentioning the taste of the fruit and the presence of the livestock, the admiral is definitely suggesting that there is profit to be made, but he also mentions the chirping of the crickets and the scented and sweet night, both pleasant but useless in a business plan. In this long entry there is also mention of tasteless periwinkles, unlike those of Spain.

Not finding any gold, and with Marco Polo's travels in mind, after November 3, the admiral starts to give the vegetation more consideration. Suddenly the vegetation ceases to be merely "very green"; the admiral is attempting to find its monetary value and also to name it. In the November 3 entry, there is mention of very leafy and scented great trees that he believed to be aromatic plants. Then on November 4 there is an attempt to use the native names for the plants and the fruit, obviously for lack of a Spanish name. The native language, or the language used to describe the fauna and the flora, is slowly making its way into the foreigner's vocabulary. There is mention of "bright red things like nuts" and a fruit called *mames*, much like carrots and with the taste of chestnuts, of *faxones* and beans "very different from ours," and of wild cotton. For lack of gold, there is perhaps profit to be made from these exotic products, just as Marco Polo profited from the spices in the Orient. But then again, the admiral is still convinced that the Spice Islands are nearby. Or is he? The question will remain unanswerable. But as the days go by, with no gold, the admiral's mind seems to be working on an alternative plan, other sources of wealth, a Plan B of sorts. The wealth can come from spices, or mastic. In the November 5 entry, there is mention of enough mastic to collect a thousand quintals every year (Dunn and Kelley 135). Then on November 6, the admiral alludes to a great quantity of cotton gathered and spun in one house. "They had seen more than five hundred arrobas, and that one might get there each year four thousand quintales [of it]" (ibid., 139). This is very close to Vogel's idea of the journal as a business plan, to Pastor's idea of literary and economic fabrication, and very far from landscape writing.

In the November 12 entry, the admiral makes reference to Pliny when attempting to describe a very large tree that very readily takes root and that has leaf and fruit like the mastic, except larger. Pliny's *Historia Naturalis* had appeared in printed form in 1469 in Venice. This is one of the rare times when Columbus makes a reference to botanical literature: "As the days pass, however, the eye becomes accustomed, nature becomes more familiar, and the first impression of violent contrast with the animals and plants of Europe gives way to a vague but significant awareness of the affinities and similarities" (Gerbi 17). On November 16, they found an animal that seemed to be a badger and a fish that seemed to be a pig, and on November 17, they found nuts and rats like those of India (Dunn and Kelley 157).

A number of conclusions can be drawn from the reading of this first encounter with the American landscape. At times this first voyage is oddly reminiscent of a Caribbean cruise with tourists coming and seeing and taking possession of the place. This would make the Niña, the Pinta, and the Santa María harbingers of the love boats and everything that comes with the love boats, including pollution and Legionnaire's disease. The modern day reader can also compare the American landscape as seen by the admiral to the landscape as it is now and determine what changes it has undergone; what plant, animal, and human species are now gone; and what plant, animal, and human species have replaced the ones that were lost.

Some conclusions, however, were already being drawn before 1550. The naturalist Oviedo wrote and subsequently published the first book on the natural history of the New World after having traveled in the Caribbean and Central America from 1514 to 1523. This publication is titled *Sumario de la Historia Natural de las Indias*. Oviedo also wrote a series titled *Historia Natural y General de las Indias* that was finished by others after his death. It is in the *Historia* that Oviedo described for the first time the opossum, manatee, iguana, armadillo, anteater, sloth, pelican, ivory billed woodpecker, and hummingbird. In that same series Oviedo also described maize, pineapples, avocados, papayas, and bananas, reported on the many products made from cassava, as well as on guayacan, used by the natives to treat syphilis. "Oviedo tried to fit the new objects into the old system of the herbals and bestiairies, but also warned of the growing number of European introductions, and European colonists' persistent dependence on imported European plants and animals" (Petersen 56). Gerbi points out that Oviedo considered Columbus to be the cause of everything that is known in the New World and that he *taught* it and discovered it for all those who enjoy it.

Although there is not yet any mention of discovery, on November 27, 1492, Columbus stops once again to contemplate the beauty of the land and marvel at how it is the *most lovely thing in the world*. At the beginning of *La Conquête de l'Amérique*, Todorov writes that he wishes to address the discovery that the "I" does of the "Other." May I add that there is also the first person singular of the admiral, and there is the third person singular of Las Casas, and they are both discovering themselves as *Other*.

Many critics argue that greed was what prompted the admiral. Nothing but greed! Greed was what made Columbus want to set out to discover what lay beyond the rim of the horizon. Greed is what made him sail from island to island. Greed is what made him try to describe the plants and the animals. Greed is what made him marvel at the beauty of the landscape and mention that it was *so very green* . . . Greed? But what about the sadness at not knowing and the vague desire to stay where he was precisely when he was beholding the beauty of the landscape before him? Todorov believes that Columbus's greatest success was his discovery of nature (20). This success is tied to the verb "to discover" being, for Todorov, in Columbus's case, an intransitive verb, intransitive in that the discovery of nature was self-sufficient; it was enough in itself. I would add that somewhere in the course of the first voyage, while writing or attempting to write about nature, Columbus discovered himself discovering nature. Obviously, he did not have a green agenda.

Vogel and Gomides believe that by imploring the Crown in the November 27 entry "not to consent that any foreigner set foot or trade here except Catholic Christians" (Dunn and Kelley 185), Columbus perceives future scarcity despite the present abundance (Vogel and Gomides 216). Vogel and Gomides subsequently point out that the desertification of Spain coincided with Columbus's adulthood. Moreover, Las Casas did title his work *Brevísima relación de la destrucción de Las Indias*, so the Indies were already in danger of destruction. As far as Colombus's pen goes, in his writing of this silent landscape Gerbi sees his pen as a brush whose delicate strokes caress the tiny islands. "With a sort of lover's awkwardness he seeks to wax poetic, and produces a flood of warbling nightingales, blossoming springtimes, May meadows, and Andalusian nights" (17).

Chapter 2

Is There Such a Thing as Too Much Water?

The Hurricanes that Foundered and the Swamps that Hindered Alvar Núñez Cabeza de Vaca

Beatriz Rivera-Barnes

This ecocritical approach to Alvar Núñez Cabeza de Vaca begins with a squall line in the near distance and ends in the coastal lowlands of the Florida panhandle. The horse has ceased to reify the conquistador and has become a hindrance. Water, too much water, gales from the north colliding with warm water expanding, the shifty nature of the Canarreos shoals between Cuba and the Isle of Pines, the Gulf Stream, the rough seas of the Yucatan channel, all elements of the inconstant weather, idiosyncratic Caribbean weather that carried the unfortunate Narvaez expedition to the inhospitable Florida coast. A one-legged god sealed their fate, and his name is *hurakan*.

It was *hurakan* who killed men and precious horses, destroyed ships, spilled wine, and did not even spare the trees, towns, houses, and churches. It was *hurakan* who propelled the Narvaez expedition east when they were trying to go west, and landed them in what Cabeza de Vaca calls a land so strange and so evil and so hopeless that it seemed impossible either to stay in it or to escape from it (*Naufragios* 103). This was a land inhabited by poor and wretched people, a land where the earth is drenched with water, where thirst always increases, and where water kills you (*Naufragios* 110).

Although more than just a regionally specific name for a strong cyclone, the triadic *hurakan* does remain regionally specific, for the

Caribbean and the Gulf will always be *hurakan*'s domain, from Cuba to Florida to Texas to Mexico to Puerto Rico. Climates and landscapes change, species become extinct, and water may soon become scarce, but *hurakan* and the swamps remain.

For the Quiché Maya, *hurakan* is the god who causes rain and flood and whose epithet in the *Popol Vuh* is *Heart of Sky, Heart of Earth*. In the beginning there was the Sovereign Plumed Serpent and the sky over pooled water, a god whose name was Heart of Sky. Then came *his* word. Heart of Sky spoke to the Plumed Serpent, the manifold begetter-knower-thinker. They talked, they thought, they worried, they agreed with each other, joined their thoughts, and the dawn of life was conceived (*Popol Vuh*, 73). For the forming of the earth, they simply said, "Earth."

The Heart of Sky trinity (Hurricane, Newborn Thunderbolt, Raw Thunderbolt) was therefore present at the origins of creation. After the earth was created, the mountains were created, followed by the trees, rivers, animals, and finally man, an experiment.

This reading of the stormy beginnings of the Narvaez expedition is about the encounter of a one-legged god (*hurakan*) with an unlucky chronicler named Alvar Núñez Cabeza de Vaca on November 9, 1527, off the coast of Trinidad, Cuba, an encounter that would ultimately produce what the critic Beatriz Pastor describes as a narrative discourse of failure (*discurso narrativo del fracaso*).

Such is Cabeza de Vaca's *Naufragios*, a rendering of the hapless Narvaez expedition that turned conquerors into mere survivors. Unlucky from the start, the Narvaez expedition was a license to conquer the entire Gulf Coast of what would one day become the United States, and the forty-year-old Cabeza de Vaca went along as the treasurer, to ensure that Charles V got his 5 percent of anything precious that Narvaez came across along the way. But there would be no 5 percent, only shipwrecks, suffering, death, and perhaps too much water.

Pastor writes that in a narrative of failure, the landscape as an aesthetic concept disappears and is supplanted by an ever hostile and threatening natural environment (204). Although the expedition went from the Gulf Coast of Florida all the way to the Pacific Coast of Mexico, this study will focus on Cabeza de Vaca's very negative rendering of Florida's Gulf Coast, the place where they arrived after all those storms.

On the ninth of November or thereabouts, Cabeza de Vaca and an officer named Pantoja arrived at the port of Trinidad with two ships. Their intention was merely to get a certain number of supplies that a gentleman named Vasco Porcalle had promised Narvaez and to leave Trinidad as soon as possible because they had been told that this was a very bad port and that many ships had been lost in the vicinity. Andrés Reséndez writes that unbeknown to the would-be conquistadors on this expedition, somewhere in the Caribbean or the Gulf, "billowing clouds and localized thunderstorms began to clash and combine with each other, and this mass of clouds, rain, and wind started to rotate around a low pressure center due to the earth's spinning motion" (65). What Reséndez is describing is a hurricane that was drifting toward Cuba.

Since *hurakan* is so regionally specific, Spanish explorers had never experienced hurricanes before reaching the American side of the world. Columbus was lucky enough to have enjoyed relatively good weather throughout most of the first voyage and was the first to describe a hurricane during his second voyage. Although quite astonished by the force and brutality of the wind and the water, Cabeza de Vaca remained unaware of what was happening. Initially, *hurakan* was too much and too foreign for Cabeza de Vaca's pen. Cabeza de Vaca simply states that the weather showed signs of becoming ominous as it started to rain and the sea became turbulent (79).

In spite of the numerous letters delivered to Cabeza de Vaca by messengers on canoes, Cabeza de Vaca insisted on staying with the ships while Porcalle and Pantoja were ashore (*Naufragios* 78). But the next day it rained even harder and the strong north wind was making the sea rough and perilous. As the storm strengthened, the sailors began to fear that they would lose everything if they remained anchored in this shallow port, and they were so insistent that Cabeza de Vaca finally ceded and took a canoe to the town in order to speed the business transactions.

Before leaving, Cabeza de Vaca warned the sailors, "que si el sur, con que allí suelen perderse muchas veces los navíos, ventase y se viesen en mucho peligro, diesen con los navíos al través y en parte que se salvase la gente y los caballos" (*Naufragios* 79).

In spite of Cabeza de Vaca's warnings about the south wind and his exhortation to scuttle the ships in a place where the men and the horses would be safe if the storm strengthened, three days later, the two ships were lost and sixty men and twenty horses had perished. Cabeza de Vaca described how seven or eight men, including him, held on to each other for dear life so as not to be carried away by the wind. "Andando entre los árboles, no menos temor teníamos de ellos que de las casas, porque como ellos también caían, no nos matasen debajo. En esta tempestad y peligro anduvimos toda la noche" (79–80).

This November hurricane is only the beginning of Cabeza de Vaca's narrative, Chapter 1 of a thirty-eight-chapter-long narrative of failure. The misadventures begin with too much water and soon transform water into a hostile element. Cabeza de Vaca's experience with Cuban waters differs greatly from Columbus's. In the October 28, 1492, entry, Las Casas mentions that the admiral had not experienced rough seas in the islands up until then. Where Cabeza de Vaca sees bad harbors where many ships are lost, Columbus sees a most beautiful island, "full of good harbors and deep rivers, and the sea appears as if it must never rise, because the growth of the beach reaches almost to the water, which it usually does not when the sea is rough" (119). It is almost difficult to believe that Columbus and Cabeza de Vaca are practically in the same waters!

Even in doubt, when the currents were against his ships, or when crossing the Sargasso Sea, Columbus never wavered. The eerie Sargasso Sea had to be a good sign; there were birds and there were crabs, so land had to be nearby! The result is that throughout the first voyage, the natural environment is always beautiful beyond description and welcoming enough to make a man wish to remain there forever (119). Far from being a narrative of failure, Columbus's journal of the first voyage was a discovery of nature, as well as a business plan, an effort to sell the Indies to the Spanish sovereigns, a 1492 version of venture capitalists who had to be convinced that they had spent their money wisely.

Naufragios differs from Cortés's first four letters from Mexico as well, in spite of the fact that the Narvaez expedition was a green vengeance. Indeed, this was Narvaez's feeble attempt to get back at Cortés for the loss of an eye as well as other humiliations, and also to quell the envy that the man who conquered the Aztec empire inspired in many other aspiring *Conquistadores.*

In the beginning of their respective enterprises, both Columbus and Cortés are boastful of their accomplishments and of everything they are seeing, discovering, and conquering. Obviously, failure ultimately awaits Columbus and Cortés. It appears that luck only accompanied Columbus on his first voyage and the various renditions of the second, third., and fourth voyages (whether they be Michele de Cuneo's, Dr. Chanca's of Columbus's, or others) could very well be considered narratives of failure. As to Cortes's Honduras expedition, it resembles Cabeza de Vaca's experiences in Florida. However, if in Greek tragedy heroes must fall from high, then both Columbus's and Cortés's narratives are tragic, as opposed to Cabeza de Vaca's *Naufragios*, which was a failure from the very beginning. If the treasurer Cabeza de Vaca wrote his narrative, it was to seek repair for eight years and five thousand miles worth of suffering. Only four out of four hundred were spared in this brutal misadventure.

Chapter 2 of *Naufragios* is short and terse. There seem to be few words to describe the weather. The heading of the chapter is Como el gobernador vino al Puerto de Xagua y trajo consigo un piloto. But the chapter is not just about how the governor came to the Port of Xagua and brought a pilot along.

On February 20, 1528, Narvaez arrived in Xagua (Cienfuegos) after having spent the winter trying to recover the men, horses, morale, and ships lost to the November storms. Cabeza de Vaca, who had been in Xagua all this time, was expecting his arrival and therefore preparing the ships so the expedition could get on its way again after a three month hiatus. With him, Narvaez brought a pilot named Miruelo because, as Cabeza de Vaca explains, he had been to the Río de las Palmas (that was in northern Mexico) and knew the north coast well (82).

Two days after Narvaez arrived, the fleet was ready. It consisted of four hundred men, eighty horses, four ships, and a brigantine that Narvaez had recently purchased in Trinidad. Another ship with forty men and twelve hoses awaited them in Havana. From the port of Xagua, they sailed west along the southern coast of Cuba for what was supposed to be a weeklong cruise. Unfortunately, they sailed straight into the sandy shallows of the Canarreos shoals, between the island of Cuba and the Isle of Pines, where they remained stuck for a fortnight.

Cabeza de Vaca does not go into details, nor does he describe the shoals; he simply mentions that they sailed into the shoals and ran aground. It is in the October 19 entry of the journal that Columbus first mentions shoals. "I tried to go there to anchor in it so as to go ashore and see so much beauty; but the bottom was shoal and I could not anchor except far from land" (101). The next day, anchored at another port he has christened Cabo Hermono, Columbus almost sails into shoals but avoids them: "and I found all of the bottom so shallow that I could not enter or steer for the settlement" (103).

It would appear that Columbus is more adept in these uncharted waters than Narvaez's entire fleet. While Narvaez sails right into the sandbars, Columbus immediately realizes that it is dangerous to anchor in these islands, "except during the day, when one can see with one's own eyes where the anchor is dropped, because the bottom is all varied, one part clear and the next not so, I stood off and on at the alert all this Sunday night" (105).

In the October 24 entry, Columbus demonstrates his awareness of these waters and his ability to read them: "This bottom is all spotty, one part rocky and another sandy, because of which one cannot anchor safely except by sight" (113).

The Narvaez expedition, on the other hand, remained stuck in the sandy mire until another type of bad luck came along, in the shape of a storm: "al cabo de los cuales, una tormenta del sur metió tanta agua en los bajíos, que pudimos salir, aunque no sin mucho peligro" (82). Free at last, they arrived in Guaniguanico where another storm awaited them and carried them to Cabo de Corrientes where they ran into a third storm.

In an article titled "Circulation of the Caribbean Sea," A. L. Gordon explains that water flows into the Caribbean Sea from the southeast and continues westward as the Caribbean current before turning sharply eastward and entering the Gulf of Mexico as a narrow current known as the Yucatan Current. It is in the Gulf of Mexico that a river of seawater whose discovery dates back to the Ponce de Leon expedition of 1513 originates. Dallas Murphy remarks that the exact site where Ponce de Leon actually landed is of no importance compared to what Ponce de Leon found when he turned around and tried to sail back south down the Florida coast: "The ships were making bow waves and leaving foaming wakes, but getting nowhere. In fact, they were going backwards" (22). Murphy then points out that this was the first ever record of the Gulf Stream.

According to Paul Schneider, this river of seawater known as the Gulf Stream is formed by the warming and expanding of water bottled up in the Caribbean behind the chain of the Greater Antilles Islands and that this warm water spills through the Yucatan channel where it expands and is ejected around the tip of Florida and up past the Bahamas. Consequently, "Gales from the north in late winter or early spring colliding with the current from the south can pile up enormous seas in the Yucatan Channel" (63).

After Guaniguanico and Cabo de Corrientes, the Narvaez fleet reached Cabo de San Anton and sailed, always with the weather against them, until they were twelve leagues away from Havana. But they never made it to Havana because another storm blew them into the middle of the Gulf of Mexico and they remained at the mercy of these waters for over a month until they finally spotted land one month later, on April 12, 1528.

Cortés had a similar experience in these waters in February of 1519, when he set sail from Punta de San Antón, the last point of Cuba, to Cape Catoche in the Yucatan. Gómara, Cortés's secretary, writes that "after Cortés had begun the passage of the strait that lies between Cuba and Yucatan, a matter of 60 leagues, a violent northwester came up and blew the fleet off its course; the ships were scattered" (26). The difference between Cortés's experience and that of the Narvaez fleet is that all of Cortés's ships save one found their way to the island of Cozumel, whereas the Narvaez fleet remained at the mercy of the Gulf waters and weather for an entire month and never reached Mexico.

Schneider points out that some scholars have recently suggested that the Narvaez expedition believed for that entire month that they were progressing toward Mexico and that this theory is not impossible to defend because in spite of their skills at dead reckoning, the currents off Cuba could confound even the best of navigators.

In other words, instead of reaching Mexico, they reached Florida on April 12, 1528. Cabeza de Vaca writes that they crossed, "por la costa de la Florida y llegamos a la tierra martes 12 días del mes de abril, y fuimos costeando la vía de la Florida" (82–83). This would seem to imply that they knew they had sailed east and reached the Florida coast.

However, in Chapter 4 of his narrative, Cabeza de Vaca clearly states that the pilot did not know where they were and that he was still hoping to find the Río de las Palmas in northern Mexico. "El gobernador mandó que el bergantín fuese costeando la vía de la Florida y buscase el puerto que Miruelo el piloto había dicho que sabía; más ya él lo había errado, y no sabía en que parte estábamos" (86).

Perhaps Narvaez should have been better able to read these waters since he had already sailed from Cuba to the Yucatan in pursuit of Hernan Cortés eight years earlier. "To go from Havana to the Río de las Palmas, all Miruelo had to do was follow a rutter and estimate his speed, plotting all of this information on a chart to keep track of his progress across the Gulf of Mexico" (Reséndes 80). Now the question is, should Narvaez and his pilot have known this much? This is followed by another question: should readers of this chronicle become overly judgmental armchair navigators and fail to take into consideration that these waters, these depths and shallows, and these weather patterns remain treacherous to this day of laptop computer navigation?

In *Admiral of the Ocean Sea*, Samuel Eliot Morison describes what must have been Columbus's experience when he navigated these exact waters on the second voyage. "Columbus, with all his good luck, missed the two greatest harbors in Cuba . . . Nipe Bay on his first voyage and Jagua Bay on the Second" (459).

It was from the port of Jagua that the Narvaez expedition sailed west along the southern coast of Cuba on February 22, 1528, until they reached the Canarreos shoals where they remained stuck for a fortnight. Although Morison makes no mention of the Canarreos shoals, there is a description of the next important bay Columbus's fleet encountered after missing Jagua, the Gulf of Cochinos (Bay of Pigs) whose northeastern shore "is noted for the subterranean streams that flow down though the limestone and break out under the sea not far from the shore" (459). Morison then adds that the most trying part of this voyage was ahead after the fleet crossed the Gulf of Cazones and left the deep water for a shallow bank and encountered a white, thick, shallow sea where they could not anchor their ships.

"No wonder the men were dismayed," Morison writes. "The Admiral had boldly sailed into a tangled archipelago . . . which are difficult enough to navigate today with chart and beacons. Moreover, the people were baffled by the different colors of the water. As they came upon the shoals . . . the water at first was clear as crystal, but suddenly turned an opaque green; then after a few miles went milk white, and finally turned black as ink" (460).

Had Columbus sailed onward instead of turning around and heading back to Hispaniola, perhaps those aboard the *Capitana* would have sighted the coast of Florida as well and been the first to experience the Gulf Stream. But although Columbus's luck was starting to show signs of failing him, he was not yet that unlucky.

Reséndez writes that the pilot Miruelo could only have had a limited understanding of the Gulf Stream and its impact on the passage he was contemplating (from Havana to northern Mexico). "Because the Gulf Stream runs in a northwest to southeast direction as it exits the Gulf of Mexico, Narvaez's ships would have run almost perfectly against it" (81). This is far from following the water! But Dallas Murphy points out that following the water is easier said than done (1). After having traveled for nearly two months, Reséndez is of the opinion that the Narvaez and Miruelo could only be certain of direction and distance, the two most important elements of dead reckoning navigation. "They had traveled long enough to cross the Gulf of Mexico, and in the right direction. The Río de las Palmas had to be farther up along the coast" (82). Little did it matter if the sun was setting on the sea rather than on land!

Cabeza de Vaca does mention Florida several times, and there is much debate and disagreement among the members of the expedition. This could have had to do with differing opinions as to their whereabouts and to decisions as to who would explore this inhospitable land. They found a shallow bay that Narvaez ordered the ships to enter when the tide was rising. Today, some scholars consider this narrow cut to be John's Pass and Boca Ciega to be the bay. Translated from the Spanish, Boca Ciega is Blind Mouth. Other scholars believe that the bay could very well have been Charlotte Harbor or Tampa Bay, an area that Juan Ponce de Leon had explored in June 1513.

In his description of Ponce's voyage to Florida, Herrera mentions several islets in the open sea with an entrance between them where Ponce's fleet stopped for water and firewood and had a skirmish with members of the local population. Robert Fuson, who states that these were the Gulf of Mexico islands facing Charlotte and Lee Counties in Florida, believes that Narvaez made a terrible decision when he elected to leave the fleet and march inland (183). The plan was to rendezvous with the ships somewhere north of Tampa Bay.

Cabeza de Vaca writes that forty men were sent inland, six on horseback: "de los cuales poco nos podíamos aprovechar" (86). Horses were of little or no use, more of a hindrance than a help in these sandy flatlands, soggy *terra firma*. The inland expedition went north until they reached what Cabeza de Vaca described as a very large bay that seemed to go far inland and that Rolena Adorno believes to be Old Tampa Bay that the Spaniards named Bahía de la Cruz.

It was the next day, after Cabeza de Vaca and the other men returned to where the ships were stationed, that Narvaez made his fateful decision to send more explorers inland while Miruelo went up the coast in search of a port that he said he knew. Although Rolena Adorno and Patrick Charles Pautz believe this port to be the Río de las Palmas, on the opposite side of the Gulf of Mexico, it could very well be that Miruelo was looking for a port on the Florida coast since he had been blown by a storm to the Florida coast sometime between 1521 and 1524. "Unfortunately, he did not bother to record the latitude nor did he even make a sketch map of the location. In other words, Miruelo did not know where he had been, and he might not have been in Florida at all" (Fuson 178).

I quote Fuson in an effort to point out how difficult, if not impossible, it is to determine where exactly Miruelo and Narvaez thought they were. Perhaps the only answer is in Cabeza de Vaca's text: "y no sabía en que parte estábamos, ni adónde era el Puerto" (86). In other words, they had no idea as to where they were.

After the fleet departed, the expedition went inland, four leagues along the coast until they encountered four Indians who lead them to their village where corn could be found. But instead of corn, what they found were crates belonging to Castilian merchants and dead bodies covered with painted deer hides in each of these crates (87). "Hallamos también muestras del oro" (87). So they asked the natives in sign language where the gold came from, and the natives gestured that it was far away, in a province called Apalache.

There is no beauty and little or no efforts to describe this land. It was on the first of May 1528 that Narvaez decided that three hundred explorers should walk inland and that the ships should travel along the coast in the direction of the Río de las Palmas until they found it. Cabeza de Vaca urged Narvaez not to leave the ships unless they were in a secure and populated port and argued that not only did the pilots not know where they were, that the horses were of no use and that they were traveling mute, but also that they knew nothing about this land and were ill prepared for this expedition (88). "Mi parecer era que de debía embarcar y ir a buscar Puerto y tierra que fuese mejor para poblar, pues la que habíamos visto, en sí era tan despoblada y tan pobre, cuanto nunca en aquellas partes se había hallado" (88).

From this point on, Cabeza de Vaca constantly uses the adjective *pobre* to describe this land, without explaining how or why he considers it to be poor. The reader of the *Naufragios* could surmise that this land so strange is *poor* in terms of agriculture, since the explorers find very little corn or, for that matter, anything else growing in the marshes. It is also poor in terms of cities, since they have not come across anything vaguely resembling Cortés's Mexico-Tenochtitlan. Often, Cabeza de Vaca alludes to this land being underpopulated, so it could be poor in terms of souls. But Cabeza de Vaca also calls this land *mala*, bad, evil, and the people wretched, an impossible land, impossible to dwell in it, and impossible to escape from it (103, 110)

Reséndez writes that the verdant expanse of the Florida interior "must have appeared to them like yet another kind of sea; the terrain was flat, endless, and, except occasional rivers and marshes, mostly featureless" (91).

Immediately, Cabeza de Vaca fears the inland expedition, but he went on this expedition all the same, preferring to risk his life than to put his honor in jeopardy (90). Very soon, Cabeza de Vaca's misgivings prove to be correct: this is a bad place.

May 1, no food, no souls, no houses, no populated areas, and at the same time this land so strange is so far away from what William Rueckert describes as an ecological nightmare "of a monstrously overpopulated, almost completely polluted, all but totally humanized planet" (113). A nightmare all the same, if there are rivers, for Cabeza de Vaca, they are hurdles: "lo pasamos con muy gran trabajo a nado y en balsas: detuvimos un día en pasarlo, que traía muy gran corriente" (91).

After having spent a day fighting against the great currents of this river, the exhausted and hungry expedition finally comes across as many as two hundred natives who informed them that they were not too far away from the sea. So Narvaez sent Cabeza and forty other men on foot to search for the port, and by noon of that same day they had set out, they came across sandbars that seemed to go far inland, and they followed them, up to their knees in water, constantly stepping on oyster shells that cut their feet. John Hoffmeister writes that the Ten Thousand Islands on Florida's West Coast geologically began from offshore mounds of quartz sand deposited by a longshore current from the north. "Upon these mounds, extensive oyster beds were formed in favorable places. When the mounds were built up to the intertidal zone, mangroves established themselves and islands were formed" (120).

When the explorers returned to the same river they had crossed with so much difficulty a few days before, they found themselves too ill equipped to cross it again. Adorno and Pautz are of the opinion that the Spaniards believed that this river was the Río de las Palmas or the Río Pánuco (61). Reséndez adds that the sight of this body of water must have been as beautiful as it was disorienting, for no European map showed a bay close to the Río de las Palmas (85). Disorienting perhaps, but nowhere does Cabeza de Vaca mention beauty, and if every place has a story to tell, this place seems to be misleading and betraying the intruders who return to where they had crossed the river beforehand and followed it downstream in search of a port that, alas, could not be found: only knee-deep water awaited them.

On June 17, the Spaniards were still walking either in search of Apalache or of the evasive port in Northern Mexico. Again, they came across natives who offered to direct them to Apalache, and again, a river is but an obstacle: it is either too deep, too wide, or too fast. "Aquella noche llegamos a un río, y la corriente muy recia" (93). They did not dare cross it on foot and proceeded to build a canoe instead. The crossing took an entire day and also a life. The current swept Juan Velasquez off his horse, and the two vanished in the waters. Many scholars believe this river to be the Suwanee River.

Reséndez writes that the terrain began to change after a month and a half of nothing but marshes. Suddenly, the trees were taller, the air cooler, and the climate more temperate (95). Cabeza de Vaca described this as "tierra muy trabajosa de andar y maravillosa de ver, porque en ella hay muy grandes montes y los árboles a maravilla altos, y son tantos los que están caídos en el suelo, que nos embarazaban el camino" (94). Twice in the same sentence, Cabeza de Vaca uses either the word *marvel* or a derivative of *marvel*. The land, in the north central portion of present-day Florida, between the Aucilla and Apalachicola Rivers, is marvelous to behold and the trees are marvelously tall. It is difficult to determine if Cabeza de Vaca is experiencing awe at the sight of this strange land, for in the same sentence he immediately mentions how their progress is hindered by the great number of the marvelously tall trees that have fallen to the ground. Many of the trees still standing had been severed in two by lightning from the great storms and tempests. Even this land so unloved by Cabeza de Vaca and his companions seems to suffer from too much water, and the Spaniards, instead of awe, only appear to be experiencing fatigue, thirst, and hunger.

By the end of Chapter 6, this place has definitely become a bad place, in the sense that it always seems to be preventing the expedition from making headway. Cabeza de Vaca writes that there are thick woods and great groves and lagoons where there are fallen trees that cause obstructions (96).

Chapter 7 begins with a description of the land as being flat and composed of sand and *tierra firme* (firm earth, solid ground). In the open woods, there are large trees such as walnut trees, laurels, liquidambars, cedars, savins, evergreen oaks, pines, oaks, and palmettos. It is interesting to note that at this moment in time, in 1528, explorers and conquerors are no longer at a loss for words when describing the American landscape. Columbus expressed his sorrow at not knowing, whereas Cabeza de Vaca seems to know what every tree is called. The trees are no longer very green, or very tall, or either like or unlike those of Castile in the springtime; now the trees all have names.

As to the water, it is ever present and always impossible. The lagoons are deep, they have sandy bottoms, and they are difficult to cross, "parte por tantos árboles como por ellas están caídos" (97).

There are also fields of maize and pastures for cattle. And the region is cold. One year after the expedition had departed from Spain, they reached Apalache, an area in the Florida panhandle between the Wakulla and Apalachicola Rivers. Between 1000 AD and 1600 AD, this region was inhabited by what present-day scholars refer to as Mississippian societies who had left small, powerful chiefdoms behind after their decline (Reséndez 98–99). It was at an Apalache chiefdom that the explorers stayed from June 25 to July 19 or 20, 1528, at which time they decided to depart because the Indians were continually attacking them wherever they went to get water. "Y esto desda las lagunas, y tan a salvo, que no los podíamos offender, porque metidos en ellas nos flechaban" (99). Here, Cabeza de Vaca is making the natives go through a process of *naturalization*, for they have become as treacherous, as inhospitable, and as impossible as their natural environment.

Fleeing the wrath of the natives, the explorers crossed the same lagoons where they had been attacked on the day of their departure, and by the end of the second day they came to a lagoon that was very difficult to cross because the water was chest-high and the presence of many fallen trees (99). Again, the natives become one with the environment, for they choose to attack the explorers just when they are chest-deep in the lagoon and unable to defend themselves. The natives and their environment seem to be working together to repel the intruder.

After a few men and horses succumbed to the natives' arrows, the governor ordered the horsemen to dismount because the horses had become such a hindrance. Even the good weapons they carried were of no use compared to the arrows that could pierce oaks as thick as a man's lower leg through and through. Cabeza de Vaca used the word marvel to express the natives' skill at shooting arrows after having seen an arrow that had pierced the base of a poplar tree the depth of two or three inches (100). A few sentences later Cabeza de Vaca uses the word *maravilla* to describe the strength and the height of the natives who have become one with this inhospitable land. Paul Schneider points out that with their weak language skills, the explorers asked captive Apalaches where they should go to find food and gold. The Apalaches pointed to the sea, to a town called Aute. The problem was that there was no getting to Aute without crossing a vast swamp (153).

After nine days of travel under constant attack by the native population, the explorers found an empty village where they rested for two days before setting out to look for the sea again and discovering a great river that they named Río de la Magdalena, which could very well be the Aucilla, the Saint Marks, or the Ochlockonee, according to Adorno and Pautz (69).

The following day, they reached what seemed a bay or the entrance to the sea where they found many oysters. For the first and perhaps only time, Cabeza de Vaca mentions pleasure as well as gratitude for having found a place such as this: "con que la gente holgó; y dimos muchas gracias a Dios por habernos traídos allí" (102). But this happiness and gratitude are short lived, for the men sent to reconnoiter the coast return with news that the bays go too far inland for passage and that the sea is very far. At this point, many of the explorers are ill, including Narvaez. Schneider describes them as being in a soggy nowhere, chest-high in hell (154). Even when the wounded, hungry, thirsty, feverish expedition finally finds salt water, they are still "in this cursed place, there was nothing but shallows and mudflats" (161).

Being in Aute, or in hell, seems about as difficult as leaving Aute, or hell. Paul Schneider points out that Aute was not a single town, but rather a collection of villages on the Wakulla River, south of

Tallahassee, in what is now the St. Mark's National Wildlife Refuge (159). The expedition was faced with the impossibility of being there and the impossibility of getting away from there. The journey was difficult to the extreme, many of the men, including Narvaez, were suffering from an unnamed illness.

There was no going forward, no going back. Cabeza de Vaca writes that anyone could guess what could happen in a land so strange, and so evil, and so lacking in everything (103). Aware that some of the explorers were considering abandoning the expedition, Narvaez seeks their opinion about "tan mala tierra, para poder salir de ella" (104). Cabeza de Vaca describes the ailing explorers' desperate attempts to leave this bad place where their sins had taken them (105). Instead of reifying or mystifying the explorers, the horses have begun to serve other purposes. In their desperate attempt to leave this bad place, the horses' hides are cured in order to make vessels for water (105–6). By September 22, all the horses had been eaten (*Naufragios* 106).

Beatriz Pastor writes that in a narrative discourse of failure such as this one, the American natural environment is always hostile and threatening. It is the most formidable enemy. Nature becomes extreme and excessive, and the European explorer feels alienated in this destructive place that he knows nothing about (204). Consequently, the question is, does biophobia have a place in environmental writing or in a corpus of ecocriticism?

The answer is yes. By taking the reader through brackish inlets in chest-deep water and into shallow and dangerous inlets that extend very far inland, Cabeza de Vaca reanimates a nature that has long ceased to exist. Ironically, there is always water, too much water, and yet the more water there is, the more their thirst increases. So much so that they are finally obliged to drink salt water: "la sed crecía y el agua nos mataba" (Naufragios 108). They were thirsty, and at the same time water was killing them. But the reader is as thirsty for a time when nature was still so formidable.

Chapter 3

Picaresque Nature

Conquistadors, Parrots, Parasites, Mimics

Beatriz Rivera-Barnes

If nature writing is what ecocriticism likes best, then ecocriticism will frown on Hernán Cortés's *Letters from Mexico* (1519–26) and José Joaquín Fernández de Lizardi's 1816 picaresque novel *El Periquillo Sarniento* (translated either as *The Mangy Parrot* or *The Itching Parrot*). While Cortés, a top carnivore, a mimic's model, pays no respect to ecological values, Lizardi's *pícaro*, a member of a lower trophic level than Cortés but a predator and parasite all the same, is always at odds with nature. Mindless of the natural world, caught in the city-jungle, well aware that no two species can occupy the same niche indefinitely, both characters—Cortés and Pedro Sarmiento, nicknamed *El Periquillo*—struggle to adapt, to survive, and ultimately to eliminate their competition. The struggle is so intense that it leaves no room for reflection, doubt, awe, or contemplation. In other words, the urgency of the moment eliminates all possibility of respect or care for the environment. Three centuries may separate those two *pícaros*, but their actions and reactions, their improvisations, and their treatment of society as wilderness—and of wilderness as society—are quasi identical. This is the picaresque; it wants to take over nature.

But how could Cortés be a *pícaro*, or worse yet a comic character in his own epistles? Coincidentally, the expression *pícaro* first appeared in 1525, the year Cortés began to pen his fifth and last letter to the king of Spain. As a noun, it barely translates into rogue or rascal, and as an adjective it can mean anything from cunning to daring to wicked, very suitable descriptions of both the conqueror of Mexico and Pedro

Sarmiento. According to Ramón Menéndez Pidal, the word itself derives from the very versatile Spanish verb *picar* (Rutherford 33). And just to enumerate a few possible translations of *picar*, there is to bite, to sting, to peck, to prick, to itch, to cut, to nosh, to nibble, to annoy, and to goad, but by no means does the list end here. It was not until the middle of the sixteenth century that the word *pícaro* appeared in the written language. Interestingly enough, Rutherford proceeds to enumerate the literary works where the word is not found, suggesting that the *pícaro* and the *pícara* already existed, but remained unnamed in the sense that they were unwritten. Among these works is Fernando de Rojas's *Celestina* (1502) and, surprisingly enough, the *Lazarillo* (1554). "¡Tantísimas situaciones picarescas sin que se emplee ni una sola vez la palabra pícaro! No cabe ninguna duda acerca dela marginalidad de esta palabra entre su aparición y su consegración en el Guzmán" (35). [So many picaresque situations without the word ever being used! This leaves no doubt as to the marginality of the word from the time it appeared to its consecration in the *Guzmán*.] By the time of its consecration, the empire of the Aztecs had long been conquered by the *pícaro* Cortés.

Rutherford points out that the expression *pícaro de cocina* first appeared in a 1525 cookbook. In this sense, the *pícaro* is the cook who cuts meat and other foodstuff into pieces (19). R. O. Jones, who alludes to this culinary origin as well, describes the typical *pícaro* as a man with no scruples and a parasite, and believes that *pícaro* has lost much of its strength in modern times (185). Joseph Meeker, in turn, considers the picaresque to be a mode of survival against odds in a society that is itself a natural environment, a wilderness (51). "His [the *pícaro*'s] world is an ecosystem and he is but one small organism in it. How he fits into the whole or what its purpose may be are beyond him, but he doesn't worry much about such questions" (ibid., 59). Meeker adds that the *pícaro* realizes that no one will help him and that both survival and failure depend solely on his actions and inventiveness.

This world where no one will be helped is precisely Cortés's and Pedro Sarmiento's world, a unique ecosystem, both figuratively and literally: high, dry forest and desert with deep underground rivers. Cortés is the archetype, the model representative of what Alexander Blackburn considered to be the "age of real heroes such as the conquistadores" where "society was teeming with those for whom heroic grandeur would inevitably and often tragically be denied" (12). But could a heroic Cortés be at the same time considered a marginal being, a trickster, an antihero like Pedro Sarmiento? Is there contradiction here? Not in the sense that the *pícaro* is a persona, a mask, and not merely, as Blackburn states, a parodistic antihero (18). Although science considers species and not individuals to be in competition for a niche, I propose that a *pícaro* is an individual caught in a competitive race for a niche. In this race there are models, mimics, and dupes or receivers, and these roles that are not written in stone. In fact, today's model can be tomorrow's mimic, only to be duped by a new mimic the following day.

As a persona, Cortés was a *pícaro* before reaching the shores of Mexico. As an eternal *buscón*, searcher-wanderer, it was precisely his picaresque nature that led him away from Spain, to Hispaniola, then to Cuba, and then to Mexico away from Velasquez. It was also his picaresque nature that made Cortés write letters to the king of Spain while on his way back to Spain, letters in which he continually justified his disobedience toward Velasquez, who represented the king's power. The same Odyssean characteristics that Blackburn sees in Lazarillo can also be found in Cortés, namely willingness, inventiveness, and adaptability (58).

An outsider and a survivor who never stops to contemplate or to question, a literary character in his own letters, Cortés was therefore a *pícaro* before Lazarillo (1554), who is often considered to be the first literary *pícaro*, before Mateo Alemán's *Guzmán de Alfarache*, who consecrated the *pícaro* (1600), before Quevedo's *Don Pablos*, the seeker (*El Buscón*, 1626) who left for the Americas, and obviously before Lizardi's Pedro Sarmiento, who was born in the city Cortés conquered.

In fact, Cortés announces both the character and the genre. Otherwise, "¿Cómo puede explicarse el hecho de que entre los conquistadores mismos no surgiera un novelista?" (Sainz del Medrano 10). [How could we explain the fact that a novelist did not emerge from the conquistadors themselves?]

In the second letter, Cortés writes that he is "crazy enough to go where [he] could not return" (63). The Spanish *conquistador* is a manipulator who mimics the societal wilderness around him in his effort to adapt, survive, and get his way in the end. "With that purpose I set out from the town of Cempoal, which I renamed Sevilla, on the sixteenth of August with fifteen horsemen and three hundred foot soldiers, as well equipped for war as the conditions permitted me to make them," Cortés writes to Charles V (50).

The year is 1519, and nothing will stop Cortés's onward march toward the unknown. At the frontier of the kingdom of Cempoal, Cortés and his army go through a pass and continue for three days through dry, cold, unfertile desert country. The descriptions of this unwelcoming natural world are few and far between, there is no sense of awe, no questioning, simply an onward thrust and a conviction that "God is more powerful than nature" (62). What lies ahead, however, is not more wilderness, nothing to nurture the pristine myth of the Americas, but rather a natural world already impacted by civilization, a totally humanized landscape.

Charles Mann points out that at the time of Cortes's arrival, 25.2 million people lived in Central Mexico, in an area of roughly 200,000 square miles (143). Cortés cannot therefore be blamed for the destruction of the Mexican natural environment. Instead of pristine wilderness, what the conquistador encountered en route to Tenochtitlán were either fortified towns built on steep slopes in defensible positions (54), or villages and hamlets of from two to five hundred inhabitants, "so that there are in all as many as five or six thousand warriors" (54–55). Nature consisted solely of impossible passes between volcanoes; nature was a world at war, as well as built-up land, frontiers, more fortresses, and more frontiers.

It was not long before Cortés made enemies and took sides, or at least pretended to take sides. A survivor, the conquistador was loyal to no one but himself. Quick to join the war in this fortress-strewn landscape, Cortés writes, "The next day I left before dawn by a different route, without being observed . . . I burnt more than ten villages, in one of which there were more than three thousand houses" (60). Barely any time was wasted adapting to this new place, or being an observer, or a transplant, and Cortés immediately seized upon the animosity and discord between different villages and saw this as an opportunity for subduing them more quickly (69–70). Even the gospels told the conqueror that every kingdom divided is brought to desolation. "So I maneuvered one against the other . . . and told each that I held his friendship to be of more worth than the other's" (70). Always convinced that God is more powerful than nature, Cortés does not hesitate to join the natives and to commit to war: in other words, to catapult himself into the heart of the action. Nearly three centuries later, Pedro Sarmiento will also act, react, and gain confidence with the certitude that God is more powerful than nature, this time in the form of *audaces fortuna juvat, timidosque repellit* (2: 512) and *Deus providebit* (2: 513). [Fortune favors the brave and rejects the timid; God will provide.]

But what is the significance of the conviction that God is more powerful than nature? This war cry and justification appears to denaturalize God and to contradict the belief in God as the creator of nature and therefore in God as one with nature. Here, just like a rogue, God is eternally at odds with nature. God is on the trickster's side, and what Cortés is disguising in this conviction that God is more powerful than nature is that he himself is God, or just as powerful. In this sense Cortés is a harbinger of his literary compatriot, Don Juan, who eternally defied God. With this in mind, it should not come as a surprise that if Cortés was catapulted into the New World, it was because of his *Don Juanesque* behavior, or of a *Don Juanesque* behavior he was announcing since the literary Don Juan did not yet exist. In other words, Cortés had to seek refuge in the New World after he was caught climbing up a married woman's balcony, just as Don Juan was wont to doing not so much for the sheer pleasure of woman but in order to better defy God. Be it mentioned in passing that Don Juan was only successful when in disguise, as a mimic pretending to be some other man.

Cortés's departure from Spain is also an act of defiance. It suggests that there was a primeval model that served Cortés and granted him this first experience of God being more powerful than nature. Some seventeen years after leaving Spain, Cortés leaves Cuba in much the same way, defying Velasquez, who represented the Spanish crown or, in other words, God. Such actions put Cortés and other explorers and conquistadors ahead of their time or of their literary time, for it was not until the end of the sixteenth century that literary *pícaros* such as Quevedo's Don Pablos and Cervantes's Felipe Carrizales in the story "El celoso extremeño" felt that Spain was shrinking for them and therefore took Cortés's path, not necessarily the path less traveled, but nonetheless the one that has made all the difference. As to Pedro, who is already in the Americas, his picaresque path will take him to Manila, and then back to Mexico.

This path led Cortés to Mexico City, a city where there is no natural world, but a city-jungle all the same. In fact, Mexico at the time of Cortés was not even a city surrounded by country; it was a city surrounded by other big cities such as Cholula and Tlaxcala. Cortés wrote that the city of Cholula, situated in a well-irrigated plain very rich in crops, was more beautiful to look at than any in Spain, but he also described the *pícaro*'s realm when he mentioned that there were as many poor people begging in the streets as there were in Spain and other civilized places.

Although the place that Cortés sought and found had already been deeply impacted by man and it was already a denaturalized place, the great city of Tenochtitlán or Temixtitan was quite different from the colonial Mexico of Lizardi's time and obviously from Mexico City in the twenty-first century. On this march toward Mexico, Cortés mentions much water, in the form of lakes. He describes the city of

Mizquic as being small and constructed entirely on the water. Another league beyond this city of perhaps two thousand souls, Cortés and his men entered upon a causeway and came upon another city, Cuitlahuac, the most beautiful he had ever seen, "both in regard to the well-built houses and towers and in the skill of the foundations, for it is raised on the water" (82). Anthony Padgen points out that the modern town of Tlahuac occupies the same site as this town but that Lake Chalco has since been drained (467).

Three leagues from Cuitlahuac, he found Yztapalapa, yet another city built on the side of a great salt lake, half on water and half on dry land, a city with many trees, sweet-smelling flowers, and pools of fresh water. At this point, Cortés is only another three leagues away from the great city of Temixtitan (Tenochtitlán), which was also built in the middle of a lake. On this final stretch of road, Cortés came across three other cities that are now neighborhoods within the Mexico City limits, Misicalcango, Niciaca, and Huchilohuchico, where there was much trading in salt that they extracted from the lake that has long ceased to exist (83).

There is no place for nostalgia in the sense that the Spaniards did not come and tear down trees or destroy the natural environment, all this had already happened. Instead of being a natural world, the city of Mexico was already, at the time of the arrival of the Spaniards, what Donald Wooster would call a technological environment (or cluster of things that people have made). Wooster considers this technological environment to be so pervasive that it is a type of "second nature" but nature all the same since that technological environment "is a product of human culture as conditioned by the non-human environment" (48). In other words, it was the natural world that conditioned man—who is also part of the natural world—to construct this technological environment.

But in spite of the human presence at the time of Cortés's arrival, perhaps there is still room for nostalgia. Eight leagues from Cortés's and *El Periquillo*'s city, there are what Cortés described as two remarkable mountains with much snow. This is one of the rare instances where Cortés expresses some curiosity as to the natural world around him and this curiosity has to do with what he calls the secret of the smoke. Cortés urged his men to climb those formidable mountains in order to discover the secret of the smoke, whence it came, and how (77).

Cortés describes the province of *Mesyco* as circular and encompassed by high and steep mountains and a vast plain almost entirely covered by two lakes. "One of these lakes is of fresh water and the other, which is the larger, is of salt water" (102). These were the lakes of Chalco and Texcoco that have long since been drained. Where there was once water, there is no more water. There is no more wooden bridge for the defense of the city "across a breach in the causeway to allow the water to flow as it rises and falls" (84). In fact, there are no more wooden bridges throughout the city of Mexico that was once built on a lake that was itself an element of the fifth evil portent in the *Codex Florentino*.

Ten years before the arrival of the Spaniards, it was recorded that the lake of Mexico rose when there was no wind, then boiled and foamed and kept rising until it washed against half the houses in the city (Leon-Portilla 9). For the Aztecs, this was a sign. The fact of the matter is that Aztec society was an animistic society that noticed, listened, and recorded something other than human language, in this case the language of water and of natural gases, and in other cases the language of the wind, sky, and animals. Instead of being silent, nature spoke, and I will eventually show how this contributed to the defeat of the Aztecs. For the time being it is important to bear in mind that instead of being animate and articulate, nature was silent for the Spaniards and this further contributed to the marginalizing and degrading of the landscape, in this case the Mexican landscape. For the Aztecs, on the contrary, there was no real distinction between nature and man; therefore nature was continually breaking its silence and interacting with the humans. Christopher Manes believes that it was by virtue of their interaction with nature that animistic societies avoided ecological destruction (18). To what extent the Aztecs degraded their environment will never be known because Cortés cut their lifeline short; they were eliminated from this particular niche before their own irreversible damage was done. Nonetheless, it was just a matter of a decade before all the water in Tenochtitlán water turned bitter (Leon Portilla 146). Obviously, this could be an allegory, but it is also an excellent opportunity to blame the intruders. Today, only Xochimilco remains, a tourist attraction, a vestige of those great lakes.

The result is that one can no longer drink the water in Mexico City where a stream of very good fresh water once flowed into the heart of the city. The causeways to this city that ran into two aqueducts are now dry and full of rats. It appears that the Aztecs had a good sense of water management and even understood how nefarious contaminated water would be to their society. For example, Cortés mentioned a channel that always remained empty and was used only when they wished to clean the first channel. It was from this water that they all drank. "Where the aqueducts cross the bridges, the water passes along some channels which are wide as an ox; and so they serve the whole city" (107–8). Parts of those same channels can still be seen in Mexico

City today, a stone's throw from the shadow of Moctezuma's palace. Not only are these relics of pre–Columbian water management genius dry, they are full of garbage and of rats feasting on garbage. Speaking of rats, everything is available for them in that pile of garbage, leftover Mexican street food, meat, chicken, corn, chips, potatoes, and perhaps there are all types of rats in the garbage, in the channels, even Aesop's and La Fontaine's city rats and country rats. The philosopher Michel Serres playfully states that it is the city rat that takes the farmer's profits and the last to profit is the country rat (3). But the rats' feast is suddenly interrupted by a noise, so the country rat is scared and scurries off, urging the city rat to accompany him to the country where they eat only soup, but quietly, with no interruption. The city rat pays no heed; he stays. He wants to finish eating his garbage. What has happened here is that another parasite has arrived and is in fierce competition for a place in the niche; the noise announces his arrival, and this is exactly what happened in Tenochtitlán when Cortés arrived.

Although Cortés was a *pícaro* before he reached the city of Mexico, it is in the city of Mexico—and at the precise moment that he encountered Moctezuma—that his picaresque nature fully developed, as if the stage had already been set. Thus, some environments are good hosts to *pícaros*, as they are to parasites:

> One parasite chases another out. One parasite (static), in the sense that information theory uses the word, chases another, in the anthropological sense. Communication theory is in charge of the system; it can break it down or let it function, depending on the signal. A parasite, physical, acoustic, informational, belonging to order and disorder, a new voice, an important one, in the contrapuntal matrix. (Serres 6)

By definition, parasites eat and thrive within the body of their host. In this case, Cortés and Pedro represent two different trophic levels of *pícaros* or parasites on an ecological pyramid, and the city of Mexico is their niche, their host. In *Parasite*, Michel Serres dedicates an entire chapter to the picaresque, because the *pícaro* is in fact a parasite. "The parasite invents something new . . . He crosses the exchange, makes it into a diagonal . . . He wants to give his voice for matter, (hot) air for solid, superstructure for infrastructure" (35). It is interesting to note that in all picaresque novels there is barter. One parasite, for example, might lend eyes for bread, as in the case of a seeing man who lends his sight to a blind man in exchange for food, in an eternal game of exchange. In Cortés's case, there was voice, translation, and language in exchange for power, whereas in Pedro's, there was example and advice, whether good or bad.

Those are forever-unjust pacts made in the city/host that Cortés conquered and where the other parasite Pedro Sarmiento arrived (was born) sometime between 1771 and 1773, a treacherous city/host/ niche where each individual, each organism, is looking out for himself, where it is necessary to beg, steal or kill in order to survive, and also a poisoned community/environment that merits what Lawrence Buell described as a toxic discourse (35). Buell points out that in their attempt to illustrate the lower depth of urban areas, authors rely on the "Virgilian mode" (43). While Eric Homberger carried this mode to New York City, Charles Dickens to London, Herman Melville to the mill towns of New England, and Hernán Cortés to the market in Tlatelolco, Lizardi carried it to the inner depths of Mexico City thus rendering it a home of lost souls, an inferno where the author finds it necessary to teach and guide the reader and to advocate social regeneration by painting a portrait of the damned.

In Lizardi's case, the author himself is the damned. Like other *pícaros* before him, Pedro Sarmiento is writing for the sake of his children, so that they will avoid his mistakes as well as his own parents' mistakes or mindless decisions. Because Sarmiento's mother was pretty, because Sarmiento's father found his wife pretty, both Sarmiento's parents decided to turn their newborn child over to a wet nurse. Immediately, Sarmiento exhorts his children never to turn their own children over to people of this sort for several reasons, the most important being "porque es una cosa que escandaliza a la naturaleza que una madre racional haga lo que no hace una burra, una gata, una perra, ni ninguna hembra puramente animal y destituida de razón" (1: 78). [Because this is a scandal against nature for a rational mother to do what no donkey, no cat, no dog, or any other female devoid of reason would do.] This comparison of women with animals is a recurring theme throughout the narrative and appears to haunt Pedro. At a given moment even hens are better mothers, as are donkeys, cows, "y todas las demás madres brutas" (ibid., 279). [And all the other brute animal mothers.]

The narrator never seems to have surpassed a memory that was not even his own but had to have been handed down to him, the fact that he was turned over to a wet nurse, something that he strongly feels denatured his parents. Lizardi, through Pedro, expatiates on the subject and insists that any female capable of nursing who refuses to nourish her young is at odds with nature. Furthermore, Lizardi alludes to a child being nurtured by a cow who risks behaving like a cow (ibid., 79). Likewise, Sarmiento's first wet nurse was evil, and this is how he explains his waywardness; the die was cast from that very moment. "Finalmente, así viví en mi casa los seis años primeros que vi el mundo. Es decir, viví como un mero animal" (ibid., 84). [Finally, that is how I lived for the first six years of my life. In other words, I lived like a mere animal.]

Interestingly enough, after having lived his first six years like a mere animal, when he goes to school wearing green and yellow clothes, Pedro will be rechristened "Perico" by his classmates. A *perico* is a parakeet or a small parrot, and were the "e" to be an "a," *perico* could easily be a scrambled *pícaro*, for the two words are as close as Pedro's last name, Sarmiento, is to the adjective *sarniento*, mangy. Nancy Vogeley affirms that the diminutive *periquillo* further ridicules the main character (83). The result is a character likened to a parrot who mimics the sounds of his biome. But this aptitude at mimicking makes the parrot a picaresque character. In the jungle, it adapts and survives by reproducing sounds. This christening renders Pedro natural and unnatural; it catapults him into the natural world and at the same time denatures him. Pedro, however, is not the only character that has been given an animal nickname. *La Zorra* and *la Cucaracha* (the Fox and the Roach) are two women who keep Pedro awake at night when he is desperately trying to be celibate (221), and *El Aguilita* (the Eaglet), is Pedro's partner in crime, "por mal hombre le llamaron Aguilita, así a mí me decían Periquillo Sarniento" (1: 417). [For being a bad man he had been nicknamed the Eaglet just as I was called the Mangy Parrot.] Both characters are bad, and both are diminutive.

So a mangy parrot entered the food web of Mexico City three hundred years after Cortés—the unnatural—found within its boundaries Moctezuma, another unnatural, another rogue, waiting for him, greeting him with open arms, showering him with gifts, and assuring him that he too was a foreigner who did not *really* belong in this niche. It took three centuries for this place to become someone's place of allegiance, and this someone was nicknamed the Mangy Parrot.

By nature, a parrot reproduces sounds devoid of meaning, words with no content that, however, sound real. In this sense the parrot could be considered an object of ridicule, a jester of sorts. The parrot is funny because it mimics, because it sounds like a human, and up until very recently, parrots have been considered somewhat devoid of intelligence. Whether or not they are is the subject of another study, but what matters here is that they are a product of their environment; in other words, they were produced by location. The location necessitated the mimicry, and they heeded this call, they adapted to the environment just as Cortés and Pedro adapted to theirs and soon began reproducing the sounds and the behavior around them. "¿Por qué hablan los pericos como la gente?" a young girl eager to hurt Pedro's feelings asks (155). [Why do parrots talk like people?]

Coincidentally, when Pedro is on his way back to Acapulco from Manila, he shipwrecks, meets a Chinese noble and experiences no difficulty in learning his language. "Yo hablaba major su idioma que él el mío, porque estaba en su tierra y me era preciso hablar y tartar con sus naturales" (2: 741). [I spoke his language better than he spoke mine since I was in his land and needed to speak to his compatriots.] Likewise, when a parrot is in a jungle, he mimics the sounds of the jungle. When he is with a human, he reproduces human sounds. Pedro mentions this very matter-of-factly; it was natural for him to pick up Chinese in no time.

Cortés too, like a parrot, listened to Moctezuma, and soon he was saying what Moctezuma needed to hear. The proof is that it took little or no effort to conquer the Aztecs with so few men. At the time of Cortés's arrival in Tenochtitlán, this land did not appear to be Moctezuma's land, since Moctezuma assured Cortés that he too came from elsewhere. In this aggressive immediacy, it is difficult to determine whether or not Moctezuma—who had let the strangers into Tenochtitlán—really believed that Cortés's arrival had been foretold, that Cortés was their lord and god who had returned, and that he (Moctezuma) was ready to obey his every command. It is at this point that Moctezuma raises his clothes, shows Cortés his body, and says, "See that I am of flesh and blood like you and all other men, and I am mortal and substantial" (Cortés 86). Moctezuma the unnatural, who shares the same trait with all other *pícaros*, a tragic view of life that makes them proud to be unnatural, is trying to reassure Cortés, the voice, the woman's voice, that he is in fact natural, and Cortés will turn around and do just the same. What has just occurred is that a new predator has just entered the food web, and he will immediately prey on Moctezuma who, until then, knew no predators.

This natural-unnatural exchange between Cortés and Moctezuma was the last leg on the road to victory over the Mexican people. In an effort to analyze this victory, Tzvetan Todorov points out that if Cortés never represented absolute evil but rather a lesser evil to Moctezuma's vassals, it was because they had already been conquered and colonized (64). By virtue of not being recognized immediately as a threat—just as an unknown virus or parasite would not be recognized by an organism—Cortés was therefore allowed to advance farther and farther into the country until he reached its heart, Tenochtitlán.

The opportunistic Cortés wasted no time in taking advantage of the ambiguous situation. Todorov adds that all the elements of Cortés's and the Spaniards' superiority, weapons, horses, and bacteria, however, are not enough to explain victory, and proceeds to explain the victory in terms of signs and communication. There exist two forms of communication: one between humans and the other between a person and the natural world. For the Aztecs the predominant form of communication was the latter (75). It was always the natural world that answered questions relative to the immediacy of the present or of the future. Cortés's arrival was interpreted as having been foretold, and Moctezuma listened to nature's prophecies. This explains the victory, but Todorov believes that this victory is bittersweet in that it deeply affects our ability to experience harmony with the world. The result is an illusion that all communication is between humans. Todorov concludes by writing that the victory was also a defeat. "En s'imposant sur toute la terre par ce qui était sa superiorité, il écrasait en lui-même sa capacité d'integration au monde. Pendant les siècles qui suivront il rêvera du bon sauvage, mais le sauvage était mort ou assimilé" (103). [By imposing himself on this land by virtue of his superiority, he destroyed any possibility of union with the land. For centuries to come he will dream of the noble savage, but the savage was either dead or assimilated.]

Such an ambiguous victory over nature and dreams of the noble savage are oddly reminiscent of Bill McKibben's thought that wilderness can survive the destruction of nature, that wilderness can survive in our minds even if the nature around us is degraded (49). Although McKibben writes at the end of the twentieth century, this degraded world was already a reality in Lizardi's time. In fact, Pedro Sarmiento was born into this degraded world; he is even a product of it. Very rarely does Pedro the Parrot sound human. One of these rare instances is when Pedro's wife, Mariana, dies in childbirth. "La ignorantísima partera le había arrancado el feto con las uñas y con otro instrumento infernal, rasgándole de camino las entrañas" (2: 622–23). [The ignorant midwife had pulled the fetus out with her nails and another infernal instrument and had scratched her entrails in the process.] For the first time, there is a sense of injustice, regret, and pity; Pedro speaks and thinks like a human; and for a few fleeting moments the *pícaro* stops to reconsider

But the *pícaro* has no choice but to step right back into his degraded world and to continue claiming the space he occupies. To this notion of a degraded world, Lawrence Buell adds that toxic discourse is by no means unique to the present day (31). By definition, Buell considers toxic discourse to be expressed anxiety arising from perceived threat of environmental hazard. If Dickens's novels could very well be considered a discourse of toxicity, so could the picaresque novel, in this case Lizardi's homegrown novel of Mexico where both society and nature are environmental hazards, where society considers nature evil, and nature has long been rendered toxic by society. Eclipses, for example, are considered to be the devil by a landowner who considers himself educated enough to be talking about the natural sciences. Just like a parrot, the landowner has heard the word eclipse and is repeating it. The problem is that he has misheard it and pronounces it *eclimpse* (156).

The natural sciences are a continuous theme throughout Lizardi's novel. They seem to give just about every character a sense of entitlement. The natural sciences do not intimidate the simple minds; on the contrary they belong to the people. A curate even advises Pedro that the natural sciences are the first step toward knowledge since they are not as lofty or as abstract as theology and jurisprudence. In Chapter 7 of the novel, the same curate tells Periquillo about the delights of studying the natural world that lead to the appreciation of the divine, a conversation that in turn leads the curate and Periquillo to a corral where they witness the branding of yearling bulls, horses, and mules. Immediately, Periquillo notices that the spectators take less pleasure in the branding itself than in witnessing riders being thrown off bulls and horses and getting hurt, which causes endless laughter. The sight of human suffering is comical, whereas the spectacle of animals suffering makes the spectators look away. When Periquillo expresses his distaste for this scene, the curate reacts by asking Periquillo if he had ever been to a bullfight, then goes on to explain how many men are either killed or seriously wounded in bullfights and that this is how it is and will be "hasta que no se olvide esta costumbre tan repugnante a la Naturaleza, como a la ilustración del siglo en que vivimos" (1152). [until we forget this custom as repugnant to nature as to the enlightenment of the century in which we live.]

In Pedro's world, as in Cortés's before him, nothing is what it appears to be. This world described in letters sent to the Spanish crown and in the picaresque genre is too fluid for truth. It is a world that calls for constant survival, for eternal action. Survival calls for defenses, and there are many types of defenses: poison, for example, or venom. There is also defensive coloration, aposematic coloration, a warning coloration, and cryptic coloration, a coloration that blends with the environment. Then there is mimicry, used by those who have no other defenses. A parrot, a *pícaro*, uses all the defenses available.

Edward O. Wilson defines a niche as, "A vague but useful term in ecology, meaning the place occupied by a species in its ecosystem—where it lives, what it eats, its foraging route, the season of its activity, and so on" (403). In this sense, a niche is not only a place, but also a potential place and a role, a verb. The picaresque world is also a verb. In conclusion, Cortés and Pedro Sarmiento are just two portraits in what Michel Serres calls the parasite gallery. Three centuries separate them, but as Raquel Chang Rodriguez points out, there is a definite relationship between the picaresque genre and the letters and narratives of the discovery, conquest, and colonization of the Americas (Ordaz 63). Although Cortés wrote his own letters and was a real character as opposed to a fictional one, he was also the main character in Bernal Diaz del Castillo's death bed confessions and at times a character fabricated by Francisco López de Gómara, his secretary and biographer. The two portraits in the parasite gallery are significant for the Mexican landscape in that by occupying this niche, they create this niche, bring it to the forefront, and tell its life story from the beginning to the end. Most parasites do not want to kill their host, and these two parasites simply exacerbated the host's carrying capacity and contributed to its toxicity. In the end, both *pícaros* lose their colorful feathers and their powers of mimicry fade. Theirs, however, is not a sentimental journey. "In the picaresque tradition, people are shown living as other animals live, confronting the present defensively and opportunistically . . . and above all adaptive to the immediate environment" (Meeker 72). Meeker adds that modern cities like Rome are messy and chaotic, and that those who flee them in search of peace are following a pastoral (73). Rome can be replaced by modern Mexico City, where undoubtedly there is still danger and opportunity for the *pícaro*, where there once was clean water and nature.

Chapter 4

Andrés Bello's "Ode to Tropical Agriculture"

The Landscape of Independence

Jerry Hoeg

In order to appreciate this extraordinary poem, titled "Silva a la Agricultura de la Zona Tórrida" (1826) in the original Spanish, one must first understand the multiple contextual elements that form the background of this particular work. The most important element to consider is the author of the poem, whose full name was Andrés de Jesús María y José Bello López (1781–1865) and who turns out to be even more extraordinary than the poem. Bello was one of the most important and influential cultural and political figures in Latin America at the beginning of the nineteenth century, a period in which the continent went from being part of the Spanish colonial empire to a collection of, eventually, ten independent republics. Indeed, at that time the term "Latin" America did not yet exist. As we shall see, many aspects of Bello's personal circumstances contributed to the creation of this poem and also to the creation of the new republics, and so before turning to the poem itself we need first briefly review pertinent aspects of Bello's life.

The author of the "Ode" was born in Caracas, Venezuela, on November 29, 1781, and lived there until 1810. His father, Bartolomé Bello, was a minor official in the Spanish colonial government, known then as the Captaincy General of Venezuela. Bartolomé died in 1804, but not before ensuring that young Andrés received a first-rate education. After elementary school, Bello studied Latin classics, especially the poetry of Horace and Virgil, under Father Cristóbal de Quesada at the Mercedarian Order's convent across the street from his home in Caracas. Both Quesada and a later teacher, Father José Antonio Montenegro, were among the leading Latinists of the day. This early training in Latin literature plays a crucial role in understanding Bello's "Ode to Tropical Agriculture." As many have observed, the "Ode" owes much to Virgil's (70 BC–19 BC) *Georgics* (29 BC), the ostensible subjects of which are rural life and farming, but which actually advocates a return to traditional Roman moral values after the fall of the republic and the chaos of the ensuing civil war. It should be mentioned here that Virgil's two other masterpieces, the *Bucolics* (37 BC), sometimes called the *Eclogues*, and the *Aeneid* (29 BC–19 BC) are also meant to be foundational narratives for post–civil war Rome. Not coincidentally, Bello's "Ode" is also a foundational narrative, in this case for the new republics of Spanish America. In line with its foundational nature, it is worth mentioning that the "Ode" has inspired many subsequent classics of Latin American literature, including Jorge Issac's *María* (1867), José Eustacio Rivera's *la vorágine* (1924), Pablo Neruda's *Canto general* (1950), and Alejo Carpentier's *Los pasos perdidos* (1953), to name but a few (Gutiérrez Girardot 232).

After finishing his studies at the Mercedarian convent, Bello went on to study at the Royal and Pontifical University of Caracas beginning in 1797, graduating with a Bachelor of Arts degree in 1800. During this period he taught himself French and English; won prizes in Spanish orthography, Latin translation, and natural philosophy; and graduated first in his class (Jaksic 7). This early interest in orthography and Spanish grammar would later manifest itself in many publications, including Bello's famous *Gramática de la Lengua Castellana Destinado al Uso de los Americanos* (Grammar of the Spanish language for the use of Spanish Americans; 1847), "written to provide linguistic unification for the emerging Latin American states, and to avoid linguistic fragmentation" (Jaksic 54) as had happened to Latin with the fall of the Roman Empire. In line with this, he also produced a number of philological studies of Spain's national epic, *El Poema de Mío Cid* (*Cuadernos de Londres* 1814–23). This poem, also known as the *Cantar de Mío Cid*, was written near the end of the twelfth century (1140, according to Menéndez Pidal) and deals with the personal fall and redemption of the hero, the Cid (Rodrígo Díaz de Vivar), who, like Bello, was also exiled from his native land but who, unlike Bello, through both heroic combat and adherence to the legal system (Bello's "temple of the law" in the "Ode") returned to unify Spain and so found a nation. Indeed, after Bello, succeeding investigators have pointed to the fact that the court proceedings in the poem follow standard Roman legal practices (Pavolic; Zaderenko), and so provide the model for later Spanish Latin American jurisprudence. Pedro Grases also points to later Spanish works that influenced the "Ode to Tropical Agriculture," especially Cervante's *Discurso a los cabreros* from *Don Quijote* (1: 11) and Lope de Vega's *El Siglo de Oro* (*La Vega del Parnaso*) (*Doce Estudios* 61–73), both for their emphasis on a "golden era."

In addition to language and literature, Bello also studied philosophy, including such writers as John Locke and Etienne Bonnot de Condillac, at a time when traditional scholasticism was feeling the impact of the Enlightenment (Jaksic 7). These and subsequent studies would play a role in his poetry and would later give rise to Bello's posthumously published *Filosofía del Entendimiento* (Philosophy of the understanding; 1881), thought to have been written in the 1840s (Jaksic 7). And concomitant with the shift in philosophy from Scholasticism to the Enlightenment and the New Science, literature too was shifting from neoclassicism to Romanticism, and Bello's poetry also reflects this trend. Addressing these changes, Fernando Vargas Bello observes that Andrés began to be "seduced by his first contacts with the romantic movement in his London years" (34), "incorporating the best of it into his own work while avoiding its excesses" (35).

During his time in Caracas, he also served as tutor to Simón Bolívar, later to become perhaps the most famous of the South American revolutionary leaders, one who, through heroic deeds, would attempt to unite Latin America. The young Bello also made the acquaintance of Alexander von Humboldt and Aimé Bonpland during their visit to Caracas from November of 1799 to February of 1800. Bello accompanied them on excursions around Caracas, and from this experience developed a lifelong interest in natural science, the influence of which is evident in the "Ode to Tropical Agriculture" (Duran 140). Later, in London, his first publication there would be a translation of Humboldt and Bonpland for the journal *El Censor Americano*, edited by his friend Antonio José de Irisarri. In the first number of Bello's own London journal, titled *Biblioteca Americana*, he would publish a selection from Humboldt and Bonpland's *Plantes équinoxiales*, and in the first number of his second London journal, *El Repertorio Americano* in which he first published the "Ode," he would publish a translation from that part of *Voyage aux régiones équinoxiales du Nouveax Continent* treating Venezuela (Duran 141). Pedro Grases lists ten such scientific translations in his bibliography of these two journals (*Tiempo* 179–218), and Mary Pratt reports that "Not an issue of the *Repertorio Americano* appeared without an excerpt from Humboldt, selected and translated into Spanish by Bello" (174). This predilection for journalism also dates to his Caracas years, when he became the editor of the first Caracas daily, the *Gazeta de Caracas*, from 1808 to 1810 (Alvarez 19). And finally, Bello's first major work in prose, and also the first book printed in Venezuela, the *Resumen de la Historia de Venezuela* (Review of the history of Venezuela; 1810), exalts the role of both agriculture and nature in Venezuelan history, and so is a direct precursor to the "Ode to Tropical Agriculture."

On July 7, 1808, in Bayonne, both Carlos IV and his son, Ferdinand VII, abdicated their rights to the Spanish throne, and Napoleon Bonaparte, who quickly had the first constitution in Spanish history approved by a compliant Spanish assembly, promptly placed his own brother Joseph on the throne. These political maneuvers, along with a subsequent occupation by French troops, caused a general uprising in the Iberian Peninsula against the French and their Spanish supporters. The net effect in Spanish America was to convert the Spanish troops stationed there, including the Captain General, into French collaborators. Hence rebellion against them became a patriotic duty (Ubieto 513–21). A Caracas junta soon formed, composed of both conservatives backing the deposed monarch and young revolutionaries like Bolívar in favor of an independent republic, but united in their opposition to the current Spanish government. With the Spanish troops no longer protecting them, the new junta needed an ally against a possible French invasion, and so it was decided to send Simón Bolívar, Luís López Méndez, and Andrés Bello on a diplomatic mission to London to secure British support and protection. Though he could not have known it at the time, Bello would never again see Venezuela.

After a couple of months of negotiations, the Venezuelans realized a permanent diplomatic presence in London was a necessity for the fledgling republic, and so when Bolívar and López Méndez returned to Venezuela, Bello, who spoke English, stayed behind in London, where he was to spend the next nineteen years working for the cause of Spanish-American independence. He would not leave until 1829 and then went to Chile, where he spent his remaining thirty-six years, during which time he founded the University of Chile, wrote the country's civil code, and was elected senator three times in succession, a position he held till his death. The years in London would be years of hardship, poverty, and personal turmoil, but also years of great scholarship. Bello passionately studied the origins of the Spanish language and more generally the origins of all the Romance languages, with an eye to understanding how the decline of Latin following the breakup of the Roman Empire had given way to the evolution of these other languages. Above all, he was interested in the parallels between the collapse of the Roman Empire and the collapse of the Spanish Empire as seen from a philological perspective. He was particularly interested in national epics such as the *Aeneid* and the *Poema de Mío Cid*, and the unifying role of language in constructing national cultures. It was Bello's intent to write a foundational epic poem for South America, which he intended to title "America" (Gutiérrez Girardot 234). Only two parts of this epic were ever written, the poem "Alocución a la Poesía" (Allocution to poetry; 1823) and the "Ode to Tropical Agriculture" (Silva a la Agricultura de la Zona Tórrida). Bello also proposed merging the two in a larger poem titled "El campo americano," and later planned placing them in a series of "Silvas americanas." Neither project was completed, and only the "Ode to Tropical Agriculture" was published under the new "Silvas americanas" title (Cussen 117–18).

Bello begins the "Ode to Tropical Agriculture" with a description of the flora of the tropics, including both cultivated and noncultivated species, often adding footnotes to give the correct Linnaean name and also place of origin. He paints an idyllic picture of the Edenic torrid zone (the tropics), that equatorial region where the sun provides for a year-round growing season. As many critics have noted, the famous first line of the poem, "Salve fecunda zona" (Hail fertile zone; this and all translations of the "Ode" from Lopez-Morillas 29–37), effectively cites Virgil's line 173 of book 2 of the *Georgics*, "Salve, magna parens frugum, Saturnia tellus" (Hail, great provider of fruits, Saturn's land; my translation), and also borrows from the opening lines of Lucretius's *De rerum natura*. He goes on to describe said fruits and assorted other tropical agricultural products, including "golden grain," "grapes to the bubbling pail," "sweet sugarcane," "the beans that overflow the foaming chocolate cup," "the dyes from cactus plants, outdoing the purple of Tyre / And the splendid dye of your indigo plan imitates the sapphires glow," all arrayed in "glorious groves, green meadows, endless plains, and snowcapped mountains" (ll. 1–20). All in all, he paints a picture of a natural paradise, filled with noble savages whose problems are those of the idle rich:

> Wine is yours, which the pierced agave
> pour out for Anahuac's happy brood.
> Yours too is the leaf that solaces
> the tedium of the idle hours, when its soft smoke
> rises in wondering spirals (ll. 22–26).

The fertile zone also supplies, free for the picking, the products of the lofty palm, the ambrosia of the pineapple, potatoes, corn, cotton, and above all the banana, which "asks no care by human arts, but freely yields / its fruit. It needs no pruning hook or plow" (ll. 44–45). But there is one amendment to the no-labor-involved clause in this golden age, because, still speaking of the banana, a nonnative by the way, the next line tells us, "No care does it require, only such heed / as a slave's hand can steal from daily toil" (ll. 46–47). Up to this point in the poem, Bello had described a prelapsarian, and preagricultural phase of human existence, life in paradise where Man was slave not to Nature but to God. But with the allusion to the "daily toil" in the above-cited line and also in a footnote to the poem, Bello introduces the hand of labor, meaning agricultural labor, into Arcadia. Effectively, this signals the fall from grace of mankind. Beginning on line 50 he traces the historic development of agriculture, from its origins among the first simple farmers to the development of vast cities and their populations that the invention of agriculture made possible. Cultivating the tree of agroscientific knowledge frees Man from bondage to God, but places him in bondage to Nature, and especially human nature and all its attendant vices. Bello writes,

> Oh, would that they could recognize the joy
> that beckons from the simple farmer's home,
> and spurn vain luxury, false brilliance,
> and the city's evil idleness! (ll. 53–56).

In the lines that follow, Bello goes on, a là Virgil in book 3 of the *Georgics*, to attribute the woes of civilization to the seductions of the city, including prostitution, adultery, gambling, alcohol abuse, teen pregnancy, and the feminization of males, "a man who curls his hair and scents himself, / and dresses with almost feminine care" (ll. 88–89), and ends by comparing, unfavorably, this behavior to that of the Roman Republic before the civil wars:

> Triumphant Rome did not thus view
> the arts of peace and war; rather, she gave
> the reins of state to the strong hand,
> tanned by the sun and hardened by the plow,
> who raised his sons under a smoky peasant roof,
> and made the world submit to Latin valor (ll. 95–99).

This criticism is, obviously, directed at the ruling classes, those wealthy enough to posses lands to abandon for the vices of the city. He also criticizes the church for appropriating these lands: "to make them [land owners] leave hereditary soil, / forsaking it to mercenary hands" (ll. 60–61). As Cussen explains, the church had a virtual monopoly on mortgage loans, known as *censos*, for hundreds of years during and even after the colonial period. The net effect of this mortgage banking monopoly was that, over time, the Church became the outright owner of vast tracts of land and held the controlling interest in many more (120–21). In this view, God has taken back paradise and Man has enslaved himself by letting his weak human nature surrender to the sins of the flesh. Where then to find freedom and virtue?

Not surprisingly, Bello's reply is "Back to Nature," or, more specifically, "Back to the country." For those trapped in the evil ways of the city, he advises, "Break the harsh enchantment / that holds you prisoner within walls" (ll. 105–6). He continues, "Do you love freedom? Go then to the country" (ll. 114), "go and enjoy the farmer's life, his lovely peace" (ll. 127), "go breath the mountain air" (ll. 135), and so on. But there are reasons for this advice that go beyond the health of the individual and touch on the health of the state:

> There too are duties to perform: heal, oh heal
> the bitter wounds of war; place the fertile soil
> now harsh and wild, under the unaccustomed yoke
> of human skill and conquer it (ll. 156–59).

Here it is worth recalling that after the wars of liberation, the economies of the new republics were in shambles. Under the Spanish Empire the colonies had never been industrialized, but rather had served as a source of raw materials and a market for Spanish manufactured goods. In addition, the mining industry was in disarray and there was not sufficient capital available to revive it (Jaksic 60). Therefore agriculture was the primary economic motor available to Venezuela in the period following the revolution. Thus, reconquering the soil mostly abandoned during the revolution was a logical cure for the economic wounds of war. And political stability depended on economic stability.

This is backdrop against which Bello calls for what sounds to modern ears as a slash and burn policy:

> Let pent-up pond and water mill
> remember where their waters flowed,
> let the ax break the matted trees
> and fire burn the forest; in its barren splendor
> let a long gash be cut. (ll.160–64)

> I hear voices and distant sounds, the axe's noise . . .
> The wild beast flees; the doleful bird leaves its sweet nest . . .
> What do I see? A tall and crackling flame
> spills over the dry ruins of the conquered forest.
> The roaring fire is heard afar,
> black smoke eddies upward, piling cloud upon cloud.
> And only dead trunks, only ashes remain
> of what before was lovely green and freshness. (ll. 177–90)

But now that wild Nature is conquered, the process of introducing various commercial crops—Bello suggests the nonindigenous cultivates coffee, sugarcane, pear, and apple trees, along with native cacao plants—can begin:

> But the wild growth of savage, tangled plants
> gives way to fruitful plantings, that display
> their proud rows and orderly design . . .
> And under the weight of plenty, the farmer's due,
> makes vast storehouses creak and groan. (ll. 192–205)

Ironically, by bringing us back to the "vast storehouses," Bello has brought us back to the city, the necessary marketplace of the new economy. The problem with the idea of abandoning the evil of the cities for the healthy joys of farm life is that cities themselves are a product of agriculture. Around the time Bello was writing, so too was the Prussian agricultural economist Johann Heinrich von Thünen (1783–1850). Indeed, his primary text on the subject, still in print, was published in the same year as the "Ode." The fundamental principles of Thünen's model of agricultural land use are still used today. They can be summarized as $r = y\,(p-c-df)$, where the rental price of land (r) is controlled by yield per unit of land (y), market price (p), and production costs per unit of product (c), as well as the distance from the production point to the market (d) and the unit freight cost per unit of distance (f). As a practical matter, this means an agricultural division of labor based on the amount of land and personal interaction necessary to maximize profit gives rise to urban centers. Crafts, government, and commerce require little space but much interaction, and so gravitate toward densely populated urban centers, while activities that require large amounts of land and little interaction such as pastoralism gravitate toward cheaper land on the outer perimeters of the total land area.

Thünen's model implies exchange between various trading partners, and the archeological record shows that self-sufficiency has never been a viable form of agriculture, nor would it serve to further Bello's aim of agriculture as an economic motor for Venezuela. Around the world, the skeletal record shows ancient farmers who were unable to trade suffered the effects of poor diets—small size, thin bones, abscesses, dental caries, knobby joints, and other indications of deficient diets (Ofek 213). The reason for this is that humans need both protein and carbohydrates in their diet, and while hunter-gatherer societies find both of these in the same ecosystem, agriculture splits the human ecosystem. The limiting factor is the sheer quantity of biomass necessary to produce animal protein or fat (Diamond 169). Acquiring sufficient plant material for grazing animals requires constantly mobile pastoral husbandry, which is incompatible with sedentary agriculture, and so a division of labor is inevitable if a healthy human diet is to be maintained. The two final products, carbohydrates and protein, must, however, be exchanged among members of society, who also presumably exchange food for nonfood items as well, and a central market location is the most efficient means of doing this, for reasons of freight costs, storage, and all the other variables in Thünen's model. In the absence of such a market, simple hunting would produce better results at less effort than herding (Ofek 222), and without protein, agriculture alone could not provide a sufficiently diverse diet.

Conversely, the archaeological record shows that a breakdown in agriculture brings a concomitant dissolution of communities. A study of the Northern Anaszai of the Mesa Verde region of the American southwest from 901 AD to 1300 AD reveals that in periods of good precipitation (propitious for agriculture), Anasazi households formed communities and exchanged corn, while in periods of drought, communities dispersed (Kohler and Van West). "Stretches of adequate-to-abundant rainfall are characterized by village formation, whereas periods of extended or closely spaced droughts signal dispersion of households and the disappearance of villages" (Winterhalder 440). Additionally, there is a process of positive feedback between agricultural production and city formation. As cities grow, they need more food, which gives rise to greater agricultural production, in turn increasing the size of the cities, and so on. There were approximately fifty thousand people alive on the planet 100,000 years ago. At the dawn of agriculture, ten thousand years ago, there were roughly five million. From that point to the present, the population has gone from five million to over six billion, with no end in sight, barring famine producing climate change, war, or epidemic (Cavalli-Sforza 94–95). Most of this demographic growth, though a result of agriculture, is sited in urban centers.

In the following section of the "Ode," Bello brings up another interesting point regarding agriculture, one that goes to the root of the origins of agriculture and also to the competitive advantages enjoyed by the "torrid zones." He says,

> Dear God! Let not the Equator's farming folk
> sweat vainly; . . .
> Let not unseasonable rains
> ruin the tender crops; let not the pitiless tooth
> of gnawing insects devour them.
> Let not the savage storm destroy,
> or the tree's maternal sap
> dry up in summer's long and heated thirst. (ll. 206–23)

In short, he brings up that topic dearest to the hearts of farmers everywhere, the weather. One of the inexplicable facts of human agriculture, both cultivation of crops and husbandry, has been the question of why it began only ten thousand years ago and then spread so rapidly in so short a period of time. For more than 90 percent of their existence, anatomically modern humans managed to survive without agriculture. Why did it spring up independently in widely separated regions of the world at almost the same time (ten thousand years ago in the Near East, eight thousand years ago in China, and six thousand years ago in the New World)? As Bello points out, the limiting factor in agriculture is the climate, or more precisely an unstable climate, the one factor shared by both the Old and the New World. Therefore it is logical to consider the advent of a stable climate as the precipitating factor in the dawn of worldwide agriculture, and evidence from ice caps of Greenland and Antarctica confirms that the climate became stable enough for agriculture only during the *Holocene*, our current interglacial and concurrent with the age of agriculture (Dansgaard). The record tells us that over the last ten thousand years we have enjoyed an exceptionally stable climate in terms of variation in climate. This stability has reduced periods of drought, frequency and strength of storms, and, of course, swings in temperature, last and first frost dates, and so on, enabling agriculture to thrive.

After initially framing agriculture in moral terms, Bello now introduces the will of God. By answering possible objections to the climate-dependent nature of agriculture by appealing to a Higher Power, Bello carries this religious theme over to the question of the aftermath of the wars of liberation. The new republics themselves participate in the agricultural metaphor as they root and thrive, much like the plants that are to sustain them, all under the watchful eye of the Supreme Being who both frees them from foreign rule and provides them with propitious growth conditions:

> For you, supreme arbiter of fate,
> were pleased at long last to remove the yoke
> of foreign rule, and with your blessing
> to raise American man toward heaven,
> to make his freedom root and thrive.
> Bury accursed war in deep abyss,
> and, for fear of vengeful sword,
> let the distrustful farmer not desist
> from noble toil, that nourishes
> families and whole countries too . . .
> We have atoned enough for the savage conquest. (ll. 224–36)

This attempt to conflate the two levels of agriculture, the real and the metaphorical, both a part of nation building, have led some to argue that the term agriculture is a code word for the Roman Republic, especially given Bello's use of the *Georgics* as a model for his own composition. One can certainly make this case, but Cussen points out that there are two possible readings of Virgil and that Bello chose that of freedom for the new republics.

In the eighteenth century, European culture was torn between two worldviews—in one, power was centralized, symbolized by the figure of Augustus; in the other, freedom predominated and individuals sought to restore the values of Republican Rome and to develop the arts and sciences under freedom. Virgil's *Georgics* became the battleground for these conflicting worldviews. Depending on which aspects of Virgil one chose or omitted—whether Octavian's apotheosis in book 1 or the simple life in book 2—one was choosing monarchy or republic, obedience to established rules or free inquiry. In his final version of the *Georgics*, Bello has suppressed Augustus and tipped the balance on the side of freedom, the higher challenge, *agricultura* (126).

Cussen bases this on a reading of the progression in Bello's description of the transformations of the people of the region from the "happy tropic's folks" aided by "a slave's hand" of the colonial period (ll. 44–47), to the beginnings of an agricultural rebirth in the aftermath of war, "Oh agriculture, wetnurse of mankind" (ll. 173), and then on to the successful agricultural freedom of the future, led by "the Equator's farming folk" (ll. 206). This reading and Bello's progression in the poem are themselves agricultural metaphors in which the seeds of freedom are planted during the colonial period, following which they subsequently weather the storms of the independence movement, and then finally bear fruit in the postcolonial period, that glowing future that successful agriculture will bring to Venezuela. In the process, Man and Nature reverse their relative positions in terms of freedom and slavery. Initially, Nature is free and supplies Man's needs without cultivation. It is Man who is a slave to Nature. But by the post-independence period, however, Nature has become a slave to Man, who is now free thanks to his control over Nature. Man is now only dependent on the goodwill of God, necessary to supply him the proper growing conditions for both plants and republics, and in the propitious climate of the torrid zone the availability of these conditions seems to be a foregone conclusion.

On Bello's plan, mankind is also free from the worst of human nature, specifically the violence inherent in human nature that has so plagued the New World in the past:

> Send down an angel, angel of peace, to make
> The rude Spaniard forget his ancient tyranny, . . .
> Let the soldier-citizen put off
> the panoply of war; let the victory wreath
> hang on his country's altar,
> and glory be the only prize of merit.
> Then may my country see the longed-for day
> When peace will triumph:
> Peace, that fills the world
> with joy, serenity, and happiness. (ll. 250–74)

Near the end of the poem he reinforces the link between conquering both Nature and human nature through cultivation, of the soil in one case and the law in the other, but both linked to a method that yields freedom from both these natures by right thinking:

> Honor the fields, honor the simple life,
> and the farmer's frugal simplicity.
> Thus freedom will dwell in you forever, ambition will be restrained,
> law have its temple (ll. 281–84).

After listing the evils of human nature, including slavery, Spanish imperial rule, the vices of the city, and the wars of independence, Bello argues for a republican form of government, *agricultura*, and the rule of law, *la ley templo*, as a way to domesticate human nature. With an eye to what he had learned from the *Poema de Mío Cid*, especially the Cid's respect for the law in the last *Cantar* of the poem, when the Cid foregoes personal vengeance and instead places his faith in the court system, he hopes that the "Ode" can also establish precedents for civic virtue and the rule of law.

Thus for Bello agriculture in the tropics comes to symbolize the complete remaking of the landscape: physically, morally, politically, and psychologically. Physically, wild nature will be domesticated and order restored to the countryside,

> but the wild growth of savage, tangled plants
> gives way to fruitful plantings, that display
> their proud rows and orderly design (ll. 192-94).

As people flee the vices of the cities for the freedom of the countryside, the urban landscape will also change for the better. And this demographic shift will have the added benefit of producing a seismic shift in the psychic landscape, for in the process human nature will also be domesticated, with the moral virtues of the country replacing the vices of the city. The bitter wounds of war will be healed and a productive economy formed by hardworking moral citizens, who will form the rootstock of future generations of Venezuelan citizens living in a free and prosperous republic.

The last few lines of the poem, however, seem to hearken back to a heroic and martial age, the epic moment of the founding of the new nations:

> Those who come after you will imitate you eagerly,
> adding new names to those whose fame
> they now acclaim. For they will say, "Sons, sons
> are these of men who won the Andes' heights;
> those who in Boyacá, and on Maipo's sands,
> and in Junín, and Apurima's glorious field,
> humbled in victory the lion of Spain." (ll. 288–94)

Although the founding hero is a necessary part of the national epic—Aeneas was a Trojan of scrupulous piety who traveled to Italy where he became the ancestor of the Romans, and El Cid, the hero of the

Spanish national epic, was equally pious and honorable—the seeming contradiction in Bello's "Ode" between a call to domestic peace through domestication and a final tribute to military glory is apparent. It appears Bello was clear on the nature of human nature, believing violence is innate in humans but susceptible to behavioral inhibition, and indeed this is the case. Although he was well acquainted with Locke's argument in *An Essay Concerning Human* that we are born with "minds like white paper, devoid of ideas" (bk. 2, chap. 1, p. 26), Bello believed all men were born with an "innate sense of beauty which is in every man" (*Obras* vol. 9, 451, qtd. in Caldera 74). This innate sense of beauty insures that "every new facet revealed to him in the ideal model of beauty thrills the human heart, created to admire and feel it" (*Obras* vol. 8, 307, qtd. in Calder 74) but that beauty is expressed "in forms which are peculiar to each country and century different ways" (*Obras* vol. 11, 281, qtd. in Caldera 74). On this view, beauty moves Man and is variable as a function of time and place. Therefore a new century can bring new ideas of the beautiful, so a vision of a cultivated land and people can replace the images of a wild land and people as an aesthetic ideal. And since art serves to produce this aesthetic response, for Bello the "Ode" makes sense as a vehicle through which to cultivate a new aesthetic for a new republic, indeed, for a New World in a new century. Before one rejects Bello's epic call to change the natural, agricultural, political, and moral landscape of Venezuela as a failed enterprise at best, it is worth noting that Bello never returned to Venezuela to implement his plan, but went instead to Chile, where he lived out his remaining years. And while Venezuela has enjoyed only brief periods of democracy, usually under literary figures such as Rómulo Gallegos (president for nine months in 1948) and Rafael Caldera (president, 1969–74, 1994–99), a Bello scholar as well, Chile promulgated Bello's *Código Civil* (Civil code) into law in 1855, and is today a prosperous democracy with a strong agricultural sector. At least in Chile, then, Bello's repainting of the Latin American landscape has indeed born fruit.

Chapter 5

"I Do Not Weep for Camaguey"

Gertrudis Gómez de Avellaneda's Nineteenth-Century Cuban Landscape

Beatriz Rivera-Barnes

"And also there are trees of a thousand kinds and all with their own kinds of fruit and all smell so that it is a marvel. I am the most sorrowful man in the world, not being acquainted with them," Columbus wrote in his journal upon reaching the island that was to become Cuba (Dunn and Kelley 105). For a few weeks, nature in the New World remained silent. Only Columbus spoke. He took possession of the islands for the Spanish crown, he named them, and he gave Spanish names to rivers and to capes, leaving other elements of the natural environment such as trees, plants, flowers, and fruit momentarily unnamed because he could not recognize them. José Martí's "Yo sé los nombres extraños/de la yerbas y las flores" (58) [I know the strange names/of the grasses and the flowers] is still in the very distant, quasi-impossible future.

But as the days passed, the admiral sailed from one island to the other, and the landscape became more familiar. Six weeks into the first voyage there is a total reversal in Columbus's attitude to nature. At this point, nature ceases to be silent in order to be silenced; the only sound is that of speculation. "The forest becomes a fleet. The virgin timber of the American woods is already raw material, merchandise for the mother country, a source of incalculable riches and naval might" (Gerbi 17–18). From foreign and inscrutable to speculative and Spanish, from manifold to binary, the environment is either similar to that of Castile in the month of April or radically different, just so the venture capitalists back home (the Spanish crown) could feel better about agreeing to underwrite this journey. The year was 1492, only the beginning.

One year later, Michele da Cuneo, who accompanied Columbus on his second voyage, is methodically tasting and testing the plants and the fruits of the New World, so as to determine value. For Gerbi, this was the "first step toward a methodically empirical investigation, that in Oviedo was to attain a high degree of scientific seriousness" (32). Just as absorbed as Michele da Cuneo in utilitarian concerns, Oviedo, however, only describes and enumerates the multitude of trees and flowers, he does not name them because "not even the Indians, let alone the Christians, know what their names are" (qtd. in Gerbi 291). Either the natives really did not know, which is doubtful, or at this early stage there is already an obvious inattention and indifference to indigenous crops and nomenclature. European natural history will soon be put in charge of classifying and naming whatever original flora remains in this natural environment that the discoverers and the conquerors will transform so very rapidly.

The impact of the Europeans on the Cuban landscape was sudden and radical. It led to the demise of the native socioeconomic infrastructure. The result is an erasure of native knowledge as well as a loss of native crops, strange vegetables that the Spanish were mostly reluctant to adopt, except perhaps manioc. Ronald Peterson writes that as early as 1520, the environment of southern Hispaniola and parts of Cuba was a wreck. "As the *conucos* [village/farms in which the Arawak people lived] were abandoned, secondary weeds arose, first as grasses and ground cover, and finally sometimes as citrus forests. Moreover, farm animals were allowed free range and multiplied by feeding on abandoned roots and the succession plants. Overgrazing was common with its predictable erosion" (148). Both the farm animals and the citrus plants were imported from Europe, whereas banana, yams, and sugarcane came from Africa, by way of the Canary Islands.

Fast-forward: it is 1841, the nineteenth-century world of commerce and industry, and a novel titled *Sab*, written by Cuban-born Gertrudis Gómez de Avellaneda, is published in Spain. Much like the earliest American naturalists such as da Cuneo, Vespucci and Oviedo, Avellaneda enumerates,

. . . golondrinas . . . el verde papagayo . . . el cao . . . el carpintero real . . . la alegre guacamaya, el ligero tomeguín, la tornasolada mariposa . . . en las ramas del tamarindo . . . del mango . . . (102–3). [swallows,

parrots, black birds, woodpeckers, macaws, etc. on the branches of the tamarind, of the mango . . .]
. . . cambutera . . . balsamina . . . astronomía . . . la azucena y la rosa, la clavellina y el jasmín, la modesta violeta y el orgulloso girasol . . . la variable malvarrosa, la aleluya . . . y la pasionaria (144). [Morning glory, jasmine, astromelia, lily, rose, pink, violet, sunflower, hollyhock, wood sorrel, passion flower.]

By the mid-1800s, the trees, birds, grasses, and flowers all have names, but the gaze has not changed; it is utilitarian, greedy, and always eager to place a monetary value. There is no innocence, only evaluation. Avellaneda's handsome young man on horseback in the picturesque countryside may stop repeatedly to contemplate the beauty before his eyes, the palm trees and the *ceiba*, but the pastoral scene is short lived. "A la verdad, era harto probable que sus repetidas detenciones sólo tuvieran por objeto admirar más a su sabor los campos fertilísimos" (102).

A la verdad, in truth, there is disjunction here; *a la verdad* could very well suggest that the Edenic opening scene was not so much a non-truth, but a wishful truth. Avellaneda is warning the readers that the young man could simply be stopping to contemplate the landscape only to get a better sense of the quality of the fields. *Fertilísimos*, most fertile, echoes Dr. Nicolò Scillacio's impressions of awe and amazement in his 1494 epistle. "The seeds never come to any harm . . . for the soil rejoices . . . and never reject anything that you throw in it; it accepts nothing without giving it back more abundantly and with great increase. And the harvest is sufficient for twenty years!" (qtd. in Gerbi 28–29). One small problem is that Scillacio never set foot in the Americas!

I propose that this idea of endless fertility, of the impossibility of future scarcity, that later morphed into a romantic, anthropocentric vision of the American natural world, is at the root of a colonial myth of Eden that has not only silenced and damaged the Caribbean landscape but has also interred a violent and unjust history that equally contributed to the degradation of this landscape. This is a vicious circle of greed and destruction taken to the twenty-first century. The idea of fertility itself leads to forgetfulness and inattention, in the sense that there was little or no environmental concern for anything that produced "huge heaps" and "ceaseless income" (ibid.). It would be there forever, for the giving, and for the taking. The result is a landscape that has been permanently altered, therefore *unhomed*, or alienated, and also degraded.

A Victim of Her Epoch

Florinda Álzaga believes that Avellaneda was a victim of her own times, and this could very well be, for a plurality of contradictory voices emerge from her text (14). However, the idiosyncratic circumstances of Avellaneda's birth could very well explain these contradictory voices. The daughter of a Spanish aristocrat and of a *criolla*, Avellaneda was both the colonizer and the colonized. Just like her protagonist, Carlota, Avellaneda was the colonizer for all the obvious reasons, for she was the privileged daughter of the slaveholding gentry; and she was the colonized because she was a *criolla*, a Cuban (although there was not yet a Cuban nationality per se), a woman, and a child of Cuba, of a subordinated people. Although the *criollos* had their own cultural traditions and history, they were handed another tradition and another history, that of a faraway motherland. During Avellaneda's youth, that faraway motherland, Spain, was struggling with her own internal problems that had little to do with life in provincial Camaguey, Cuba. Napoleon had been ousted, a liberal constitution had been written, and soon, all the American colonies would declare their independence from Spain, one after the other, except Cuba and Puerto Rico, which would remain Spanish colonies for another eighty years or so. With the Spanish history and drama being imposed on the *criollos*, their own history, their *criollo* history, was repressed. Consequently, when Avellaneda left for Spain at a relatively young age, this repressed history was buried in the psyche and replaced by a more immediate layer of Spanish history. It is likely that Avellaneda soon began to think like a Spaniard and construct the Cuban environment just as a Spaniard would, in terms of natural landscape, virgin, untouched, most fertile.

The relationship between Spain and the colonies, in this case Cuba, resembled that of the capitalist and the working class. For one, Cuba was Spain's private property, and Spain was making a profit not only on the land and its raw materials but also on the labor of the *criollos* and the natives. As a result, the life of the *criollo* was in itself estranged; he was much like the small landed proprietor Marx referred to when he wrote, "The small landed proprietor working on his own account stands to the big landowner in the same relation as an artisan possessing his own tool to the factory owner. Small property in land has become a mere instrument of labor" (61). The same applies for the relationship between the *criollos* and the natives or the slaves, in this case, the *criollos* being the capitalists.

Well intentioned, these contradictory voices speak for the landscape, but they misunderstand it, just as they speak for the slave and undermine him. In fact, the slave and the land are often interchangeable. While there is a constant effort to have consideration for the natural world and for the slave, they are nonetheless used and discarded, valued and subsequently destroyed. There is concern for them; indeed, an innocent girl does not hesitate to step forward and demand that all slaves be manumitted. But unfortunately this stepping forward does not change anything because the girl understands nature about as much as she understands slaves. Little does it matter if the harm she does was unintentional. According to the critic Hugh Harter, Sab, the protagonist, the slave, is a melancholy neurasthenic, and Carlota, his beloved, seems to us today like a sentimental schoolgirl "either too shortsighted or too short-witted to see the reality before her eyes. Oblivious to the overpowering passion she has inspired in Sab . . . She is, by today's standards, insipid, shallow, and, in her emotional myopia, inconsiderate of the needs and feelings of those around her. She was not created in our day, however" (128). In this sense both Sab and Carlota are also victims of their epoch.

The result is that the mouthpiece for slaves and nature, Carlota, could very be a study of inattention, of good intentions that pave the way to hell. From these good intentions emerge a Babel of voices all trying to have the last word, Spanish, African, Indian, colonizer, colonized, *criollo*, landed gentry, oppressor, oppressed, as well as virgin landscape, acculturated landscape, degraded landscape, for the Cuban landscape is character in this text.

Avellaneda was not in Cuba when she wrote *Sab*. She was in Spain and clinging on to an idea or a memory of Cuba. She was born in Cuba in 1814, but she left when she was twenty years old, with no real intention of ever returning. In this sense, Avellaneda was much like Dr. Nicolò Scillacio, who was in awe of nature in a faraway New World. On the other hand, Avellaneda does know the strange names of the grasses and the flowers and the Cuban-ness of the landscape she left behind. "No solo desfilan por el libro descripciones bellas y apacibles. También surge la naturaleza cubana con toda la fuerza iracunda de una de esas tempestades" (Álzaga 98). [Not only is the book rife with beautiful and peaceful scenes. There is also the Cuban natural world with all the irate force of one of those storms.] Avellaneda calls these harbingers of storms symptoms of the tempest, very familiar to all the Cubans. "Estos síntomas de tempestad, conocidos de todos los cubanos" (131). These symptoms include suffocating heat, total stillness, no breeze, an atmosphere charged with electricity, dark gray clouds, the fearful silence of nature, bands of vultures, and even dogs that sense the imminent rage of nature (130–31).

Alternating between quietude and rage, nature in Avellaneda's text echoes human emotions. "La naturaleza se embellece con la presencia del objecto que se ama y éste se embellece con la naturaleza" (149). [Nature is enhanced by the presence of the beloved just as the beloved is embellished by nature.] Avellaneda also establishes a parallel between the voice of the beloved and the whispering of the branches of the trees in the breeze. In this particular case the beloved is a foreigner. Enrique Otway is embellishing nature and, in turn, being embellished by nature. The foreigner—in Carlota's eyes who see nothing but the foreigner—is also he who never experienced this immense, powerful life until he reached Cuba, and who should never search for this vitality in other lands because it does not exist elsewhere.

Again, this novel was not written in our times, and it constantly falls victim to its own times, thus the contradictions. Kirkpatrick points out that "the fact that she [Avellaneda] wrote the first Hispanic antislavery novel as a vehicle for an oblique feminist protest points to something less predictable: Gómez de Avellaneda found it easier to express abolitionist sentiments . . . than to broach directly the issues of sexual inequality" (158). Kirkpatrick then concludes that Avellaneda was more fearful of openly representing female rebelliousness than she was of acknowledging the justice of Sab's anger with her own class and race.

The Foreigner

The relationship of Spain with the Anglo-Saxon world, first England and then the United States—the new foreigners—also comes into play, particularly in regard to Cuba's natural resources. Initially, the Spaniards were the foreigners—they came, they named, they conquered, and they unhomed the natives—but when the British became the intruders in the seventeenth century, the Spaniards were suddenly *less* foreign, just as imported crops such as bananas and sugarcane had by then become an integral part of the landscape.

This much said, it should not come as a surprise that the young man on horseback in the beginning of the novel has blue eyes and golden hair. This means he cannot possibly be from *here*, here being the torrid zone. No, the brutal sun of the torrid zone would never have allowed for such delicate white skin, such white features. The foreigner in Avellaneda's text who comes to alienate all those who approach him is of British origin, but he came to Cuba by way of the United States. At this point, however, the harm has already been done. Avellaneda is not announcing what is to come; everything has already happened.

It is this same young man who stops to contemplate the late afternoon rays of sunlight that give the virgin fields (*"campos vírgenes"*) of that young natural world (*"joven naturaleza"*) a melancholy hue (102). Obviously these are not virgin fields, for these are sugarcane fields, and sugarcane is not even native to Cuba. It was Columbus who introduced sugarcane to the Indies in 1493. From that point on, sugar cultivation spread rapidly and the first shipments back to Spain occurred in 1516 (Petersen 142). Coincidentally, both sugarcane and slaves are transplants, imported from Africa.

As early as the 1650s, North Americans began to consume tropical sugar from the Caribbean. Consequently, in Avellaneda's world, sugarcane was an old crop that had not only shaped Cuban society but had already transformed the Cuban landscape as well. Richard Tucker points out that in many locations, primary forest was cleared expressly so as to plant cane. In other instances, cane replaced native field crops and pastures. "Where cane grew, the cornucopia of flora and fauna was eliminated, replaced by wide acreage of only one species" (8). Moreover, the cultivation of sugarcane necessitated a transport system that further impacted the natural environment. After 1812, U.S. investments in Cuban sugarcane expanded, only to peak around the time that *Sab* was published.

Antonio Benítez-Rojo points out that there were periods in the nineteenth century in which the annual increase in sugar production was 25 percent. "The ecological cost, however, cannot be measured in money. Perhaps one could make a very general estimate of the wood that was lost, but how can one put a value on the irrecoverable disappearance of plant and animal species, the quick evaporation of the soil's moisture to the point of sterility?" (41)

Writing about the Cuba she left behind, Avellaneda sees nothing but fertility. Moreover, Avellaneda is a romantic, and consequently the virgin fields she is describing belong more to an emotional geography than to a factual one and coincide with the interiority of the characters. If they are happily in love, nature reciprocates; if they are not, nature reciprocates as well. This is the Cuba Avellaneda remembers while in Spain, a Cuba of virgin soil, a young natural world. Nonetheless, the alienating, foreign economic presence is already in this text that pleads for a natural landscape that no longer exists.

But perhaps Avellaneda did sense that an untouched natural world was one of her creation when she wrote in an 1842 poem "Despedida a la Señora Da D. G. C. de V" that the mountains, the forests, and the fields no longer exist (for her).

Bosques espesos, do jamás penetra;
La sabanas de inmensos horizontes,
No existen para mí (qtd. in Álzaga 100).

This could very well be Avellaneda's way of letting go of a Cuba that has sold itself to the foreigner, the same foreigner who is portrayed in the novel *Sab* as having no qualms about asking the country fellow (another foreigner), "Dice Ud. Que pertenecen al Señor de B—todas estas tierras?" (Did you say that Señor de B—owns all of this land?) he asks. "Parecen muy feraces" (They appear to be very fertile). "Esta finca debe producer mucho a su dueño?" (This farm must bring its owner a good income?) he suggests (105–6). At this point both Señor de B— and his land are being evaluated as commodities by this foreigner, this capitalist. Without this newcomer, however, Señor de B— is the capitalist, the slave-holding landed gentry.

The country fellow, who is a native in the other foreigner's eyes, explains that there was a time when this plantation produced far more than now, "dice mil arrobas de azúcar cada año, porque entonces mas de cien negros trabajaban en sus cañaverales" (106). [some three hundred thousand pounds of sugar every year, because then more than a hundred blacks worked in the cane fields (Scott 29).]

The foreigner's reaction is one of studied concern over the difficult life of a plantation slave. The country fellow agrees that it is truly a terrible life and expatiates on the subject. Here, Avellaneda is in fact describing alienation just as she describes the landscape, in a romantic way. The country fellow expresses how the sun burns the slave's skin, the slave who works all morning without rest and whose only pleasure in life consists of two hours of sleep every night and a very frugal meal. "Cuando la noche viene . . . el esclavo va a regar con su sudor y con sus lágrimas al recinto donde la noche no tiene sombras" (106). [When night comes . . . the slave with his sweat and tears waters the place where night has no shadows.]

The country fellow concludes this diatribe by exclaiming, "¡Ah! sí; es un cruel espectáculo la vista de la humanidad degradada, de hombres convertidos en brutos, que llevan en su frente la marca de la esclavitud y en su alma la desesperación del infierno" (106). [Oh, yes! The sight of this degraded humanity, where men become mere brutes, is a cruel spectacle. These are men whose brows are seared with the mark of slavery just as their souls are branded with the desperation of hell (Scott 29–30).] Estrangement and alienation are continually suggested with words and expressions such as degraded humanity, brutes, cruel, seared, branded, desperation, and hell. Marx affirms that when the worker sinks to the level of a commodity, he becomes the most wretched of commodities and begins to confront the product of his labor as something alien. Labor, in turn, appears "as a loss of reality for the workers; objectification as loss of the object and object-bondage; appropriation as estrangement, as alienation" (71). Consequently, the laborer denies himself, feels unhappy, coerced, and begins to mortify his body and torture his mind. "He is at home when he is not working, and when he is working he is not at home" (74). His labor, however, defines him, but he denies that definition. The characters in Avellaneda's text, including the landscape, all represent different stages of alienation.

The foreigner, Enrique Otway, represents the mercantile world (Servera 66–67); Sab and sugarcane are the transplants, both shaping and degrading the environment; and Carlota, the *criolla*, yet another intruder, is the inattention that also leads to destruction of human life and of natural environments.

Eve without the Apple Tree

Harter suggests that Carlota is "another aspect of la Avellaneda herself, the innocent and beautiful young Cuban girl, untouched and untainted by the flesh or the practical realities of the world, Eve without the apple tree" (127). In fact, Carlota's relationship with the foreigner, Enrique, mirrors the British–U.S.–Cuban relations in the nineteenth century that had everything to do with the exploitation of slaves and the cultivation of sugarcane, its peak, and its downfall.

"Sabido es que las riquezas de Cuba atraen en todo tiempo innumerables extranjeros" (119). [It is well known that Cuba's riches attract many foreigners.] One of these foreigners was George Otway, Enrique's father. It was George Otway who decided that Carlota, the heiress, would be a brilliant match for his son. Carlota's family, however, was not of the same opinion. Little did it matter if the elder Otway was now a Roman Catholic; he had once belonged to another religion and was therefore called a "heretic." Of course, Carlota loved Enrique all the more when her family opposed the marriage.

So Carlota fell gravely ill with suffering and despair, and her father gave in, to the family's great dismay. Subsequently, Carlota's uncle changed his last will and testament in favor of other nieces and nephews in order to take away from Carlota all hope of her inheritance. For Enrique's father, this meant that Carlota, the commodity, was no longer the woman he wanted for his son. If Enrique arrives unexpectedly in the beginning of the story, it is to determine whether or not Carlota is still sufficiently rich. This is why he is assaying the fertility of the fields.

Obviously Carlota feels an odd feeling of discomfort, and her unease is a harbinger of the unhomely moment into which Enrique will soon catapult her, simply by not loving her the way she thinks she needs to be loved. In this case, the man and the woman are taking on the roles of the master and the slave. However, the feminist critic Susan Kirkpatrick believes that Otway's case presents "an interesting reversal of male Romantic narratives, his role is that of object—the a priori object of feminine desire. As if his desirability were a universal given. Carlota and Teresa are already both in love with him when the novel opens" (148). In this case, Enrique is a commodity as well, a sexual commodity.

Carlota has just begun to experience a moment of terror. She will soon be alienated by her unrequited love for Enrique. Kirkpatrick would describe this moment as "the fall from the illusions of the passionate imagination to the bitter knowledge of alienating reality" (149). Consequently, it is not by accident that Enrique is a blue-eyed foreigner whose gaze *alienates* or unhomes everyone it falls on, whether Spanish-born, *Criollo*, Black, *Mulatto*, or *Indio*. Homi Bhabha writes that the *unhomeliness* is the condition of extraterritorial and cross-cultural initiations:

> The unhomely moment creeps upon you stealthily as your own shadow and suddenly you find yourself with Henry James's Isabel Archer, in *The Portrait of a Lady*, taking the measure of your dwelling in a state of 'incredulous terror.' And it is at this point that the world first shrinks for Isabel and then expands enormously. As she struggles to survive the fathomless waters, the rushing torrents, James introduces us to the unhomeliness inherent in that rite of extra-territorial and cross-cultural initiation. The recesses of the domestic space become sites for history's most intricate invasions. In that displacement, the borders between home and world become confused. (9)

In Avellaneda's text, the shrinking and the expanding announce Enrique's *unhoming* of all the other characters and even of the natural world before him, a natural world that, coincidentally, almost kills him twice. This is a step toward Homi Bhabha's *beyond*. "It captures something of the estranging sense of the relocation of the home and the world—the unhomeliness . . . To be unhomed is not to be homeless" (9). Consequently, it is not that Enrique feels no love for Carlota, but his feelings of love or tenderness are being counterbalanced by another passion: greed (69). Enrique remonstrates with himself for "no ser bastante codicioso para sacrificar su amor a su interés, o bastante generoso para posponer su conveniencia a su amor" (134). [being neither sufficiently covetous to sacrifice love to self gain nor sufficiently generous to defer his personal advantages to his love (Scott 50).]

Likewise, it is not so much that Carlota feels no love for Sab or for the Cuban landscape, but her feelings of love and tenderness are also being counterbalanced by another passion, the passion for the intruder-foreigner, and what this intruder has to give. This too is a form of greed. In this sense there are no victims; like the woman, the landscape was there for the taking, or perhaps these are all victims of their epoch.

Nature Unhomed

Just as Sab gazes into the innermost recesses of his rival's heart, the storm breaks. Nature has been so subjugated that it now mirrors human emotion. Sab feels hatred, and the storm breaks. Enrique's horse bolts, causing Enrique to fall and be hurt, and it rains harder. Suddenly, Sab is given the opportunity to kill Enrique. The slave can now decide to kill the master. The slave decides against it, for the love of a white woman.

When they return to the plantation the next day, Sab becomes a hero for having saved Enrique's life and is instantly granted freedom by Carlota. But even this manumission unhomes him, as if it were too late, just as it is too late for the landscape; both have been used to the point of degradation. "Su mirada era triste y tranquila, y serio y melancólico su aspecto" (140). [His gaze was sad and calm and his appearance serious and melancholy (Scott 53).] Susan Kirkpatrick points out that Avellaneda "colonized the mulatto slave's subjectivity to suit her own purpose when she represented him as willing to sacrifice both his freedom and his people to his impossible love for a white woman."

This explains why the words against slavery are sentimental, illusory, and impractical. "¡Pobres infelices!" Carlota exclaims (146). [Poor unfortunate souls!] "Cuando yo sea la esposa de Enrique . . . ningún infeliz respirará a mi lado el aire emponzoñado de la esclavitud. Daremos libertad a todos nuestros negros. ¿Qué importa ser menos ricos? ¿Seremos por eso menos dichosos?" (146). [When I am Enrique's wife . . . no unhappy soul around me will breathe the poisonous air of slavery. We will give all our blacks their freedom. What does it matter to be less wealthy? Will we be any less happy because of it? (Scott 57)]

In this monologue, not only is Carlota feeling sorry for the slaves, but she is also calling for their manumission, and renouncing wealth.

These are all good, progressive feelings that suggest that Carlota can somehow see clearly, but somehow they point to her blindness as well. She is totally oblivious of how her lifestyle depends on slaves, wealth, and plantations, as well as of Enrique's financial concerns, of his conditional love for her, and also of Sab's suffering. Her inattention that unhomes Sab causes Sab to curse nature before he realizes that nature is no less the slave's mother than the white man's (206). Nature, in fact, has been unhomed, defiled, and these characters are a portrait of this unhoming of nature.

This is a world full of good intentions that produce an uncanny effect. Both Sab and Carlota seem to have been robbed of their eyes; they see, but they do not see. Freud quotes E. Jentsch, who affirms that one of the surest devices for producing this effect is to leave a "reader wondering whether a particular figure is a real person or an automaton" (135). Freud then explains that with this observation Jentsch is referring to Hoffmann's story, "The Sandman." In the novel *Sab*, Enrique Otway could very well play the part of the sandman from the very beginning. He throws sand in Sab's eyes as well as in Carlota's. In Carlotas's eyes for all the obvious reasons, love makes her blind. She also appears unreal at times, a crying doll of sorts. When it comes to Sab, Enrique plays the role of the sandman in a more subtle way. First, he prevents Sab from seeing himself as a person of value. Then, more importantly, the jealousy Enrique arouses in Sab, the sexual jealousy—since Enrique is *he* who will ultimately possess Carlota, the angel of heaven—renders Sab all the more blinder in his passion. Enrique, in turn, is just as blind, for he cannot see beyond personal gain. In this case, it is his father, George, who has played the part of the sandman, by not allowing Enrique to see value anywhere but in riches. The uncanny effect here is now being produced by each character possibly being another or any other character's double. Carlota and Sab are just as blindly in love. Carlota and Enrique both see each other as commodities. Carlota and Teresa, in turn, represent the shallow and the profound, the *said* and the *unsaid*, the virgin and the ravaged landscape; they are recurring counterparts.

Coincidentally, Sab is officially declared a free man just as he comes into the lottery money. Freud points out that the uncanny effect arises with the double, as well as when "the boundary between fantasy and reality is blurred, when we are faced with the reality of something that we have until now considered imaginary, when a symbol takes on the full function and significance of what it symbolizes . . . This is at the root of much that is uncanny about magical practices" (150–51). His entire life, Sab fantasized about freedom and wealth, and the moment they are granted, he pushes them away; they scare him. Freedom and wealth belong to the realm of the imagination; Sab is more at home in his slave state. The harm has been done to Sab just as it has been done to the landscape. The native crops are gone, and sugar, the intruder, is Cuban; it is difficult or impossible to imagine Cuba without sugar. Even the intruder Spain was replaced by another intruder, thus making Spain *homelier*, an uncanny effect.

"CUBA, MI AMOR, TE AMARRARON AL POTRO" (NERUDA, CANTO 146) [CUBA, MY LOVE, THEY TIED YOU TO THE RACK]

In their excursion into the Cuban countryside, the protagonists—Sab, Carlota, Enrique, Don Carlos, Teresa, and Carlota's siblings—encounter Martina, a descendant of the Indian race, "aquella raza desventurada" (169) [that unfortunate race]. Martina happens to be a prophet, a seer. One of her prophecies has to do with the future of the oppressed races of Cuba. "La tierra que fue regada con sangre una vez lo será aún otra: los descendientes de los opresores serán oprimidos, y los hombres negros serán los terribles vengadores de los hombres cobrizos" (169). [The Earth which once was drenched in blood will be so again: the descendants of the oppressors will be themselves oppressed, and black men will be the terrible avengers of those of copper color (Scott 73).]

Instantly, Carlota weeps, and Enrique makes fun of her tears, for how could she possibly weep over a story that possibly never existed, except in that woman's imagination? "No, Enrique," Carlota retorts. "No lloro por Camaguey ni sé si existió realmente" (169). [I do not weep for Camaguey nor do I know if he ever really existed.] With tear-filled eyes, Carlota explains that whether or not a cacique named Camaguey ever existed, she is nonetheless weeping for is a past that is no more, a time when the "unfortunate people" were the peaceful owners of this virgin soil where everyone lived in happiness, a virgin soil that did not need to be watered with the sweat of slaves to be productive. Unintentionally, Carlota is attempting to convey a form of colonial oppression or a time when oppression did not exist. She does suggest, however, that it is possible that this time never really existed. The ecofeminist Andy Smith argues that "most forms of oppression did not exist in most native societies prior to colonization" (22). In this instance, Carlota is being less dogmatic than Smith who adds that with colonization "begins the domination of women and the domination of nature" (ibid.). However, in light of Smith's text, it could be argued that if Carlota takes this stance it is because sexism is Carlota's primary form of oppression, not colonization, although Carlota does feel more at home expressing colonial oppression, never sexist oppression. What Carlota is describing is a paradise lost, or a lost home, and she appears to be well aware of it. This primitive lost home is precisely the place she longs for, and the mere thought of it makes her both fearful and sad. But why would home arouse these negative feelings in her? Freud writes that "the uncanny is that species of the frightening that goes back to what was once well known and had long been familiar" (124). He then goes on to explain under what conditions the familiar can become uncanny and frightening. For example, once Don Carlos is through acquainting Enrique with all the property he owns, Enrique is surprised to find the low value of his holdings, and his attitude toward Carlota changes dramatically, so much so that Carlota begins to feel that Enrique is keeping something from her. Because of this, the countryside, which seemed so homely and familiar the day before, begins to make her sad, and she cannot explain why. This melancholy state, in turn, makes her blinder. In her blindness she speaks like an automaton. She is so blind as to tell Teresa that she cannot possibly understand what she (Carlota) is going through, for Teresa has never loved. After this incident, Carlota cries herself to sleep. The oh-so-familiar sandman has made his rounds again.

Likewise, Sab speaks like an automaton when in the throes of indignation. Then slowly he comes to the realization that nature is no less the mother of the blacks than of the whites. Human society, however, has not listened to nature, who considers all men brothers. "Imbécil sociedad," Sab concludes, "que nos has reducido a la necesidad de aborrecerla, y fundar nuestra dicha en su total ruina!" (133). [Idiotic society, which has reduced us [blacks] to the necessity of hating it and of founding our happiness on its total destruction! (Scott 97).] From indignation to clarity and back to indignation, Sab becomes blind once again. It is unclear at this point whether Avellaneda is protesting against the horrors of slavery or describing the pangs of passionate, unrequited love:

> ¡Mi vida! ¿sabeís vos lo que es mi vida? . . . No tengo tampoco na patria que defender, —porque los esclavos no tienen patria; —no tengo deberes que cumplir, porque los deberes del esclavo son los deberes de la bestia de carga . . . Si al menos los hombres blancos, que desechan de sus sociedades al que nació teñida la tez de un color diferente, le dejase tranquilo en sus bosques, allá tendría patria y amores . . . porque amaría a una mujer de su color . . . Pero ¡ah! Al negro se rehúsa lo que es concedido a las bestias feroces (145).

[My life! Do you realize what my life is? . . . I don't even have a country to defend, because slaves don't have a country; I don't have responsibilities, because the duties of a slave are that of a beast of burden . . . If the white man had at least left those born with dark skin in their woods, there, they would have loved a woman of their own color . . . But no, the black man does not even have the privileges given to wild animals (Scott 107).]

In this monologue, Sab could very well be Avellaneda's double. Avellaneda began writing the novel in Bordeaux, shortly after having left Cuba, and finished it in Galicia, "apparently as a means of passing the time in a period which was a difficult one for her" (Harter 125). She has left home (Cuba) behind to come and live in the mother country, which was supposed to be the real home in the first place. But the departure from Cuba, however, turns Cuba into a lost home and consequently renders Spain *unhomely*. Like Sab, Avellaneda has no country. Like Sab, she has not the privileges given to wild animals because at that moment in time, because society is coming between her and the man she loves (Ricafort). This marriage did not take place, for her stepfather refused to give her inheritance. With this broken engagement, perhaps Avellaneda feels that she will never love or be loved again.

Sab, too, feels the same way when he utters, "Ninguna mujer puede amarme" (146). [No woman can love me.] What he is in fact saying is that no "white" woman can love him. But he is wrong. Suddenly Teresa declares herself to be that woman who will love him. Sab's reaction is, "¡Tú me prodigarías consuelos cuando ella suspirasede placer en brazos de un amante!" (147). [You would console me when she is sighing with pleasure in a lover's arms!] It is this jealousy that will kill him, for Sab dies at the same hour that Enrique and Carlota receive their nuptial blessing. "Five years later, the romantic heroine is a tearful and unhappy middle class wife, suffocated in a mercantile and speculative atmosphere that has destroyed all her youthful illusions . . . romanticism has given way to realism" (Harter 134–35). Normally, it is the unknown that should be frightening, but what could possibly be more familiar—or less threatening—than this middle class couple?

By taking into consideration the different meanings of the word *homely*, Freud points out how the term becomes increasingly ambivalent "until it finally merges with its antonym *unheimlich*. The uncanny (*das umheimliche* [the unhomely]) is in some way a species of the familiar (*das heimliche*, the homely)" (134). This paradox, however, does not express a tautology. Rather, this slipping and sliding of meaning suggests the identity of a difference and the difference of an identity. The terms never fuse, they remain apart, and this being apart allows them to come in contact with each other at different moments in time. Unhomely is the way of being at home in the world, and also at home, in privacy. Homely is the way of not being at home in the world.

The result is sheer terror and anxiety; this homely couple, Enrique and Carlota, one a species of the other, two intruders who have become natives living in the interstitial immediacy of the "post," of the future, much like sugarcane. This is the aftermath that *homes* the past. Enrique and Carlota have apparently arrived there unharmed. They are still alive. The only problem is that Carlota is unhappy, but then again, she was always unhappy; she could very well have a pattern of suffering. This is the virgin who yearned for the virgin soil of Cuba, who is a virgin no more, and whose virginity cost Sab his life. Perhaps this is her nature, and perhaps indeed this angel of heaven is also a weeping diabolical doll that brings death and destruction to those who love her, and wealth to those who do not. The only time Carlota admits that she is happy is after she has lost her father, her brother, Teresa, and Sab. She asks Enrique, "¿Qué son todos al lado de tu amor?" (178). [What are all of them compared to your love?] This was the future. Carlota did not weep for Camaguey nor did she know if he ever existed. Never having been acquainted with Camaguey, Carlota forgot, and because she forgot about this cacique whose name and the landscape are the same, I will take liberties with Columbus's journal entry and evoke the time when there, in that same landscape, were trees of a thousand kinds and all with their own fruit and all smelling so that it was a marvel. Now I am the most sorrowful of all, never having been acquainted with them.

The Aftermath

In spite of the fact that Avellaneda writes about a Cuban natural world that had long been altered, transformed, and degraded, to read Avellaneda is to feel nostalgia for nineteenth-century Cuba, a Cuba that one has never known unless one is over one hundred years old. Perhaps this Cuba remains in those inalterable moments before the storm, in the sugarcane fields, and in what is left of the natural world. After independence came what Benítez-Rojo refers to as the Republican Machine that made Cuba a single-industry country with colossal sugar mills that were producing six million tons in 1959 and had diminished the forest to 14 percent of Cuba's surface.

Chapter 6

Rebellion in the Backlands (*Os Sertões*)

The Darwinian Landscape

Jerry Hoeg

Euclides da Cunha's (1866–1909) *Os Sertões* (*Campanha de Canudos*), first published in December of 1902, is considered a classic of Brazilian letters and is still very much alive today; witness Mario Vargas Llosa's recent rewrite of it under the title *La guerra del fin del mundo* (The war of the end of the world; 1981). Translated to English (Samuel Putnam 1994) as *Rebellion in the Backlands*, the original title, *Os Sertões*, means simply the backlands, the harsh, barren landscape of the impoverished northeast of Brazil. In order to fully understand the universal appeal the book holds for the Brazilian and, indeed, Latin American imagination, it is important to understand the context surrounding its creation.

The manifest subject of the book is the violent repression, by the Brazilian army, of a breakaway backwoods religious group led by the fanatic Messiah Antônio Vicente Mendes Maciel, commonly known as Antônio Conselheiro. The campaign began in October of 1896 and ended with the complete and total destruction of the rebel city, Canudos, in October of 1897. During this period, four separate campaigns were launched against Canudos. Euclides dropped his job as a civil engineer in the public works department of the state of Sâo Paulo and, in the company of the Sâo Paulo battalion, covered the last of these expeditions as a reporter for the Rio de Janeiro newspaper known as the *Estado de Sâo Paulo*. It is important to note that he arrived in

Canudos in September of 1897 (Fernandes 60) and so spent only two weeks on the ground before the conflict ended. Therefore, as Marco A. Villa notes, "the major part of the observations of Euclides . . . were formed not from his own eyewitness observations, but rather were reconstructed based on interviews, diaries, books, and various annotations . . . and when no such data were available, Euclides availed himself of literary license to reconstruct events" (260–61; my translation). So while the book purports to be a factual account of the campaign by a civil engineer, a scientific account if you will, it is also a literary account.

Several important circumstances form the background to Euclides's book, especially the intellectual and sociopolitical climate of the period. Brazil had achieved independence from Portugal in 1822, but as a monarchy under Emperor Dom Pedro I, whose father, Dom João VI, had returned to Portugal the previous year to resume the throne there. In 1824, Dom Pedro I decreed a constitution that included passages from France's 1789 Declaration of Human Rights, and this perhaps unintended commitment by the absolutist emperor empowered and inspired reformers and modernizers, especially abolitionists. The attendant social protest produced a series of rebellions in the newly formed nation, including a series of regional separatists movements in the 1820s, 1830s, and 1840s—the Confederation of the Equator, the Farroupilha Revolution, the United Provinces of the Rio de la Plata, and so on. These separatist movements reflected the divisions that existed between both the north and the south, and the coast and the interior of Brazil. The issues raised in this period, such as slavery, national unity, and modernization, would still hold center stage in Brazilian politics at the time of the Canudos campaigns.

On April 7, 1831, Dom Pedro I abdicated, leaving five-year-old Dom Pedro II to succeed him in 1840 (a regency ruled in the intervening period). In 1852, Pedro II defeated the Argentine dictator Juan Manuel de Rosas and then, in a triple alliance pact signed with Argentina and Uruguay on May 1, 1865, fought a devastating five-year war with the Paraguayan dictator Francisco Solano Lopez, which Brazil eventually won. These wars forced Brazil to enlarge the army, partly through the inclusion of many slaves, who fought well and were given their freedom in return. The increased number of army officers, with the consequent decline in opportunities for advancement in peacetime, combined with Pedro II's absolutist actions during the war, caused many military officers to become involved in Brazilian politics, generally supporting a republic.

In November of 1889, a military plot led by Marshall Deodoro de Fonseca demanded the abdication of Pedro II, who promptly left for Portugal, and the republic was proclaimed the next day, November 15, 1889. The republican movement had its intellectual roots in the Brazilian positivists, a group of progressive thinkers influential among the sons of the upper classes, especially in the military colleges. They followed Auguste Comte's idea that everything was explicable by means of scientific laws, which were in turn obtainable through experimentation. Scientific study would enable "social engineers" to replace anarchy with order, and reactionary politics with progress, hence the theme of both positivism and the new Brazilian flag, "Order and Progress."

The positivist movement began in Brazil and started with Luis Pereira Barreto's *Três Filosofias*, in part an attack on the Brazilian Catholic Church. Importantly, the issues raised therein, such as separation of church and state, civil marriage, and divorce, would also play a role in the Canudos campaign. Let us recall that Antônio Conselheiro was a religious mystic and penitent who had roamed the backland for twenty years railing against ungodly behavior and rebuilding churches and cemeteries, all the while awaiting the coming of the millennium and the Day of Judgment (Levine 2). And because ungodly behavior included separation of church and state, Conselheiro was painted in the press as a reactionary who vigorously opposed the new republic and sought a return of the monarchy, whatever his actual opinions on the matter might have been.

From the 1850s on, positivism rapidly became the guiding intellectual theory in higher education in Rio de Janeiro, particularly in the military school where Benjamin Constant Botelho de Magalhaes, the leading positivist thinker of the day, taught a math-centered Comtism, and so garnered a wide following among military officers and civil engineers. As a student of Magalhaes, Euclides read Comte's six volume *Cours de Philosophie Positive* (1830–42), *Synthèse Subjective* (1856), and the *Gèomètrie Analytique* (1843) (Amory "Euclides," 90). According to Luiz Costa Lima, "Cunha's years in the military school gave him an initial exposure to positivist teachings and to the passionate republican dream" (156).

In 1881, again prefiguring the events in Canudos, a breakaway sect of positivists, the so-called Apostolate, founded the Positivist Church, the dogmatic, intolerant, and near fanatic quasi-religiosity that drove more scientific-minded moderates such as Benjamin Constant and Euclides to disassociate themselves from this spiritual-mystical faction. Indeed, following this early period, Euclides moved from positivism to Darwinism: "Da Cunha nonetheless really outgrew both French and Brazilian Positivism in his maturity, through his adherence to

Darwinian principles of evolution . . . As the philosophy of the age in Brazil, Comtean Positivism itself was no longer competitive with evolutionary social Darwinism" (Amory "Euclides," 89). It is this English evolutionism, rather than French positivism, that comes to provide the bulk of the intellectual framework of *Os Sertões*. Costa Lima writes, "Euclides da Cunha's generation was formed in the scientific tradition, of which Comte, Haeckel, and Spencer were the high priests . . . Cunha received the influences of positivism and, albeit more gradually, of evolutionism as well" (155).

Although Charles Darwin himself spent four months in Brazil, in 1832, during his voyage around the world, and Henry Bates and Alfred Russel Wallace spent years in Brazilian Amazonia, it was not until 1864 that Darwin's ideas bore fruit in Brazil. In that year, Fritz Müller, a German immigrant living in present-day Florianópolis, published *Für Darwin*, a far-reaching scientific work that corroborated Darwin's theory through embryological studies of crustaceans and confirmed Earnst Haeckel's biological "law" that ontogeny recapitulates phylogeny. Haeckel's notion that development of the individual repeats the evolution of its species is seen in *Os Sertões* in various allusions to atavism, or biological and/or psychological reversion. Such was its impact that Darwin later had Müller's book translated from German to English (1869). It is worth noting that because it was written in German, Müller's book had a very limited reception in Brazil.

During the 1870s, Darwinism took off in Brazil. Public courses were given at the Museu Nacional in Rio and public lectures, such as "Conferencias Populares da Glória," offered to debate Darwinism (Lopez Cid). A central figure in defense of Darwinism was Agusto Cesar de Miranda Azevedo Collichio. Importantly, he used Darwinism to attack the emperor, who was a staunch critic of Darwin, aligning himself as he did with the French school of anthropology led by Quatrefages de Brèau and Paul Broca, a school that explained racial and cultural differences through craniometry and anthropometry. In the one extant palestra, or talk, he gave at the "Conferencias Populares da Glória," "Darwinismo" (the other five or six are lost, according to Waizbort) Miranda Azevedo asks, "Would it not be more advantageous to accept the consequences of Darwin's theories than to formulate stupid military laws which only serve the caprices of despotism?" (qtd. in Bertol Domingues 79). Miranda Azevedo also called for the Darwinian education of youth to better democratize the republic.

In Miranda Azevedo, one can see the beginnings of social Darwinism, a movement later championed by Euclides. According to Frederic Amory, "Euclides was the foremost exponent, in Brazil" of Spencer's evolutionism ("Historical source" 675). The impact of Spencer's Lamarkian-influenced ideas (the inheritance of acquired characteristics), which included psychological and social traits along with biological traits as heritable factors of given races, can be seen throughout *Os Sertões*, especially in the treatment of race and environment. Much later, thanks to Darwin's cousin Francis Galton, who coined the term "eugenics," biology would be driven from the human sciences, and an anthropological mediation originating in the cultural relativism of Franz Boas would hold sway in the latter half of the twentieth century. As Renata Wasserman, speaking of Vargas Llosa's rewrite of *Os Sertões*, observes, "Vargas Llosa's greatest departure from his predecessor's text is in removing from the start that faith in the power of science to explain" (467). But for Euclides, science did indeed have that power to explain, "for he [Euclides] never abandons the notion that biology is the *scientia princeps* of sociological interpretation" (Costa Lima 161). Importantly, as we shall see, scientific developments in the twenty-first century have vindicated many of his ideas.

Os Sertões itself is divided into three main parts, "The Land" (*A terra*), "The Man" (*O homem*), and "The Rebellion" (*A luta*) (González Echevarría translates this last heading as "The Struggle," which seems slightly more accurate, 131). And in fact, much of the story concerns the struggle between "civilized" man and the primitive backlands environment. Conversely, the inhabitants of the backlands struggle not with their environment, indeed quite the opposite, but rather with "civilized" man. The first part, "The Land," is a description of the Brazilian landscape on which the actions of the campaign against Canudos will take place. Writing as a geologist and civil engineer, Euclides goes from the general to the specific in giving us the lay of the land. His first subsection, "Preliminary Observations" (3), begins with the central plateau of Brazil, which "descends, along the southern coast, in unbroken slopes, high and steep, overlooking the sea; it takes the form of hilly uplands level with the peaks of the coastal mountain ranges that extend from the Rio Grande to Minas" (3). He goes on to describe the "segment of seashore between Rio de Janeiro and Espíritu Santo" (3), and then follows the coast past the fifteenth parallel, whence comes "an attenuation of all these characteristics . . . until, as one comes out on the coast of Baía [*sic*], his gaze is at last freed from the rampart of mountains which up to now have repelled and hemmed it in and may wander at will to the west, plunging into the heart of the broad-sweeping land that slowly emerges in a distant roll of highland plains" (3). And wander to the west we will, for there, far out past the horizon, lie the backlands and Canudos.

As we move from the coast to the interior, Euclides highlights the geology and hydrology of the region, from the "gneiss-granite masses . . . on the extreme south" (3–4) to "extensive plains . . . consisting of horizontal layers of clayey sandstone, intercalated with juttings of limestone, or *dikes* of basic eruptive rocks . . . stretching away to the northwest" (4). These geological formations give rise to "a most original hydrographic network . . . [that] readily break through these strata in uniform beds" (4). Overall, he speaks of "three different geological formations, of ages hard to determine, one supplanting another or the three intermingling in discordant stratifications, the predominance of one or two or the combination of all three going to form the variable features of the earth's physiognomy" (3). It should be noted that his geological description highlights geological time. The gneiss-granite formations are much older, igneous formations produced in a period of volcanic activity. The sandstone and limestone are sedimentary, one from inorganic materials and one from organic materials, deposited from bodies of water that later overlaid the more primeval igneous material. The hydrologic features of the harsh environment break through the more recent strata to reveal the underlying, previously hidden, geologic history, much as the harsh environment will later break through the thin veneer of the soldier's civilization to reveal their older psychological formations: "The only comparison one can think of here is that of geologic strata, which not infrequently are disturbed and inverted, with a modern formation beneath an ancient one; so the moral stratification of peoples likewise may show an inversion and confusion of layers, with undulating furrows and abrupt synclinals, breaking out in faults in the form of ancient stages through which the race has long since passed" (280).

This same method of combining from basic formations, often with "intermingling in discordant stratifications," will later be used to describe the human physiognomy of the region as well, with emphasis on the timeline, from older to newer formations, always with an eye out for atavistic reversions: "The Indo-European, the Negro, and the Brazilian-Guarany or the Tapuia represent evolutionary stages in confrontation; and miscegenation, in addition to obliterating the pre-eminent qualities of the higher race, serves to stimulate the revival of the primitive attributes of the lower" (85). Keep in mind that it was only in 1830 that Charles Lyell had published his *Principles of Geology* (3 vols., 1830–33), in which he argued for uniformitarianism, the theory that geological processes such as mountain building and continent formation are the end results of slow-working geological processes that still go on today. This went against the prevailing creationist or catastrophist view that the earth was created suddenly some six thousand to ten thousand years ago. Darwin, who began his scientific career as a geologist, took volume 1 with him on the *Beagle* (he received volume 2 during the voyage), found corroborating evidence, and so first became interested in biogeography (the study of the geographical distribution of plants and animals), an interest that later progressed to evolutionism. Euclides applies these concepts to human subjects as well.

In the first part of *Os Sertões*, Euclides demonstrates his interest in geological uniformitarianism and biogeography. As we advance from the coast to the interior in "The Land," we eventually reach "Terra Ignota" (The unknown land): "Our best maps, conveying but scant information, show here an expressive blank, a hiatus, labeled Terra Ignota, a mere scrawl indicating a problematic river or an idealized mountain range . . . This strange region, at a distance of less than a hundred and sixty-five miles from the ancient metropolis [Bahia], was destined to be absolutely forgotten throughout the four hundred years of our history" (9). The land is so primitive that it cannot outgrow its fundamental nature, and even life-giving rain causes atavistic reversion rather than progress: "The torrential rainfalls characteristic of such a climate of alternating flood and drought, coming of a sudden after protracted dry periods and beating down upon these slopes, carrying away all the loose mantle, have left largely exposed the older geologic series of these last mountain spurs . . . forming pictures which give the landscape here its impinging and tormented aspect" (13). In the following pages, Euclides gives us the geological history of the region, from the Silurian to the Tertiary period, from the Middle Paleozoic to the Cretaceous, and from the elevation of the Andes to the joining of the two Americas.

Next comes a description of the climate, "an alteration of very hot days and frigid nights" (23), including the cycle of droughts that have afflicted the region as far back as data are available. He then offers various hypotheses regarding their origin. Strangely, he refers neither to Hadly cell circulation (George Hadly 1735) nor to Louis Aggazis's work on ice ages, this latter work confirmed by Darwin's observations in 1839 and 1842 (Calvin 212), both of which would have been available to him. Nevertheless, he does correctly correlate environmental change with adaptation in living organisms, hence with natural selection. Unfortunately, he fails to apply the appropriate time scale, geological, to both, thus creating one of the sources of error for his theories on race. Another is his lack of knowledge of genetics. Although an obscure Augustinian monk, Gregor Mendel (1822–84), had published his paper "Experiments on Plant Hybridization" in the little-known *Journal of the Brno Natural History Society* (1866), in which he explained his discovery of "transmission factors," now called genes, the prevailing theory in genetics at the time was blending, the idea that factors contributed by both parents fuse in the offspring, and it was to this theory Euclides subscribed. Indeed, Mendel's work was rejected by the blending theorists, and would not be rediscovered until the twentieth century (in 1900 by Hugo de Vries and Carl Correns).

Had Euclides known then what we know now, about mitochondrial Eve, for example, he would have realized how genetically alike are all humans and how cultural differences were simply external manifestations of the same genetic propensities. Knowledge of Eve comes from studies of motochondrial DNA that count the number of mutations that differentiate two living individuals, and so can identify when their last common ancestor lived (Ayala 118–19). The last common ancestor of all living humans today was a female who lived in Africa approximately 143,000 years ago. This same method shows the last common ancestor of chimps and humans lived approximately six million years ago (Cavalli-Sforza 77–80). This means chimp DNA has had far more time than human DNA in which to mutate. This explains why two randomly selected chimpanzees from neighboring bands are likely to be more genetically different than two humans from opposite ends of the earth (Kaessmann, Weibe, and Pääbo). It also means that all living humans are very genetically similar, more so than any other species. Our superficial differences are climatically induced—dark skin for the tropics, light skin to produce more vitamin D in northern latitudes, eyes protected by fatty folds of skin in Siberian climates, and so on. Additionally, leaving aside these climate-related adaptations, there are no genetically "pure" or homogeneous human populations (Cavalli-Sforza 11–13). But, of course, Euclides could not have known this and so, as we shall see, he is forced to attempt to finesse the differences between cultural and genetic evolution.

In the following subsection of *Os Sertões*, Euclides begins to outline his theory of the relation between environment and natural selection. His first example is the *caatinga* or scrub-forest. These plants have adapted to their harsh desert environment (*sertão* means desert, from *desertão*, deserted). In a reversal of Darwin's observations of the finch population of the Galapagos, but still in the vein of descent with modification, Euclides observes, "Through an explicable effect of adaptation to the cramped conditions of an unfavorable environment those very growths which in the forests are so diversified are here all fashioned in the same mold. They undergo a transformation and by a process of slow metamorphosis tend to an extremely limited number of types, characterized by those attributes which offer the greatest capacity for resistance" (30). So where earlier environmental factors had removed the thin veneer left by the passage of time on the earth, revealing the ancient strata, here the flora reveal "the stigma of the silent battle that is going on" (31) with the environment. He gives numerous examples of adaptations to environmental factors, including one type of "enormous tree that is wholly underground. Lashed by the dog-day heat, fustigated by the sun, gnawed by torrential rains, tortured by the winds, these trees would appear to have been knocked out completely in the struggle with the antagonistic elements and so have gone underground in this manner, have made themselves invisible, with only the tallest shoots of their majestic foliage showing aboveground" (32). He also describes social networks of plants, formed by necessity under the prevailing harsh conditions:

> When, contrary to the cases mentioned, the species are not well-equipped for a victorious reaction, arrangements which are, perhaps, still more interesting may then be observed. In this case, the plants unite in an intimate embrace, being transformed into social growths. Not being able to weather it out in isolation, they discipline themselves, become gregarious and regimented . . . Their roots, tightly interlaced beneath the ground, constitute a net to catch the waters and the crumbling earth, and, as a result of prolonged effort, they finally form the fertile soil from which they spring, overcoming, through the capillarity of their inextricable tissues, with their numerous meshes, the insatiable suction of the strata and the sands. And they do live. "Live" is the word—for there is, as a matter of fact, a higher significance to be discerned in the passivity exhibited by this evolved form of life. (33)

He goes on to give other examples, such as the Joaz and Umbú trees, this latter "the most apt example of the hinterland flora" (37), but with the examples already given, the parallels between the reaction of the flora and that of the population of Canudos to their respective environments begins to be seen. For the backlanders too tried to go underground and make themselves invisible in the Terra Ignota of the desert, united to form a social growth, and exhibited a higher significance in the passivity of their evolved form of life. An important difference is, however, that the flora exhibits genetic adaptations and the residents of Canudos cultural adaptations, though even these cultural adaptations were, obviously, made possible by previous psychological adaptations through the course of human evolution.

In the following subsection titled "The Land," Euclides makes clear his environmental determinism. He cites Hegel as outlining "three geographical categories as comprising the basic categories which . . . react upon man, creating ethnic differentiations" (39), and seeks to add a fourth, the Brazilian backlands. Now, in a sense, he is correct, in that certain geographic features serve to isolate various groups, creating what are known in population genetics as refugia, and produce certain lifestyles. He mentions the *llanos* or savanna of Venezuela as producing "a society of wandering herdsmen" (40) and that topography does lend itself to this type of usage. What he does not get right is the time scale necessary for natural selection to allow for genetic adaptations to the savanna environment. The African savanna was indeed the environment of evolutionary adaptation of the human race, but the process took millions of years. The last common ancestor of humans and chimpanzees lived some six million years ago (Corballis), about the time ice age cooling converted rain forests to savanna in Africa, at which point our ancestors left the trees for a more upright lifestyle. The savanna is indeed our environment of evolutionary adaptedness, and up until about 10,000 years ago, before the invention of agriculture, our species continued to live a hunter-gatherer lifestyle. But natural selection is backward looking, and our adaptations come from savannas past, not savannas present.

Importantly, our adaptations are not only purely physical but also psychological. In order to survive on a predator-filled savanna, physically weak but psychologically powerful humans evolved into the most social animal of all, and those mental adaptations are also still with us today. They are the ultimate causes of the proximate cultural formations Euclides details in the backlands, especially among the followers of Antônio Conselheiro. Because all humans are so genetically similar, these same psychological predispositions are universal, found across all cultures (Brown), which is what Euclides finally realizes at the end of *Os Sertões*, when he appears to reverse his previous distinctions as to who represents civilization and who represents barbarism: "Despite their three hundred years of backward development, the sertanejos by no means carried off the palm from our troops when it came to deeds of barbarism" (439).

He returns to his concept of "regressive evolution" (42) in the subsection on "How a Desert is Made." Emerging from the original Tertiary sea, the backlands have regressed to their current desert state due to a relation of positive feedback between climatic circumstances and the regressive evolution of the flora of the region. The harsher the climate, the more the flora shrink in response, and so the less the flora protect the backlands from it; the less they protect the land, the harsher the climate becomes—the more evaporation, the more exposed soil surface—causing the flora to adapt by regressing to fewer and more basic species. To this Euclides adds one more element, human intervention: "There is one notable geologic agent that we have overlooked—man. The truth is, man has not infrequently exerted a brutal reaction upon the earth and, especially among us, has assumed, throughout the long course of our history, the role of a terrible maker-of-deserts" (43). He traces the process through various cultures: "All this began as the result of a disastrous native legacy. In the primitive agriculture of the aboriginal forest-dwellers the basic implement was fire" (43). They would slash and burn areas of once luxuriant forest, cultivate it to exhaustion, and abandon it, leaving a *caapuera*, or "extinct forest" in the Tupi language (43). He continues, "The aborigine went on burning and clearing fresh plots, widening the circle of devastation with new *caapueras* . . . desert tracts whose stunted growth was ill adapted to cope with the external elements, and which, as they grew wider in extent, merely added to the rigors of a hostile climate" (43). And finally he describes how the process was repeated on a much grander scale by colonizers looking for grazing land, gold, and slaves: "Came then the colonizer and copied the same procedure . . . huge tracts were opened up, common grazing lands . . . by the free use of fire . . . which swept across vast spaces . . . the hardy backwoods pioneer, who, lusting for gain, had come in search of gold and the Indian . . . the hiding-places of the Tapuia . . . he destroyed by setting fire to it . . . He attacked the earth stoutly, disfiguring it with his surface explorations, rendering it sterile with his dredges . . . precipitating the process of erosion . . . And he left behind him tracts forever sterile now . . . where not even the humblest of plants could thrive" (44). Interestingly, he goes on to mention that the colonial governments, from 1713 on, issued a series of decrees to limit these practices, appointed a judge-conservator for the forests in 1796, and disseminated royal letters of that same year reproving the destruction of "precious forests . . . which formerly did so abound" (45), all to no good effect.

Although these early, and failed, efforts at conservation in Brazilian history appear to have set the tone down to the present day, Euclides counters with examples of successful efforts, in similar circumstances, taken from thousands of years earlier. In the following subsection, "How the Desert Is Extinguished," he analyses Roman civil engineering labors on the edge of the Sahara, specifically on the Tunisian plain between Béja and Bizerte. Essentially, he says, the Romans imposed erosion and sediment control through a system of dykes and retention storage ponds that increased hydrologic infiltration and decreased runoff, "changing the climate for the better" (46) to such an extent the area became the "granary of Italy" (46). He goes on to describe how the French later used these same tactics in Tunisia to achieve the same results: "Thus is this historic region, freed of the inert Moslem's apathy, transformed, to resume once more that aspect which it bore of old. France is saving what remains of the opulent heritage of Roman civilization" (47). And finally, he adds, "Now a mere glance at the hypsometric map of the northern backlands will show that use could here be made of an identical expedient, with equally certain results" (47).

The above reference to the ability of civilization, and more specifically civil engineers, to change nature for the better, along with the reference to "the inert Moslem's apathy," is a synopsis of his positivist view on civilization versus barbarism. In the next section of the book, "Man," Euclides will go on to explain what he believes are fundamental distinctions between races and how the natural environment dictates both the physical and the psychological traits of most races, save for those civilized, modern, and progressive enough to dictate to nature. He explains that, in Amazonia, "Natural selection in such an environment is effected at the cost of grave compromises with the central functions of the brain, in a most prejudicial inverse progression between intellectual and physical development . . . Acclimatization in such a case means a regressive evolution" (61). He goes on to explain that the tropical climate weakens the European race to the point where "the inferior race, the crude savage, dominates him; in league with the environment he conquers him, crushes him, annihilates him" (61). Fortunately for the European, "this does not occur in a good part of central Brazil and throughout the southern regions" (61). There then follows a discussion of the effect of climate on various racial and ethnic combinations, which he calls subraces, all of which reflect his Lamarckian outlook on the inheritance of acquired characteristics. These include, among many others, mestizos, mulattos, and the inhabitants of "the mud-walled Troy" (Canudos), the jagunços. Effectively, he walks a thin line between cultural evolution and genetic evolution, all the more remarkable because until Mendel's work was rediscovered in 1900, the mechanisms of hereditary transmission were unknown, even to Darwin. Euclides concludes, "Agreed that environment does not form races . . . Through the very diversity of the conditions of adaptation, it prepares the way for the appearance of different subraces" (66).

Nevertheless, throughout *Os Sertões* Euclides confounds the two types of evolution, speaking continuously of "the evolution of their character" (78), "the evolutionary manifestations" (145) of their dwellings, and always defining anything he considered barbaric, that is, nonmodern, nonprogressive, as "retrograde" (134), or reverse evolution, "recessive atavism" (221), "a remote phase of evolution" (119), "a backward flow" (161). In contrast, he always emphasizes a teleological view that modern, progressive, scientific civilization and knowledge are the end product of evolution. Speaking of Antônio Conselheiro's system of belief, Euclides summarizes, "It is a splendid example of the identity of evolutionary stages among peoples. The retrograde type of the backlands reproduces the aspect presented by mystics of the past . . . He is a being out of our time" (134).

This view recalls the Comtean perspective that orders intellectual history into the successive epochs of theology, metaphysics, and positivism (i.e., science). This also explains Euclides's solution to the problem of backlands backwardness, one still popular today, and just as effective—education: "There was a more serious enemy to be combated, in a warfare of a slower and more worthy kind. This entire campaign would be a crime, a futile and barbarous one, if we were not to take advantage of the paths opened by the artillery, by following up our cannon with a constant, stubborn, and persistent campaign of education, with the object of drawing these rude and backward fellow-countrymen of ours into the current of our times and our own national life" (408). A good part of the book is written in a scientific tone that exemplifies such an educational bent. But the last section of the book veers a bit off course, for just when all the observations necessary to corroborate the geographic and environmental determinism of his racial views are in place, actions on the ground in the final days of Canudos serve to overthrow his predetermined views. To his credit, Euclides remains ever the scientist and follows his observations where they lead him, which is to the realization that all humans possess the same propensities for civilization and barbarism.

Euclides begins the final section, "The Rebellion," with an explanation of relation between the physical environment of the backlands and the human population that inhabited it. When the original "desert-makers" had at last "washed all the pebbles and had got to the bottom of their stock of furs, there was little else for them to do but turn bandits if they wished to go on living as they had been accustomed to live. The jagunço, pillager of cities, thereupon took the place of the *garimpeiro* [diamond hunter] who pillaged the earth for diamonds" (173). And the jagunço is perfectly adapted to his harsh environment, and even in the worst of times, "the land comes to his assistance" (175). The jagunço represents that "phase of human civilization in which man was governed by the earth and his identity was determined by it" (xx) in the words of Afrânio Peixoto in his preface to *Rebellion in the Backlands*, which he calls "an always impressive document of man's struggle with the earth—an earth that bestows upon him its own direct imprint" (xx).

And indeed, the struggle between the jagunços and the government troops is a story of two relations with the earth, in which the land is the outsiders' worst enemy, while at the same time it "comes to the assistance" of the jagunço. In the first of the four campaigns against Canudos, the government sent, on November 7, 1896, one hundred troops against the thousands of able-bodied men in Canudos. "They did not posses the indispensable equipment for a march of one hundred and twenty-five miles across a barren and unpopulated countryside; but, nevertheless, they went" (181). Due to the heat and the equipment they carried, they could not march after 10 AM. There was neither shade nor water, and maps were nonexistent. After many days of forced march, the exhausted troops straggled into the desert village of Uauá. Two days later the jagunço forces attacked at dawn, catching the troops asleep. After a four-hour battle, both sides withdrew, the sertanejos back to the desert, the troops back to the city of Joazeiro. For Euclides "two things were evident: the rebels were in large force and they had in their favor the wild nature of the region where they had sought shelter" (189).

A second expedition, of 560 troops, set out in December of that same year to avenge the defeat at Uauá. The plan was to adopt the small group tactics of the jagunços, fighting in small detachments that "would be able to adjust themselves better to the rugged terrain" (189). It is here that Euclides begins to admit a grudging admiration for the jagunços, who have a more effective, though primitive, in the sense of a throwback to earlier evolutionary stages, relation with the land: "It was, without a doubt, a throwback to primitive warfare; but, if the brave and shrewd jagunço did not lead us to adopt it, then the exceptional character of the terrain which served as his protector certainly should have induced us to do so" (190).

But in the end the government troops could not abandon their European military theories, "the mechanical precision of the mechanized soldier" (206), and so they fall victim to a series of ambushes while marching double file through the scrub forests, the caatingas: "With all this, the caatingas are an incorruptible ally of the sertanejo in revolt . . . For the invader they are an impenetrable wilderness; but they have numerous paths by which they are accessible to the backwoodsman, who was born and grew up there" (191). In true guerilla fashion, the jagunços use the terrain to their advantage, wearing down the government troops and living off the land. For while the government force "has to contend not merely with man but with the earth itself" (194), the backlander is at home in the desert: "These trees are for him old companions. He knows them all. He and they were born and grew up together, like brothers . . . The umbú tree will quench his thirst . . . the araticú, the verdant urucuri, the shapely marizeiro, the quixabeira with its tiny fruit—all will give him enough and more then enough to eat and drink" (195). On January 12, 1897, in perfect formation the civilized army set out across the primitive backlands for Canudos, a three-day march. On January 17, still wandering in the desert, their provisions ran out. The next day they were ambushed at Mount Cambaio, "a mountain in ruins . . . splitting under the periodic lash of sudden tempests and scorching suns, cleft and disjointed—in a slow and age-old disintegration" (211), and two days later they were in full retreat. They were followed closely by the jagunços, whose leader, Pajehú, was "a fine example of recessive atavism, with the retrograde form of a grim troglodyte, stalking upright here with the same intrepidity with which, ages ago, he had brandished a stone hatchet at the entrance to his cave" (221). Again, the rebels use the earth to their advantage, tumbling boulders down off Mount Cambaio onto the fleeing troops: "The expedition had completely lost any semblance of discipline" (221). And so a second expedition was destroyed by the primitive nature, and natives, of the backlands.

On February 21, yet a third expedition of 1,281 men under Colonel Moreira Cesar set out for Canudos. And yet again, they were unable to deal with the harsh conditions of the backlands. After days of forced marches through the blistering desert, facing soaring temperatures and constant ambushes, they finally arrived at Canudos, which they promptly attacked, only to be routed and sent fleeing in defeat once again. The eight hundred survivors abandoned their arms and equipment and dispersed across the backlands, the survivors eventually making it out days and weeks later. The jagunços collected the corpses of the soldiers, decapitated them and burned the bodies, and then lined the road to Canudos with the heads. This disaster inspired, of course, a fourth expedition.

On June 16 and June 19, 1897, two columns totaling 4,283 troops set off for Canudos. By now the rebellion had become a national news item, an international conspiracy to destroy the republic was feared, and mobs in Rio burned the offices of the monarchist journals. Euclides mentions this and other incidents in the capital "to call attention in passing to a certain similarity between the scene in the Rua do Ouvidor [an important street in the capital] and a disturbance in the caatingas, one equaling the other in savagery" (279). It is here he begins to realize there is a distinction between cultural heredity and genetic heredity and that nurture cannot always cancel out nature. Speaking of the incidents in the capital he says, "Here, as in all places and in all ages, the portentous force of heredity, out of the most advanced environment, was producing—gloved though they might be and with a thin veneer of culture—thoroughgoing troglodytes" (279). The thin veneer of civilization would come off completely in Canudos.

As usual, the troops set off with half rations, slowed by siege cannon, marching in close formation, and in brightly colored and hot European-style uniforms. And also as usual, they met ambush after ambush from rebels using the terrain to their advantage, while it continued to be the enemy of the civilized government army. By the time they reached the approaches to Canudos, with its 5,200 dwellings (475) and twenty thousand inhabitants (346), their rations and ammunition were exhausted, they were pinned down by enemy fire, men were deserting, and another disaster seemed imminent. Euclides describes the Old Testament feel of the situation: "And all this was set in a biblical landscape, against the infinite melancholy of the barren hills, where no trees grew. A river without water, winding about the town, was turned into a long and dusty highway. And in the distance, dominating the four corners of the compass, an undulating row of mountains, likewise deserted, and standing out sharply against the brightness of the horizon, like the giant frame of this strange picture . . . The settlement itself—"four-square," like the cities in the Bible—completed the illusion" (346). But on July 13, just before the apocalyptic moment, a new supply column finally arrived, and the mass productions of modern technology began to overcome the nature of the terrain, though not the nature of the men. From this point on, more and more men and materials arrived, until eventually the resistance was ground down, and on October 5, the last four defenders of Canudos were killed, and the battle ended, though not before the government troops had been reduced to the same savagery as the rebels, "those extraordinary representatives of civilization who exhibited so lamentable a degree of barbarism toward semibarbarians" (479).

Throughout, Euclides uses the landscape in three ways. Firstly, his description of it is couched in scientific terms with an eye to the educational programs he advocates. *Rebellion in the Backlands* is, in a certain sense, a popular science book, though it was also praised in the specialized geological literature of the day (Bueno 14). Secondly, he uses the multiple strata of the earth as a metaphor for the multiple strata of the human mind. In this, modern brain science concurs with him. The human brain is built of newer layers overlaying older constructions. David Linden, professor of neuroscience at Johns Hopkins University, compares it to an ice cream cone: "Through evolutionary time, as higher functions were added, a new scoop was placed on top, but the lower scoops were left largely unchanged . . . When new, higher functions were added, this did not result in a redesign of the whole brain from the ground up: a new scoop was just added on top. Hence, in true kludge fashion, our brains contain regions . . . that are functional remnants of our evolutionary past" (21–22). And so our brainstem is not very different from that of a frog, nor our limbic system from that of a rat, and when environmental conditions penetrate the thin veneer of our neocortex to reveal these regions, primitive emotions, and actions, do surface.

Thirdly, Euclides realizes that environmental changes such as climate change produce adaptations through natural selection. But without knowledge of the human genome and other advances in molecular genetics, Euclides, in some cases, gets the time frame wrong. He also, for the same reasons, is not clear on the distinction between cultural, social, and genetic evolution, a distinction that is only now beginning to be properly understood (Clark and Grunstein; Linden; Levinson and Jaisson). Nevertheless, in all these areas his insistence on staying true to his scientific principles has been demonstrated by later empirical research to have been the proper decision.

CHAPTER 7

YUYOS ARE NOT WEEDS

AN ECOCRITICAL APPROACH TO HORACIO QUIROGA

Beatriz Rivera-Barnes

The *yuyo* is, in fact, a weed. But the literary critic Emir Rodriguez Monegal recalls that Horacio Quiroga once told him that the *yuyo* was not a weed, but rather a plant that was not in its natural place. Rodriguez Monegal concludes that away from the jungle Quiroga felt like a *yuyo*, and in the jungle he became a colossal tropical plant (11).

In an initial attempt to conceptualize place-connectedness and to argue for the importance of place sense in literary imagination, Lawrence Buell alludes to a passage in James Joyce's *Portrait of a Young Man* where Stephen Dedalus scribbles in his geography textbook first his name, then his class, his school, his county, his country, his continent, and finally the world and the universe (*Writing for an Endangered World* 64). This is Buell's first model for place-connectedness in a fivefold analysis. Regardless of the fact that he soon declares that first model to be partially obsolete, if a similar expanding and contracting succession were to be applied to Horacio Quiroga, it could be much like this: Horacio Quiroga, his house, his patch of land between the Upper Paraná River and the town of San Ignacio, Misiones Province, Argentina, South America, the world, the universe. But the succession that interests me here begins with the province of Misiones and ends with Horacio Quiroga and his sense of place, that particular place.

From 1903 until he took his own life in 1937, Quiroga was obsessed with a place, Misiones, the Argentine tropical frontier. Thus, his stories bring this landscape to the reader at a given moment in time and allow the reader to focus on its existence, power, pull, past, socioeconomic issues, environmental problems, and consequently, its fragility. For that reason alone Quiroga warrants an ecocritical approach.

Before proceeding any further, I would like to mention that as far as terminology goes, I hesitated between *ecocriticism* and *environmental criticism* upon reading that "ecocriticism still invokes in some quarters the cartoon image of a club of intellectually shallow nature worshippers, an image slapped on the movement during its salad days" (Buell, *The Future of Environmental Criticism* viii). Counting on those salad days being over, or nearly over, I finally opted for *ecocriticism*.

In broad terms, Cheryll Glotfelty defines ecocriticism as "the study of the relationship between literature and the physical environment" (xviii). So the ecocritical approach to Horacio Quiroga begins with this relationship. Initially, there is Quiroga's relationship with nature, an intense and obsessive one, and the stories that are the result of this relationship. The stories, in turn, portray not only the conflicts and dynamics between man and the physical environment, as well as how nature responds to man's presence in the jungle, but also, as Jennifer French affirms, "the intense relationships among land, labor and capital in the colonial jungle, where the power exerted by metropolitan capital extracts surplus value by deforming beyond all reason the 'natural' interaction between local people and their environment" (54–55).

For example, in the story titled "El regreso de Anaconda" (The return of Anaconda; 1925) it is not so much the local farmer, but rather the logging company that represents the power of capital. But the spirit of the place is not always aware of this imbalance of power, so the animals quickly come to see one dying laborer as representative of all the exploiters. Politically speaking, all the animals except Anaconda end up confusing labor and capital. But in spite of the animals' confusion and of the need to separate labor from capital, it is important to keep in mind that the local farmer cannot help but do his share of cutting and burning and of making a fragile environment all the more fragile.

In fact, the tourist who is merely there to see and the preservationist who is there to protect also have their impact on the environment. These impacts can be measured either with scientific rigor or with metaphors. Nature can respond any number of ways: with erosion, storms, floods, droughts, and deluges. Quiroga conveys this by having the animals of the tropical zone plotting against man and planning to blockade the Upper Paraná River.

In other words, nature can respond with anthropomorphic metaphors, by becoming man's mortal enemy. Anaconda alludes to the first man who arrived in the jungle, "con su miserable ansia de ver, tocar, y cortar," and then to the other men who followed, "sucios de olor, sucios de machetes y quemazones incesantes" (Quiroga, *Desterrados* 47). [with his miserable urge to see, to touch, and to cut; dirty-smelling, with dirty machetes and incessant burnings.]

Anaconda's discourse, however, does not limit these jungle stories to the dialectics of the greedy capitalist and fragile nature, or pitiless nature and the hapless tract farmer. The dynamics between man and the physical environment are explored in depth through the different perspectives, for this Argentine tropical frontier was peopled by Brazilian squatters, all kinds of drunken foreigners, pioneers like Quiroga himself, large-scale loggers and farmers, colonial oppressors, peons, as well as charismatic anacondas who use labor union language, impulsive caimans, and concerned, insightful fox terriers. "In fact, by 1881, the Argentine public had begun to think of Misiones as a sort of international refugium peccatorum—quite a contrast with the thriving centers of Indian agriculture and industry that had supported some 50,000 people in the Campo during Jesuit times" (Eidt 82).

If Quiroga first ventured into the tropical forest, it was *to see*. He was considered to be a dandy at the time, a dandy from Uruguay, a country that lacked native culture or local color, as the critic Perez Martin points out (91). This is an important detail in that it reflects Buell's second model for place sense. "To understand fully what it means to inhabit place is therefore not only to bear in mind the (dis)connectedness between one's primary places but also the tentitcular radiations from each one" (Buell, *Writing for an Endangered World* 66). In other words, it is necessary to keep in mind that Quiroga was not from the region that obsessed him. He came from somewhere else; his identity was ineluctably entangled with other places.

The first encounter with the jungle would change the dandy's way of seeing the world. Instantly, the place moved Quiroga deeply, and he must have felt much like Paul Bowles when he first arrived in Algeria, his own magic place that he felt would give him "wisdom and ecstasy—perhaps even death" (125). From that moment on, Quiroga's works would be imbibed with what he saw, and with his desire to return. What Quiroga saw in the jungle, be it the jungle itself or his own self in the jungle, attracted him, deeply so; but before long, he was as anxious to touch and to cut as was the first man who ventured into the jungle. So the question may very well be, does man invariably do this to a beloved place? But it can also be, what is it that a beloved place does to man?

The opportunity to see first came to Horacio Quiroga in June 1903, when his friend, the poet Leopoldo Lugones, was sent by the

Argentine Ministry of Education to the Jesuit ruins of San Ignacio in the province of Misiones, and Quiroga decided to accompany him as a photographer. The two friends went up the Paraná River to this place that would forever have an impact on Quiroga. This is where Quiroga's lifelong attraction to the jungle begins. "Para Quiroga significó el primer contacto con un mundo en que existía otra escala de valores, un mundo que lo facinaba por su aparente impenetrabilidad, que desafiaba su espíritu competitivo" (Rodriguez Monegal 79–80). [For Quiroga this was the first contact with a world where another set of values existed, a world that fascinated him because of its impenetrability that challenged his competitive spirit.]

In spite of his insufferable attitude during the entire expedition, Quiroga discovered almost immediately the spirit of Robinson Crusoe within himself. Henceforth, the environment would play a crucial role in his writing. Not only was Quiroga intent on making the tropical forest his habitat, but also on telling its stories. In this way Quiroga is much like his protagonist Juan Brown whose initial intention was to see the ruins of San Ignacio and who ended up spending the next quarter century of his life there. "Así Juan Brown, que habiendo ido por sólo unas horas a mirar las ruinas, se quedó veinticinco años allá" (*Desterrados* 65). [So Juan Brown, having gone for just a few hours to look at the ruins, wound up staying there twenty-five years.] In other words, the act of seeing made both Quiroga and his protagonist want to touch and appropriate; to do so they had to cut and burn.

But in 1903, Quiroga's eyes are only seeing, and seeing for the first time. No need to touch, not yet. There are the columns of the ruins and the gigantic roots of the canopy trees growing together, forming what Rodriguez Monegal calls mestizo structures, half-tree, half-column, which the natives called "corazón de piedra" (80) [heart of stone]. These particular ruins are the vestiges of one of eleven settlements or missions established by the Jesuits between 1609 and 1767 and which account for the name of the province. But the Jesuits were not the first to see and to touch this subtropical area of land in northeast Argentina nestled between three rivers, the Upper Paraná to the west, the Iguazú to the north, and the Uruguay to the south.

In 1525, Sebastien Cabot was sent there by Charles V in search of a legendary, wealthy "White King" of this region inhabited by the Guaraní people. This expedition was followed by Pedro de Mendoza's in 1536. Then in 1541 Alvar Núñez Cabeza de Vaca also explored the area. He navigated down the Upper Paraná River, past Misiones, all the way to Asunción, Paraguay. "During the next forty years settlers in Asunción kept the Paraná-Paraguay river system open to shipping and gradually probed south and east toward the densely forested region of Misiones" (Eidt 35). The presence of the native Guaraní, the initial European settlements, and the arrival of the Jesuits reflect Buell's third dimension of place-sense. For "places themselves are not stable, free-standing entities but continually shaped and reshaped by forces both inside and outside. Places haves histories; place is not just a noun but also a verb" (*Writing for an Endangered World* 67).

The geography proves to be just as fluid as the cultural artifacts and the history. Eidt writes that the terrain, soil, climate, and vegetation all emphasize the transitional nature of this region. For example, "Level to rolling lands of the Campo rise to hills and mountains in the Selva" (Eidt 7). It is to this seemingly virgin forest that Quiroga will return almost immediately, this time in order to touch and to cut.

It is not to the province of Misiones, however, that Quiroga returns in 1904, but to the Argentine Chaco. Rodriguez Monegal sees a subtle error in Quiroga's choice of place and explains this as Quiroga's need of a false acculturation before discovering the true one. In other words, the discovery of his true habitat or country could only be the result of trial and error. Rodriguez Monegal considers the Chaco to be the threshold, an error (82).

So Quiroga spends almost all his inheritance, around seven thousand pesos, to buy six hundred acres of land to plant cotton. The encounter with the selva, the seeing, almost immediately made Quiroga want to own and to touch; once he does own, he proceeds to exploit the land as well as the natives, to burn and to cut, like the other settlers in Argentina's tropical frontier. Jennifer French sees a similar triad, this time formed by land, labor, and capital, where "land itself becomes the basis of the action and interaction of his characters in the colonial jungle" (54).

In other words, by wanting to establish himself on the frontier, Quiroga was willing to play the role of the colonizer, or the conquistador, and little did it matter if he succeeded or failed in this attempt. His relationship with the natives sheds light on his relationship with the environment, for if the natives are not only a product of the environment but also at times the environment itself, just like the fauna and the flora, Quiroga's resentment toward them could easily be likened to his conflicts with nature, in this case the Argentine frontier. "Estos indios son de lo más vil, ladrones y sin palabra que hay, y me hallo muy dispuesto a vengarme de todas las que me han hecho" (Rodriguez Monegal 86). [These Indians are of the vilest kind, they are thieves and liars and I'm quite ready to get back at them for everything they've done to me.] Since the natives know nothing about numbers, Quiroga decides to steal from them each time they weigh the cotton that they have harvested. He tries it several times, and succeeds, but this makes him feel so guilty and so angry that he soon quits these dishonest schemes.

In the same way, it could very well be that Quiroga's initial intention, as a businessman, was to bleed the Argentine Chaco and, here again, because of moral issues, he finds himself unable to do so. A year later, the whole enterprise has failed. Quiroga returns to Buenos Aires in 1905, having lost his inheritance.

Rodriguez Monegal sees in the Chaco experience a dialectic relationship between the colonizer and the colonized. The Indians are the exploited ones. The colonist determines the price of cotton, and then cheats the Indians before turning around and calling them liars and thieves. But all this is fiction, in Rodriguez Monegal's opinion, for the Indians have no choice but passive resistance that Quiroga qualifies as laziness. Quiroga, however, never does become the colonist by virtue of his rebellious nature and radical anarchism (87). In fact, Quiroga's failed financial enterprises in the jungle kept him from joining the ranks of the dirty-smelling men with dirty machetes who followed the first man, the one who was simply eager to see, touch, and cut.

Because of a guilty conscience, because of a sense of honesty, or of rebellion, of refusing to emulate the other colonists or exploiters, or perhaps just because of bad luck, conquering the frontier proved to be quite a difficult task. This time around the land won, Quiroga lost, so the relationship with nature evolves and intensifies, a relationship that will be as ambivalent as Anaconda's relationship with man. "Quiroga ama y conoce la naturaleza como por un desafío hecho contra sí mismo y no por un descubrimineto placentero o místico" (Jitrik 102). [Quiroga knows and loves nature as a challenge, not because he finds in it pleasure of mysticism.]

So if Quiroga was attracted to the jungle, it was not because he saw in it an Eden or a paradise lost; he is neither sentimental nor romantic. Rodriguez Monegal even points out that he avoided the colorful niceties such as the fauna, flora, waterfalls, and even the ruins (80). In his stories set in the jungle, Quiroga does not allude to the beauty of the place; this is not a reification of nature. However, in Quiroga's stories nature is not only a backdrop, it is an entity, a catalyst, and a protagonist. The tropical forest is *el ambiente*, a formidable challenge; at times it is a death wish. This is Quiroga's elusive place. Finally, it is the Selva (*el ambiente*, the jungle, the environment) that provides Quiroga with the means to construct a dialectical representation of nature.

In spite of his failed attempt at becoming an aristocratic planter and his return to Buenos Aires, Quiroga is not altogether through with the Chaco. Time and time again, he returns there whenever he gets a chance, to see. In a letter dated February 6, 1908, Quiroga describes the jungle as something that has been nailed perpendicularly into his skull and regrets how what was once his property has changed, how the *yuyo*, a weed, has invaded what was once a *tabula rasa*. (Rodriguez Monegal 88) What he regrets, in fact, is the Horacio Quiroga who lived in the Chaco. Rodriguez Monegal believes that Quiroga encountered in the jungle the possibility to begin from scratch (the *tabula rasa* invaded by the *yuyo*) and also to experience and observe his actions and reactions in a hostile environment. "En la soledad del Chaco, en un mundo que podía pensar como salido de su mano, Quiroga debió creerse Diós" (Rodriguez Monegal 89). [In the solitude of the Chaco, in a world that he could consider to be his creation, perhaps Quiroga thought he was God.]

It is in 1906 that Quiroga returns to the province of Misiones, this time around in hopes of making a fortune cultivating *yerba mate*. Fearful that the frontier will be taken over by Brazilian squatters, the Argentine government is forever facilitating and encouraging colonization. Already with the Land Act of 1903, the Argentine government "hoped that the formation of new settlements in Misiones would help to guard the important international frontier zone from possible repetition of a wave of invaders with less peaceful motives than those who had swept westward from Brazil a few years earlier, as well as from the dangers of increased contraband in a region so difficult to police" (Eidt 96).

That Quiroga's 1906 business venture fails is beside the point; what matters are Quiroga's descriptions of the tropical forest. Rodriguez Monegal writes that he is seeing and describing the green core of America. What Quiroga sees is nothing but Selva, with no clearing, all the way north to the Amazon, all the way east to the Atlantic, all the way west to the mountains, and all the way south to Corrientes. Rodriguez Monegal writes that this is the compact and primitive world that tempts him and attracts him (120). Again, this reflects Buell's third dimension of place-connectedness: "A basic, sometimes fatal error made by discoverers and explorers of old as well as by tourists today is to fantasize that a pristine-looking landscape seen for the first time is so in fact—as if it hadn't been changing for eons before they set eyes on it, certainly from natural causes and probably anthropogenic ones as well" (*Writing for an Endangered World* 67–68).

So the Selva does not remain stable, and neither do people. Quiroga, for example, was born in Uruguay, lived in Argentina, traveled to Paris, traveled to Misiones, lived in the Argentine Chaco, returned to Misiones, then returned to the city where he will continue thinking and rethinking the Selva. Buell's fourth dimension of place-connectedness has to do, precisely, with all the places that have been significant to a person, "like a coral reef or set of tree rings" (ibid., 69). Back in the city of Buenos Aires, Quiroga is determined to return to Misiones once and for all, but the return to the Selva keeps being put off until his marriage to Ana María Cirés on December 30, 1909.

Rodriguez Monegal affirms that Quiroga hoped to find in Ana María a companion for the life in the Selva, his most ardent dream (135). Early in 1910 the couple sets out for San Ignacio eager to build a life there. San Ignacio is not in the jungle; Quiroga describes it as a cluster of huts, some houses, a few stores, and a bar (Jitrik 25). Quiroga's dwelling stands between the Upper Paraná River and the town, on what Jitrik describes as inhospitable tableland with a magnificent view. The living conditions are rough in their small wooden bungalow, the roof leaks, and they spend their nights shifting the bed from one room to the other. Rodriguez Monegal believes that Quiroga wishes to prove himself once and for all against nature, "que no premia ni perdona, la naturaleza que él necesita pero que será (como para Vigny) madre implacable" (136) [that neither rewards nor pardons, nature that he needs but that will be (as for Vigny) an implacable mother]. Rodriguez Monegal adds that Quiroga "se hunde en la selva, la posee y la fecunda, para que de esa monstruosa unión nazca (renazca) el verdadero Horacio Quiroga" (137) [sinks into the jungle, possesses it and fecundates it, so that from that monstrous union the real Horacio Quiroga may be born, or reborn].

William Rueckert points out that in Margaret Atwood's ecological novel, *Surfacing*, there is a relationship between the ways in which men treat and destroy women and the ways they treat and destroy nature (117). I am alluding to this because in many ways it is reminiscent of Quiroga's relationship with his wife and family at this particular moment in time, and subsequently could point to his relationship with nature. Because childbirth was something natural, Quiroga insisted on serving as midwife himself and on Ana María giving birth to their first child in their bungalow, in the wild, with no modern amenities. The result is that Ana María suffered terribly and would never fully recover from the trauma. Even if, the following year, Quiroga finally allows her to go to Buenos Aires to give birth to their second child in a hospital, with the help of doctors, his relationship with his wife and children will continue to be as exacting as the relationship he maintains with the natural world around him.

From the moment they were able to walk, Quiroga insisted in taking his children to the jungle: "Los arrimaba al peligro para que, a un tiempo, tuviesen consciencia de él y aprendieran a no temerle . . . Eran, en efecto, experiencias inauditas, como la de dejarlos largo tiempo solos en una espesura del bosque, o la de sentarlos en el borde de los acantilados con las piernas balanceándose sobre el abismo" (Jitrik 126). [He took them to the edge of danger so that eventually they would become conscious of it and learn not to fear it . . . These were incredible experiences, such as leaving them alone in the depths of the forest for greats lengths of time or having them sit at the edge of a cliff with their feet hanging over the abyss.]

Likewise, Quiroga is obsessed with rendering his place in the Selva habitable. This means working the land and constantly trying to improve his dwelling. To make matters all the more taxing, Quiroga insists on doing everything himself, with his hands. Not only did he struggle with the climate, the heat, and the unfertile land but also, as Rodriguez Monegal points out, with the people around him and with his own physical limitations (140).

Initially, Quiroga came to see, but now he wants a better view of the river, and to do so he needs to transform the mesa on which his house stands and also to cut and clear the jungle. "Para penetrar en ella, para irla domesticando de a poco, Quiroga abre picadas que mantiene viables a fuerza de machete. Es una lucha diaria con la naturaleza que no da tregua" (Rodriguez Monegal 140–41). [In order to make inroads into the jungle, to tame it little by little, Quiroga wields machete and makes clearings. It is a daily struggle with nature that gives no respite.]

The daily struggle with nature made Quiroga all the more determined to struggle with the environment and make it succumb to his will. He turned a deaf ear to his wife's protests and insisted on living a primitive life; little did it matter if civilization was a few miles away, in the town of Posadas, or in Corrientes. Rodriguez Monegal points out that the demands he made on his wife were tyrannical and incomprehensible to anyone who didn't share his fantasies of life in the wild (156). This is how Quiroga manages his family, his dwelling, his house, and then the world around him, the ecosystem and the large house. For the *eco* in ecosystem, economy and ecology comes from the Greek *oikos*, house.

In the house, in this case a bungalow, Ana María, spends her days weeping and complaining, because she cannot acclimate to life in the wild. The couple has violent arguments. Ana María attempts suicide several times and finally succeeds in December 1915. Rodriguez Monegal believes that Ana María went mad in the jungle, and also that Quiroga felt responsible for her having felt so desperate that death seemed to be the only salvation (168). Eventually, Ana María's absence renders life in Misiones unbearable and less than a year later, Quiroga returns to live in Buenos Aires. "Abandona el paraíso tan penosamente levantado con sus manos, se refugia en el caos (ajeno, monstruoso, indifference) de la gran ciudad del Sur. Vuelve" (Rodriguez Monegal 171). [He abandons the paradise that he so laboriously built with his own hands, and takes refuge in the alien, monstrous and indifferent chaos of Buenos Aires. He returns.] This remains the fourth dimension of place-connectedness. For the next ten years he will return to Misiones regularly, only for brief stays, for in spite of it having been the scene of so much grief, it remains, according to Rodriguez Monegal, a point of reference for Quiroga's creativity and also a stimulus for his narrative work (183). In 1925, Quiroga will attempt once again to live in Misiones, only to fail again.

The years spent in the city, thinking and rethinking the Selva, were to be Quiroga's most productive period. In 1918, under Kipling's influence, he published *Cuentos de la selva para niños* (*Tales of the Jungle for Children*), a collection of stories he had written for his children where jungle animals speak and think and feel, much like man, and are given anthropomorphic attributes. Rodriguez Monegal analyses Kipling's influence on Quiroga and points out that for Kipling, the jungle was a literary theme and not a personal experience. For Quiroga, on the contrary, the Selva was his natural environment (186). Rodriguez Monegal adds that Quiroga was not a displaced person or an exile in the Selva, on the contrary, and this touches on the fifth dimension of place-connectedness. From the moment Quiroga first set foot in Misiones, he was home, this was his habitat, and he knew that this was where he would put down roots (11).

Three years after the publication of *Cuentos de la selva para niños*, Quiroga was still exploring the possibility of seeing the Selva through the animal's perspective and also of speaking on behalf of all the disempowered, not only the animals, so he published *Anaconda*. Rodriguez Monegal considers some of the stories in this collection to be a much more elaborate collection of jungle stories for children. The story that gives the collection its name, for example, describes the struggle between all the serpents of the region and the men from the *Instituto de Seroterapia Ofídica*. All the snakes are the residents of a laboratory where their venom is being studied. It was to stories such as these, where animals are allowed to articulate speech, that Jorge Luis Borges was alluding when he told Rodriguez Monegal that Quiroga wrote the stories that Kipling had already written better. Rodriguez Monegal recalls how dismayed Quiroga was to hear Borges's judgment, a judgment that he considered unfair (222). But it could very well be that Rodriguez Monegal misunderstood Borges, for Borges did not necessarily say that Kipling's stories were good, only that they were better than Quiroga's. Perhaps what Borges was questioning was not so much Quiroga's talent, but rather the animal stories themselves. In Lawrence Buell's opinion, with the imagined miseries of beasts "Anna Sewall's [sic] *Black Beauty* becomes the so-called *Uncle Tom's Cabin* of the horse" (229).

With "El regreso de Anaconda," Quiroga attempts once again to see the Selva through the boa's perspective and thus to expose riverine environmental problems caused by humans. "El regreso" constitutes the first part of the collection titled *Los desterrados* (*The Exiles*), the second part being made up of seven stories all set in the Misiones Selva. Quiroga's most productive years come to their apex precisely with the publication in 1926 of *Los desterrados*. He has not yet returned to the Selva and will not do so until 1932, to live the last chapter of his life. According to the critic Arturo Sergio Visca, the Quiroga who returns to Misiones on January 10, 1932, is not the same Quiroga who first went there in 1903, or the one who returned there in 1904, and again in 1910. Visca believes that this time around, the return to the Selva is an escape of sorts (9–10).

The first months of life in the jungle are idyllic, according to Rodriguez Monegal. It is not long before the natural environment takes Quiroga back into its fold, as if he were returning home. There is an incident with an enormous snake that Quiroga kills with a machete. Rodriguez Monegal believes that the city man died at the very moment that he wielded the machete and chopped off the snake's head. Quiroga is home, and once again, he sets out to forge the world around him. He chops wood, he hangs his collection of anaconda skins on the walls, and he cultivates his garden.

The idyllic existence, however, is short lived, for in a May 10, 1936, letter to his friend Asdrubal Delgado, Quiroga confides that he is determined to divorce María Elena, his second wife, since she cannot tolerate life in the jungle, and he, in turn, will not return to the city (Visca 49). In a May 21, 1936, letter to Ezequiel Martínez Estrada, Quiroga expresses the extreme attachment he has to his habitat in the Selva by writing, "He de morir regando mis plantas, y plantando el mismo día de morir. No hago más que integrarme en la naturaleza, con sus leyes y armonías oscurísimas aún para nosotros, pero existentes" (Visca 103). [I should die watering my plants, and I should be planting the day I die. I do nothing more than become part of nature with its laws and harmonies that remain obscure for us, but nonetheless existent.]

It is obvious that his relationship with nature has evolved through the years. The Quiroga who tries to cheat the natives and to make a fortune farming, the Quiroga who kills vipers and collects anaconda skins, who incessantly returns to the jungle in search of creative energy, is also the Quiroga who once attempted to see the tropical jungle through Anaconda's eyes and who, toward the end of his life, wishes to become one with nature. This final return to the jungle was indeed an escape of sorts, an escape from the city, but also, according to Visca, a reencounter with himself and with nature. "Reencuentra la naturaleza que, en verdad, nunca había abandonado del todo, pero a la cual ahora va a amar en su última y más profunda y pura desnudez, sin pretender forzarla para que le dé temas literarios" (Visca 11). [He encounters nature all over again, but then again he had never left it altogether, except that now he is going to love it in its ultimate and most profound and pure being, without wanting to extract from it ideas for stories.]

The battles with the land have been fought, some have been won, others have been lost, the stories have all been written, and coming to its end is the life of a man who carved the Argentine tropical frontier into South American literature. As a conclusion, I would like to approach "El regresso" with some questions in mind, questions put forth by Cheryll Glotfelty, such as how nature is represented in this story, what role the physical setting plays, what values are expressed, and whether or not these values are consistent with ecological wisdom (xxiii). Perhaps these questions will supply some answers as to why Quiroga belongs in the ecocritical canon without, however, having to be labeled an environmentalist saint.

Visca writes, "Quiroga no vió sólo en la naturaleza un objeto de contemplación, sino también una fuerza fraternalmente enemiga—admítase la paradoja—con cual era necesario luchar para subyugarla. Esa lucha es, para el salteño, un puente tendido entre la intimidad del espíritu y la intimidad de la naturaleza" (3). [Quiroga not only saw in nature an object of contemplation, but also a fraternally inimical force—in spite of the paradox—that needed to be contended with and ultimately subjugated. The struggle itself is, for Quiroga, a bridge between the intimacy of his spirit and the intimacy of nature.]

The juxtaposition of the words *fraternalmente* and *enemiga* (*fraternally* and *inimical*) are reminiscent of the "sombría fraternidad" that unites the monkey, the serpent, the crocodile, the bird, the rat, and the anaconda at the beginning of "El regreso." What precipitates this somber fraternity is the drought. It has not rained in the jungle for months; even the morning dew has disappeared, the "ambiente" is rapidly drying up. Three factors come into play with this drought: logging, farming, and bad luck. Since two of those three factors point to man, Anaconda and the other animals will hope for better luck—a rainfall—while they struggle against the effects of logging and farming in the area.

The common enemy, man, brings the animals together in a somber fraternity. They hold a meeting. Anaconda prompts the animals as well as the spirit of the place to action, "Todos somos iguales, pero juntos. Cada uno de nosotros, de por sí, no vale gran cosa. Aliados somos toda la zona tropical. ¡Lancémosla contra el hombre, hermanos! ¡El todo lo destruye! ¡Nada hay que no corte y ensucie! ¡Echemos por el río nuestra zona entera!" (50). [We are are equal, so long as we are united. Each one of us alone is not worth much. United we are the entire tropical zone. Let us set out against man. Man destroys everything, there is nothing that he will not cut and soil. Let us throw our entire zone into the river!] Doing so, Anaconda hopes to blockade the river and take it back.

In the heart of the story, nature is man's enemy, perhaps even a formidable enemy, at least for a short while. Eventually, it starts to rain and the river floods. Once again, the deluge rages against mankind; it is the answer to a prayer from nature. Satisfied, Anaconda allows herself to be carried by the waters of the Paranahyba for days, until she comes across a shack floating adrift, and a fatally wounded laborer in the shack. As soon as the serpents become aware of the wounded man, they decide to kill him because he is an enemy of the jungle. Immediately, Anaconda orders the serpents to move back. "He tomado a ese hombre enfermo bajo mi protección. ¡Cuidado con la que se acerque!" (54) [I have taken this man under my protection. I dare any one of you to approach!]

Although unsure as to why she has decided to protect this man, her enemy, Anaconda is adamant that she will kill any animal that dares to approach. Initially, the wounded man could have been a symbolic result of the tropics agreeing to unite against the intruder, but soon enough Anaconda's uncanny decision to protect the man points to a certain ambivalence. Anaconda is aware of her ambivalent feelings and stops to question them, only to convince herself that this man is not worth the thought; he is about to die. Her unwillingness to delve into this matter will, obviously, lead her to her untimely death. Before she is shot and killed by other men, she lays her eggs next to the dead man's body.

Jennifer French is of the opinion that by adopting the perspective of the boa, "Quiroga explores a relationship with the environment outside the assumptions underpinning capitalism's exploitation of natural resources" (66). The silenced voices are speaking, and the silenced minds are thinking. French never questions this decision to make the boa speak and think like a human, and takes it for granted that Quiroga is simply trying to overcome anthropocentrism. He very well could be, and Christopher Manes sounds convincing enough when he writes, "Nature is silent in our culture (and in literate societies generally) in the sense that the status of being a speaking subject is jealously guarded as an exclusively human prerogative" (15). By simulation, Quiroga could very well be treating the ecosystem as a silenced subject and allowing it to speak.

Nonetheless, the boa and all the other animals are speaking and thinking in man's language, in this case Spanish. Not only are they being ascribed human attributes, but human feelings and values as well. The logger does not care about the river, but the boa does. The boa cares. The boa even cares about one dying laborer. Then again, perhaps there is no other way, no way to know the animal's language and perspective, whatever that may mean. So Quiroga worked with what he had, his emotions, his values, and his language, in order to bring awareness to the fragility of the natural world.

Quite similar to "El regreso" is Barbara Gowdy's novel *The White Bone*, which Lawrence Buell judges as "a bold attempt to imagine how elephants think and feel" (232). Soon, Buell comes to the conclusion that the "result is a far less reader-friendly text than *Bambi* or *Babar* or *The Year of the Whale*" (233). So now that the question of how nature is represented has lead to an aporia, perhaps it is wiser to analyze how nature is *not* represented in "El regreso."

For one, "El regreso" is not a pastoral. It does not fall under any of the definitions of pastoral that Terry Gifford proposes. "El regreso" is neither a classical pastoral nor a romantic one, nor does it contrast the city with the country, or even idealize nature. Without man, Quiroga suggests that the jungle would not necessarily be a harmonious machine, for the animals are in fierce competition against each other, they are enduring a drought that simply has to do with bad luck, and they find balance and fraternity when they unite against the common enemy, man. This suggests that were man to be eliminated, perhaps the animals would go back to the way it was, with each one fending for survival of the species.

"El regreso" does not fall into the category of wilderness narrative either. Much like the pastoral, the wilderness narrative is at the very beginning of the triad: to see, to touch, and to cut. Both the pastoral and the wilderness construction have much to do with seeing. The nature Quiroga is representing is quite a distance away from Thoreau's and Muir's idea of sublime nature. Never does Quiroga attempt to describe a sublime landscape untainted by man. On the contrary, this is the jungle, it is closer to the bog than to the mountaintop, and man is always present. In this sense, Quiroga steers clear of the trouble with wilderness, this trouble being, as Greg Garrard suggests, that nature is only pure and authentic if man is absent from it. (70)

Greg Garrard adds that "a further problem is apparent: the ideal wilderness space is wholly pure by virtue of its independence from humans, but the ideal wilderness narrative posits a human subject whose most authentic existence is located precisely there" (70–71). Nearly a century ago, when the historical perspectives of ecocriticism were not yet defined, before the time of political orientations, before deep ecology, casual environmentalism, and ecological hysteria, Quiroga was exploring possible answers and solutions to the questions and the issues. He sensed that literature had a role to play and, by virtue of living there, he was privy to the political and economical dimension of this matter.

For environmental problems do indeed require analysis in scientific terms, but also personal and artistic ones. By making the animals speak, Quiroga was exploring ways to give nature some independence without assuming righteous moral positions, and without being sentimental or romantic. What he could not avoid, however, was using man's language and man's perspective. But he is well aware of this. After all, not only does Anaconda choose against the other animals to protect one dying laborer, but she also lays her eggs next to his body. Without providing specific solutions, this serves several functions. First of all, it points to the political and *eco*nomical dimension, the presence of man, who will not be eliminated. It also points to the different types of men, the laborer, the logger, the pioneer, the man in search of a dwelling, and so on. In other words, it refers to those who are there to touch, to cut, dirty-smelling with their dirty machetes, and who will not be made to leave, for it is too late, the jungle has been discovered, in this particular case, the Argentine tropical frontier.

Quiroga expected to die in the jungle, watering his plants, being one with nature. His life was that of a man obsessed with a place, a place that happened to be the subtropical jungle. By virtue of this obsessive relationship with the Selva alone, Quiroga merits an earth-centered approach. But eventually all of Quiroga's stories set in the jungle should be included in any historical inquiry of literary works having to do with man's attitude toward the natural world.

Regardless of whether or not Quiroga's stories have a moral, green or political agenda, they also deserve consideration in modern attempts to study the relationship between literature and ecology. The reason for this is that by virtue of their contents and of their artistic value, these stories bring the awareness to the place, in this case, the South American tropical jungle before it resembled a square fragment of rain forest left standing on land cleared for pasture.

Quiroga expected to die in Misiones watering his plants, but he did not. Misiones remains, however, the place where he rehearsed his death over and over again, in his letters and his stories. On the Sunday he arrived in Buenos Aires and asked his nine-year-old daughter for a kiss, before kissing him she told him she never wanted to return to Misiones (Rodriguez Monegal 282). So the magic place where he became a colossal tropical plant had become his daughter's unloved place. A few months later, Quiroga died in Buenos Aires. A medical report would say that he did not die of natural causes.

Chapter 8

The Landscapes of Venezuela

Doña Bárbara

Jerry Hoeg

Venezuelan author Rómulo Gallegos's (1884–1969) novel *Doña Bárbara*, first published in Spain by Araluce in 1929, then extensively rewritten with a second, definitive version in 1930 (again Barcelona, Araluce), is generally characterized as a *novela de la tierra*, one that treats the Latin American countryside both in the sense of being about the land but also in the sense of coming from the *tierra*, or land. And indeed, *Doña Bárbara* is a novel of the land in both senses: firstly, because it is set in the then-untamed Apure region of Venezuela, an expanse of *llanos*—savanna or plains—between the Colombian border and the Orinoco River drained by the Apure, Arauca, and Cunaviche rivers (Vila 9–13), and secondly, because this landscape plays a central role in the novel, symbolizing as it does wild and primeval nature, including human nature, which issues forth from it. In Gallegos's conceptualization, the uniqueness of the land and people make both Venezuelan literature and Venezuela itself distinctive, unmatched by any other. The protagonist of the novel, Santos Luzardo (in Spanish, *Santos* means "saints," and *Luzardo* means "I am a burning light"), brings the enlightening, domesticating, and pacifying effects of civilization from the city onto this wild landscape and its equally wild and untamed inhabitants, setting up the novel's primary conflict, that of civilization versus barbarism.

At one level, the novel can be read as an effort on the part of Gallegos to create a new cultural vision for Venezuela. By the time of the novel's publication, Venezuela had ceased to be a rural nation with timeless village life run by local caciques or caudillos, and had begun to modernize and industrialize and, importantly, to urbanize, in large part due to advances in the petroleum industry (Liscano 141; Pino Iturrieta 37–40). Indeed, the *llano* Gallegos describes in the novel is the *llano* of the past, for by Gallegos's time, railways, motor launches, and motor cars, such as the one Gallegos used to visit the *llano*, were already in place on the savanna. Gallegos avails himself of this semi-mythical past—most of the characters, place names, and incidents in the novel are based on real people, places, and incidents Gallegos discovered on his visit to the *llano* (Shaw 14–15)—to orchestrate a new solution to the problems engendered by the barbarous behavior he sees as ubiquitous in Latin America, namely the anarchy, civil war, and despotism that had followed close on the heels of political independence. Historically, the problem had been posited in terms of racial types—Argentine author and later president Domingo F. Sarmiento's (1811–88) *Facundo* (1845) began the discussion, which runs through Latin American letters up to the present day—and writers did and do debate the merits of various races and mixes thereof. Although Gallegos advocates education over superstition, altruistic cooperation over self-serving competition, and written, codified law over the "law of the plains," which in the novel appears quite red in tooth and claw, he still blames a hereditary, racial component for part of the problem. "Corregir nuestro sistema de educación . . . no baste a extirpar . . . muchas de las condiciones que tienen su origen en las raíces mismas de la raza, haciendo desaparecer las herencias perniciosas" (*Una posición* 61–62). [Correcting the educational system isn't enough to eliminate many of the troublesome conditions, the origins of which are rooted in race, nor will said correction eliminate these pernicious racial inheritances.] And the final line in the novel prophesizes a new utopian mix as the final solution, "una raza buena." But, as we shall see, human nature is a hereditary component of all races and plays a key role in the novel, fluctuating between imposing civilization and opposing the impositions of civilization.

At another level, one can recognize in the novel the same factors that have always troubled human civilization since the domestication of plants and animals and so the advent of herding and agriculture, some 10,000 years ago (Cavalli-Sforza 53), namely substantial population growth and consequent urbanization. This in turn occasioned the need for cooperation at a massive level in a species whose very nature is to cooperate only at the level of band and village society, and then only with closely related conspecifics, and always to compete with outsiders (Bridgeman 175–93). The problem and its possible solutions are still with us today, and as elusive as ever, though books such as Peter Singer's *The Expanding Circle* offer reason for optimism.

Effectively, *Doña Bárbara* treats the problems caused by human nature in the move from the hunter-gatherer lifestyle in which humans existed for over 95 percent of our natural history to civilized, urban society. The landscape in *Doña Bárbara* describes how our specific human nature evolved over the course of some six million years (Bridgeman 41). In the opposition between civilization and barbarism, the barbarism is not so much the natural landscape as the human psychological landscape that evolved to survive in the natural environment of the savanna but must now survive in another, quite different, modern environment. Humans are a grassland species, adapted to an opportunistic economy of hunting and gathering. We know humans evolved in a savanna environment both from the fossil record (Bridgeman 61) and from universal human preferences for certain kinds of landscapes. Gordon Orians and Judith Heerwagen interviewed a large number of people from a broad range of ages and cultures and found a universal preference for a savanna or *llanos* type environment: short grass with a few trees and shrubs, gently rolling hills, and some standing water. This is our environment of evolutionary adaptedness (Plotkin 93, 101).

Of course, one might argue these preferences are simply learned preferences to one's surroundings. But for the vast majority of those surveyed, the savanna landscape is not their native landscape. Additionally, were these learned preferences, we should expect them to strengthen with age and experience, but the exact opposite occurs. The savanna preference is strongest in young children, and with age, people develop an additional parallel preference for their current environment (Balling and Falk). There is even a preference for certain tree shapes, specifically those grown in ideal savanna conditions, and studies of landscape art reflect the same tendencies (Orians and Heerwagen; Repton). In the artificial environments we create for ourselves—the short grass of the traditional American yard, water features in the home landscape, golf courses, parks, suburban sprawl, and the suburbs themselves—we continue to exhibit this preference (Orians and Heerwagen 62–63; Kaplan).

That these preferences are instinctive is not surprising; indeed, many things previously thought to be learned—language, narrative, emotional responses, food preferences, sexual preferences, sibling and parent rivalry, and on and on—have been shown to have an innate basis, albeit always in a general form. We are not born blank slates, though our innate predispositions both fashion and are fashioned by culture (Pinker). This interior landscape of innate propensities—variously called in Spanish *alma de la raza, genio de la raza*, or *modo de ser*—is precisely what both Gallegos, as educator and later president of Venezuela (1948), and Santos Luzardo, as protagonist in the novel, seek to redirect in order to bring about a civilizing racial and social synthesis in an effort to overcome the traditional Latin American problems of violence, corruption, injustice, and despotism.

In the novel, Gallegos paints the conflict between civilization and barbarism as a landscape portrait, one in which civilization triumphs by "modifying nature" (54), that is, by converting the natural environment into a civilized, cultured, and legally demarcated—subdivide and conquer—countryside. He then goes on, in a kind of environmental determinism, to equate civilizing the land with civilizing the people. Both the savanna and doña Bárabara are "devadoras de hombres" (devourers of men). Santos's cousin Lorenzo Barquero, whom Santos finds living in alcoholic misery after having been destroyed by the seductive wiles of doña Bárbara, says, "Esta tierra no perdona . . . ! La maldita llanura, devadora de hombres!" (This land doesn't forgive . . . ! The damned savanna, devourer of men!), to which Santos replies, "Realmente, más que a las seducciones de la famosa doña Bárbara, este infeliz ha sucumbido a la acción embrutecedora del desierto" (62). [Truth be told, it wasn't so much to doña Bárbara that this poor bastard succumbed as it was to the brutalizing power of Nature.] Even people are described in terms of nature. The voice of the first of doña Bárbara's henchmen that Santos meets is "blanda y pegajosa como el lodo de los tremedales de la llanura" (2) [smooth and sticky like the mud from the quagmires of the savanna], but Marisela, the noble savage cousin he meets soon thereafter, is "todavía silvestre, como la flor del paraguatán" (64) [still wild, like the flower of the paraguatan tree]. Indeed, D. L. Shaw believes "the key-sentence of the whole novel is Lorenzo Barquero's assertion (142): 'Es necesario matar al centauro que todos llaneros llevamos por dentro'" (71). [It's necessary to kill the centaur that all plainsmen carry inside.] Doña Bárbara is also described as a sphinx, a woman's head on a lion's body. Both these descriptions indicate the animal origins of our human nature, and the battle between civilization and barbarism that exists within each of us.

In this view, barbarism is endemic to nature, as seen in the swamp fevers, deserts, droughts, floods, wildfires, and other natural disasters that abound in the savanna. For Gallegos, if you eliminate those, you will eliminate the barbarism of the inhabitants of the land. Implicit in this idea is a version of development theory, the idea that material progress will solve sociopolitical problems, an example of which we see in Santos's implementation of cheese production, the *queseras*, which serves to tame both the people and the animals of the *llano*: "La quesera comenzaba así la civilización de la barbarie del ganado" (104). [Cheese production began the civilization of the cattle business.]

And, just as in countless Hollywood Westerns, by the end of the novel the *llano* is finally tamed by barbed wire, paid for, ironically, by the collected plumage of wild birds (*Casmerodius albus*), nature commercialized: "Llegó el alambre de púas . . . y de los innumerables caminos . . . el alambre comenzaba a trazar uno solo y derecho hacia el porvenir" (198). [The barbed wire arrived . . . and of the innumerable paths on the savanna . . . the wire began to delineate one, unique and straight, toward the future.] As Marco Aurelio Vila reports, this commercialization nearly led to the extinction of these birds in Venezuela (43), their salvation coming from early ecologists and a shift in women's fashion away from hats. So when Santos wins the legal battle with Mister Danger and doña Bárbara over the use of fencing to delineate property lines, the road to civilization is clearly marked by the legal and physical division of the landscape. But whether human nature was tamed in the process is quite another question.

The novel opens with Santos's return to the *llanos* after years studying and living in Caracas. Traveling in a small boat up the river into the heart of darkness, he allows a suspicious character, "uno de esos hombres inquietantes, de facciones asiáticas, que hacen pensar en alguna semilla tártara caída en América . . . Un tipo de razas inferiores, crueles y sombrías, completamente diferente del de los pobladores de la llanura" (1) [one of those unnerving types, with Asiatic features, that made you think of a transplanted Mongol . . . Somebody from an inferior race, cruel and dark, completely different from the settlers of the plains] to travel along for part of the way. This stranger turns out to be one of doña Bárbara's henchmen, the evil Melquíades Gamarra, alias *el Brujeador* (the warlock). This is another example of the hereditary determinism Gallegos advocates, and it includes Santos Luzardo himself, given that Santos was born on the savanna and, as the characters never tire of repeating, "Llanero es llanero hasta la quinta generación" (104). [A plainsman is a plainsman until the fifth generation.] When Santos's inner anger shows through his civilized exterior, a ranch hand rejoices, "Tenemos hombre . . . La raza de los Luzardos no se ha acabado todavía" (34). [We have a man . . . The bloodline of the Luzardos lives.] It also extends to doña Bárbara, who is herself of mixed blood, with a white father and Indian mother, hence her propensity both for violence and for guile: "Las indias la iniciaron en su tenebrosa sabiduría toda la catevera de brujos que cría la bárbara existencia de la indiada" (23). [The Indian women initiated her into their dark knowledge, the whole throng of witches that produced the barbarous existence of the tribe.]

Initially, Santos's purpose in traveling to his boyhood home, the ranch known as Altamira (in Spanish, *Altamira* means high sights, Johnson 457) located in the farthest reaches of the Arauca region, is to meet a buyer for the property. But when the prodigal son returns, the *llano* strikes a mysterious chord deep in his heart and he finds he cannot sell. The ranch had been founded in the remote past by a blood relative, Evaristo Luzardo, an itinerant herder, "uno de aquellos llaneros nómadas que recorrían—y todavía recorren—con sus rebaños las inmensas praderas del cajón del Cunaviche" (12) [one of those nomads who used to roam—and still do—with their herds the immense vastness of the plains]. Reprising the human species' move from nomadic hunter-gatherer to herdsmen to village life, Evaristo's descendents, "true llaneros," continued to enlarge the holding until it became one of the most important of the region, multiplying and enriching the family in the process. This population growth sowed discord in paradise, generating much sibling rivalry. The final patriarch of the original Altamira was José de los Santos, who bought out all the other relatives in order to eliminate the discord and consolidate the property, but on his death his two children, José and Panchita, decided to divide the ranch in two, with José's part conserving the original name of Altamira, and the other taking that of La Barquereña, after Panchita's husband, Sebastián Barquero. Unfortunately, the document that specified the dividing line stated that the line should run up to the palm grove known as La Chusmita (in Spanish, *la chusma* literally means the crew of a slave galley and, by extension, the rabble, the mob), without stating on which side the palm grove should be included. Because neither side would cede the grove to the other, it was agreed that the palm grove should be fenced off and become a sort of no-man's-land, with entry therein prohibited to both sides.

With reference to José and Panchita, it should be noted that in natural populations on the savanna, sibling rivalry is common. It has been documented in mammals, birds, amphibians, fish, insects, and even plants (Mock and Parker 74; Mock 212–17). In animals it is instinctive. African black eagles lay two eggs to increase the odds one hatches. Siblicide is obligate, so the first to hatch always pecks the second to death (Mock 50–51). In humans siblicide is rare, but the instinct for violent competition is not. It comes not from bad parenting, but rather from human nature. Children are most violent in toddlerhood; it comes to them naturally, and only later are they partially behaviorally inhibited, or civilized (Holden 580–81).

In the center of the grove was a riverbed that, although normally dry, became a swampy, quicksand-filled quagmire in the rainy season, a *tremedal* in Spanish, swallowing up anything that entered, including one day a barquero cow. Upon seeing the cow drowned in the quicksand of the swamp, José Luzardo accused Sebastián Barquero of violating the terms of the prohibition agreement and a fight ensued, which in turn resulted in José killing Sebastián. While at the international level, Spain and the United States were fighting over land Spain had seized in the remote past, in the *llanura* the family feud over land seized in the remote past likewise continued, until finally don José fought and killed his own son Félix and then killed himself. A few days later, Santos, the only survivor of the family feud save for Lorenzo Barquero, fled with his mother to Caracas. The income from Altamira provided living expenses and Santos's education as a lawyer. But over time corrupt administrators at the ranch and the predations of the neighboring landowner, one doña Bárbara, ate into both the income and the property itself, hence Santos's return some thirteen years later to sell the troubled and unprofitable land.

Santos's first visit outside Altamira was to the home of Lorenzo Barquero in an effort to end the family feud. The home, reduced to a ruin, was located in La Chusmita, now literally home of the rabble. As the reader will recall, this was the zone that was included in neither part of the division of the original Altamira property, an oversight that had occasioned the family feud that nearly eradicated both sides. La Chusmita, a palm grove that covered a depression in the savanna, was named after a small blue heron found in the grove. According to legend, the heron represented the tormented soul of the daughter of the chief of the Yaruro, the tribe that had been living there when Evaristo Luzardo first arrived with his flocks. Evaristo exterminated the Indians in order to take the land for himself, but before the chief died he cursed the palm grove, saying that the invader and his descendents would find only ruin and disgrace in it until the Yaruros returned to power. And indeed, "Era un lugar maldito: un silencio impresionante, numerosas palmeras carbonizadas por el rayo y en el centro un tremedal donde parecía, sorbido por el lodo, cuanto ser viviente se aventurara a atravesarlo" (54). [It was an accursed place: stunningly silent, full of palms charred by lightening, and in the middle a quagmire whose oozing mud devoured anything living thing that dared try to cross it.]

Lorenzo Barquero was the youngest son of Sebastián Barquero, and it was he who had instigated Félix Luzardo the day of the tragic confrontation with José Luzardo. Lorenzo had inherited La Barquereña and moved to Caracas, but then returned to the *llano*, where he soon fell under the evil spell of doña Bárbara, who bore him a child, drove him to alcoholic ruin, and then forced him to sign away La Barquereña. Shortly thereafter he, now an "ex hombre," and their daughter Marisela were exiled to La Chusmita, to pass his remaining days in "una vivienda miserable, mitad caney, mitad choza, formada ésta por cuatro paredes de barro y paja sin enlucido . . . la negra y ya casi deshecha techumbre de hojas de palmera . . . chinchorro mugriento" (56) [a miserable shack, half cabin, half mud hut, made of four windowless, adobe walls, partially roofed with palm fronds . . . and furnished with a filthy hammock]. According to Lorenzo, "Esta no es una casa; esto es el cubil de una bestia" (57). [This isn't a house, it's a cage for a beast.] For him, La Chusmita was a living hell.

When Santos arrives, Lorenzo tells him, between slugs of aguardiente, that in Caracas he realized the rational veil of civilization that covered city life, and especially university life, was false, a self deception that hid the hereditary cancer of the plainsman, the call of nature, human nature: "La sentí agazapado en fondo de mi corazón . . . la úlcera latente del cáncer hereditario. Y comencé a aborrecer la Universidad y la vida de la ciudad" (62). [I felt crouched in my heart the latent ulcer of our hereditary cancer. I began to abhor the university and city life.] So he returned to the savanna and was powerless to resist the enchantments of doña Bárbara and the "maldita llanura" (62) [the damned savanna], both "devoradoras de hombres" (devourers of men). Throughout, Lorenzo believes he and Santos are fated to succumb to nature as personified by doña Bárbara. Conflating the two, he tells Santos, "Esta tierra no perdona. También has oído la llamada de la devoradora de hombres. Ya te veré caer entre sus brazos" (61). [This land doesn't forgive. You too have heard the call of the "devourer of men." And you too will fall into her clutches.] D. L. Shaw sees Lorenzo as a "symbol of the older generation of Venezuela's landholding élite. This generation recognized the need to save the country from *barbarie*, but failed to carry out the task. In practice they supported the dictator Juan Vicente Gómez as a 'gendarme necesario' and saw the country's resources fall further into the power of foreign interests" (64). Interestingly, at the end of Part I, Santos brings Lorenzo and Marisela to his home, thus saving them from the clutches of the local foreigner, the American Mr. Danger, who has designs on one of the region's prime natural resources, Marisela. And at the end of the novel, when Santos finally civilizes the *llano*, the process includes the exit of the foreigner, Mister. Danger.

On his way back to Altamira, Santos runs into the local peasant girl he had asked directions from on the way into La Chusmita. But now, having been told by Lorenzo of her birth, he recognizes the dirty, barefoot, and half-wild peasant girl dressed in rags as his now fifteen-year-old cousin, Marisela. The chapter in which the meeting takes place is titled "La bella durmiente" (Sleeping Beauty), and it is an apt summary of their relation over the course of the novel, as would be "Marisela Dolittle" (Levy 120). Marisela, who represents wild nature, coming as she does from La Chusmita, also represents the racial mixture that Gallegos seeks to reconcile, civilize, and socialize in the new Venezuela. Remember, Marisela's mother is doña Bárbara, who is *mestiza*, while her father is a white *criollo*, descended from the conquerors of the land. And remember also the original curse on La Chusmita—a name that represents the tormented soul of the daughter of the chief of the tribe who cursed the palm grove—prophesizing that the invader and his descendents would only find ruin and disgrace in it until such time as the native people returned to power. Marisela represents those native people of the land—"una personificación del alma de la raza, abierta, como el paisaje, a toda ación mejoradora" (93) [an incarnation of the soul of the race, open, like the landscape, to all actions for betterment]—perhaps even the tormented soul of the chief's daughter, and she does indeed return to power at the end of the novel as the civilizing efforts of Santos tame her wild nature and that of doña Bárbara, which allows her to inherit the former La Barquereña, now El Miedo under doña Bárbara, marry Santos, and so reunite the divided Altamira. This scenario embodies Gallegos's vision of racial unity and social cooperation through the civilizing effects of education. On this view, people adapt not to the environment, but rather they adapt the environment to themselves. But in order to achieve this unity, not only must Marisela's Edenic nature be tamed, but she must also tame Santos's *llanero* instincts. And who is to tame doña Bárbara's evil nature?

In the case of Marisela, by moving to Altamira she is not only transformed through education into a civilized person but also falls in love with Santos, which appears to be a result of the civilizing process. Later, feeling unrequited and vying with her own mother for the affections of Santos, she attempts to return to La Chusmita but finds she can no longer live its primitive lifestyle. The horse La Catira symbolizes the difference between the former wild-child, animal nature of Marisela, "bestia arisca, báquiro" (a wild, surly beast), and her new, civilized self. Arriving back at La Chusmita on board La Catira she sets the mare free and, after a moment of doubt, the horse "se convenció de que realmente era libre y, despidiéndose de la dueña con otro relincho, se perdió de vista por la sabana inmensa. Mas si la *Catira* podía volver a la libre vida del hatajo, no así Marisela a la simplicidad de su antigua situación montaraz" (144) [convinced herself that she really was free and, saying goodbye with a last whinny, she disappeared from sight out onto the savanna]. She now knows that the education in civilization she received at the hands of Santos has changed her forever.

Meanwhile, left at the moment to his own devices, a grieving Santos feels the call of the *llano* and his inner *llanero* begins to break through the thin veneer of civilization, first in the *doma* (bronc bustin') and *vaquería general* (roundup) after which he begins to think, "Bien estaba la llanura, así, ruda,y bravia. Era la barbarie; mas . . . la barbarie tiene sus encantos, es algo hermoso que vale la pena vivirlo, es la plenitud del hombre"(190). [The savanna was good, just like it is, rough and tumble. It was wild; but . . . the savageness has its charms, it's something wild that makes life worth living, that brings out the man in you.] Next, frustrated by the lack of law enforcement as a viable recourse to the crimes inflicted on him and his family, he takes the law into his own hands. But in the end, Marisela's love for him saves him from his natural, innate barabarism, returns him to civilized ways, and he finds the good within himself and also within others, including doña Bárbara, whose instinct for love in the end overcomes her instinct for revenge. And so while the *llano* appears to embody both good and evil, "bello y terrible a la vez" (47) [both beautiful and terrible at the same time], in reality the problems in the novel come from the conflict between human nature and the efforts of civilization to overcome those fundamental drives adapted over millions of years to a different *llano*, and now dysfunctional in a modernizing Venezuela. And this same term, "bello y terible a la vez" (29) is applied to doña Bábara as well.

Doña Bárbara, like Santos, arrived via the river. She is first described as "fruto engendrado por la violencia del blanco aventurero en la sombría sensualidad de la india, su origen se perdía en el dramático misterio de las tierras vírgenes" (19) [fruit of the union of the violence of the white adventurer inflicted on the dark sensuality of the Indian maiden, her origin lost in the dramatic mystery of unknown lands]. She worked on a pirate boat on the river, until one day a new crewman came on board, a certain Asdrúbal. He taught her to read and write, much as Santos does later with Marisela, but was killed by the savage, mutinous crew who then raped Bárbara. That same night, the boat's pilot spirited her away to his Indian village, where her beauty caused enough jealousy that she was forced back to the river and her encounter with Lorenzo Barquero (in Spanish, *barquero* means boatman or ferryman), and her subsequent installation in El Miedo (The Fear). In this initial phase she is characterized as a murderess seeking revenge on all men for what the crew did to her. She is described as avaricious, a sorceress, and lacking in maternal instinct for abandoning Marisela, all in the embodiment of evil save for a spark of love left deep in her soul, *el alma de la raza*: "lujuria y superstición, codicia y crueldad, y allá en el fondo del alma sombría una pequeña cosa pura y dolorosa: el recuerdo de Asdrúbal, el amor frustrado que pudo hacerla buena" (29) [lust and superstition, greed and cruelty, and in the inner most recess of her dark soul a tiny thing, pure and painful, the memory of Asdrúbal, and the frustrated love that could have made her good]. But her bitterness over the murder and rape still required "sacrificios humanos" (29).

As the novel progress, however, this view starts to change, and she begins to evolve into the doña Bárbara who at the end of the novel overcomes her "instintos rapaces" and cedes both Santos and El Miedo to Marisela. This change occurs because Santos awakens in her heart "sentimientos, nuevos en su vida" (feelings, new in her life), and a desire for the lost love and purity of her childhood. Here the parallels with Marisela are obvious, save for the fact that Santos saves Marisela from the clutches of Mr. Danger, and so from the loss of her purity and innocence. Indeed, toward the end of the novel, doña Bárbara thinks about shooting Marisela, her rival for Santos, but is deterred by the recognition of herself in Marisela: "En la mira . . . de la muchacha [Marisela] . . . doña Barbara se había visto, de pronto, a sí misma . . . pendiente de las palabras de Asdrúbal . . . ¡Por fin el amor de Asdrúbal . . . se reposaba en un sentimiento noble!" (195). [In the look . . . of the girl . . . doña Bárbara had seen, suddenly, herself . . . hanging on Asdrúbal's words . . . she contemplated this noble sentiment!]

By Part II of the novel, doña Bárbara is struggling between "el hábito de mal y el ansia del bien, lo que ella era y lo que anhelaba ser" (193) [the habit of evil and the desire for good, what she was and what she wanted to be]. Finally, after much vacillation, "sentimientos contradictorias," she decides to change her ways, "A todo estaba dispuesta: a entregar sus obras y a cambiar de vida . . . Seré otra mujer" (159). [She was prepared to do anything: to mend her ways and change her life . . . I will be another woman.] And all this was part of the civilizing work of Santos, with whom "por primera vez se había sentido mujer en presencia de un hombre" (104) [for the first time she had felt herself to be a woman in the presence of a man].

By the end of the novel she has changed, and in a final scene, she rides to Altamira to kill Marisela but, as noted above, she cannot do it. That same night she disappears from El Miedo for good, on her face "la calma trágica de las determinaciones supremas" (196) [the tragic calm of final decisions], making the ultimate sacrifice and leaving everything to Marisela. Passing La Chusmita on the way, she sees something strange in the *tremedal*. The aquatic birds of the swamp are flying about in terror. Doña Bárbara spies a young cow on the shore of the swamp struggling in vain to free itself from a giant constrictor (*Eunectes murinus*, Vila 49) that has latched on to its lower jaw. On the day she herself disappears, doña Bárbara comments, "—Ya esa no se escapa—murmuró doña Bárbara. Hoy come el tremedal" (197). And indeed, much as the drowned Barquero cow began the tragic division, this sacrificial calf ends it. "El tremedal agitado recuperó su habitual calma trágica" (197). [The agitated swamp recovered its tragic calm]. Also, "Según una antigua superstición . . . cuando se fundaba un hato se enterraba un animal vivo . . . El de Alta mira era un toro araguato que . . . enterró Evaristo Luzardo" (44). [According to an ancient superstition . . . when a ranch is founded an animal is buried there alive . . . In the case of Altamira it was a tawney-colored bull that . . . Evaristo Luzardo buried.] And this new animal was also buried alive in the swamp to commemorate a new beginning. Finally, "llegó el alambre de púas" (198) [the the barbed wire arrived] authorized by the triumph of legal code over the law of the plains that might makes right, and the many paths of the plains become "uno solo y derecho hacia el porvenir" (196) [one unique and straight path to the future].

The implication is that both the land and the people—including the animals, various minor characters like Paiba, as well as Marisela and doña Barbara—have been civilized by the written word, education in general and legal code in particular. The sacrifice of doña Bárbara, as symbolized by the final sacrifice of the calf to the heart of nature's dark side, the *tremedal*, is a theme treated by René Girard in his classic *Violence and the Sacred. In that work* he argues that to break the chain of reciprocal violence, the endless eye for an eye, tooth for tooth of the Luzardos and Barqueros, for example, a sacrificial victim, not a member of either side but whose death will propitiate both sides, is needed to end the violence. This third party—he gives Jesus as one example, the *pharmakos* as another—can be determined by religious or legal authority or by the author of a novel.

Doña Barbara's self-sacrifice also returns her to the bounds of human nature. Earlier, she had been prepared to kill her daughter, a very unhuman thing to do. Studies show over 90 percent of murders of one family member by another involved nonblood relatives (Daly and Wilson). Additionally, she abandoned an only child, and according to Daly and Wilson (75), infanticide is widely practiced in traditional societies, but none condones the killing of the first child. And finally, in most cultures the mother raises the children. A study of traditional societies in Mexico, Java, Peru, Nepal, the Philippines, and other regions showed fathers spend about 8 percent of their waking hours on child care, while mothers average 85 percent of theirs (Barash and Lipton). When only one parent raises the child, it is the mother in 90 percent of the cases.

And finally, parent-sibling rivalry in all species is based on competition for resources among parents and multiple offspring, but there was no such competition in this case. To put a finer point on it, in nature parent-offspring conflict is generated by the need of parents to maximize the number of surviving offspring and the need of the individual offspring to maximize the number of their own offspring, which means they themselves must first survive to reach parenthood, at which point the roles will reverse. Put simply, each offspring wants to monopolize all the resources, while the parents must divide the resources among multiple offspring to ensure the survival of more than one (Trivers 162). But there was only Marisela, so doña Bárbara should have been naturally inclined to provide her with the material resources to continue the bloodline. The fact that she did not demonstrates how unnatural were her inclinations. She did not so much represent the terrible side of nature as she did the presocialized side of human nature. It is not so much that nature is violent until civilized, but rather that human nature is violent until civilized. The savanna does indeed produce savage animals, all of which need to be domesticated if they are to live among humans. And of all the animals that evolved on the savanna, the animal most in need of domestication is the human animal.

Chapter 9

"It didn't work, Mother. You should have let me stay here."

Alegría's and Flakoll's *Ashes of Izalco*

Beatriz Rivera-Barnes

"It didn't work, Mother. You should have let me stay here, let me shift the blame to Santa Ana" (67). The mother is dead, and the words are Carmen's, the daughter in Claribel Alegría's and Darwin Flakoll's novel *Ashes of Izalco* (1966). Now that Carmen has returned home to make all the necessary preparations for her mother's funeral, she comes face to face with the past, childhood memories as well as borrowed memories. So she addresses her mother while she walks around the house with her mother's bunch of keys at her waist and deals with the heat; the earthquake weather that reminds her of the eruption of Izalco, another memory that has just resurfaced.

But what is it that didn't work? The simple affirmation suggests a plan, a plan that failed, expectations that come with a plan, and illusions lost because the plan was no more than a wrong turn. The plan involved not staying *here*, here being home, and home being the town of Santa Ana in El Salvador. What did not work was leaving home. There is lament in the statement and also blame. *You should have let me* implies that someone, in this case, the mother, made a decision for Carmen and that Carmen had no say in this matter. Even if life had worked out differently for Carmen—if her departure had turned into a *happily ever after*—Carmen would have remained disempowered, for she was not the one who opted to leave.

In her musings, Carmen remembers that Santa Ana started to shrink for her before she turned seventeen. She "began to feel the gray weight of it, the irritating, fenced-in feeling . . . the tepid, somnolent monotony of it" (16). At the same time, however, Carmen equated departure with death (52). Consequently, the feeling of spite for Santa Ana, the egotistical conviction that her hometown just was not good enough, could have been handed down from her mother who always complained about feeling that she never belonged in Santa Ana and "died imagining Paris from what she had read" (52).

In fact, Isabel dreamed of Paris her whole life and taught her daughter Carmen French in hopes that she would one day study at the Sorbonne, but Isabel never saw Paris and she never forgave her husband for having visited Paris without her. It is not clear whether Alfonso refused to take Isabel along, but Paris is at the root of the contempt and uneasiness in Isabel and Alfonso's marriage, for Isabel never got over the resentment. Whenever Alfonso reminisced about Paris, Isabel would "turn to furious stone" (18). On the other hand, when Frank Wolff—the North American, the foreigner—alludes to Paris, Isabel immediately turns to him and pleads, "Tell me something about Paris" (42). Such attitudes leave the reader wondering why Isabel never went to Paris, since she was free to travel and did travel to the Yucatán with Carmen when Carmen was fourteen and to Washington, D.C., to visit Carmen after Carmen was married to Paul (57, 66).

These issues with home that Carmen inherited from her mother—this conviction that home just is not good enough and the center of the world is elsewhere—soon convinced Carmen that the solution was to pack her bags and leave home. Departure was experienced as liberation. Instead of turning her attention to home and gaining a new understanding of it, Carmen preferred to turn her back on Santa Ana without even asking herself why she felt Santa Ana was shrinking. She is experiencing "the grass is greener syndrome": if the world was shrinking in Santa Ana, then it had to be expanding somewhere else.

But unfortunately life went on; just as there was an event that preceded departure, departure itself was an event, followed by yet another event, the arrival. Then there was the day after the arrival, and the time it took to realize that life in Washington, D.C., could be just as restricted as life in Santa Ana, with no one to blame but Mother who did not let Carmen stay in Santa Ana (27). With Mother tucked away in El Salvador, soon enough it is Paul, Isabel's dutiful husband, who is to blame. "Ah, Paul, there's nothing spontaneous about you, my monosyllabic friend, dutiful husband, unimaginative helpmeet" (ibid.).

So what do these pampered, unfulfilled, economically privileged women have to do with ecofeminism?

My initial intention was to find a link between women and nature in this text, in hopes of bringing the Salvadoran landscape to the forefront and establishing a solid relationship between the literature written by women and the ecology of Central America. This was to be both an ecocritical and a feminist reading. In spite of her many years spent in exile, Claribel Alegría always remained connected to a place that witnessed many upheavals and massacres, to a place with many wounds as well as serious ecological problems such as the loss of topsoil, water and soil contamination, and the progressive destruction of the tropical rain forest. Through her writings and her own sense of place and of loss, Alegría speaks for El Salvador, a country whose fragile ecosystem could easily be representative of its political, economic, and social frailties, as well as of its treatment of women.

The promise at the end of the reading and the research was a nice, tidy analysis. But my view of the characters slowly shifted until I found myself questioning the characters, their unfulfilled lives, the constant blame, and finally ecofeminism itself, or at least the unilateral judgment of Third World women by First World intellectuals. (I say First World because if there is a *Third* World, then there must be a *First*.) This is why I am suggesting two readings of *Ashes of Izalco*, the second reading being a retracing of the first and a glimpse into the pitfalls of blame, pity, and self-pity. Ultimately, it all leads back to home, the *oikos*, the *eco* in ecology and in ecofeminism.

THE FIRST READING

All the ecological elements are present: water, air, vegetation, and fire. And of these four elements, fire is the most prevalent in *Ashes of Izalco*; it includes heat, ashes, passion, silencing, secrets, volcanoes, and volcanic eruptions. Moreover, *Ashes of Izalco* is a novel written by two people, Claribel Alegría and her husband, Darwin Flackoll, but nowhere in the novel is the reader ever told who is doing the writing, nor does it really matter. In an interview with the scholar Consuelo Meza-Márquez, Alegría explained that she and her husband decided to write this novel together so that it would be both a masculine and a feminine text. To do so they played out the Frank-Isabel love affair and apparently had bitter arguments while writing and constructing the novel (Meza Márquez). This of course implies all the more heat and fire.

Written sometime before 1964, *Ashes of Izalco* marks a transition from poetry to the novelistic form. Not only is it considered to be a feminist and political novel, but it is a testimony as well. Nancy Saporta Sternbach points out that this is a testimony of a woman imprisoned in a man's text. I may also add that this has everything to do with the structure of the novel because throughout the novel Carmen is reading and responding to a man's diary that her mother has bequeathed her.

The man is Frank. In the beginning Carmen simply refers to him as Frank, and the reader later discovers that Frank is Frank Wolff, an "ex-drunk and sometime writer" in search of something to do, of something vital (81, 101). Fresh out of the sanatorium, Frank made a spur-of-the-moment decision to spend some time in Central America after having read a letter from a friend who had become a lay preacher in an evangelical sect and subsequently a missionary in El Salvador (62). While some of the Santa Ana townspeople referred to Frank as a Communist, others considered him a liar for having pretended to be a novelist working on a novel set in the lush tropical jungles of El Salvador. But it is Frank Wolff who knows himself better than anyone else when he writes in his diary, "I'm a man with no occupation, a victim of mental and emotional bankruptcy" (81). He is no dupe. At that point, his only truth is that he will not start drinking again, but he is conscious "that's a negative resolution, not a program of action" and also that the pages in his diary are "listless, narcissistic introspection: certainly no hint that the great American novel is germinating in some unused recess of my brain" (ibid.).

Since the novel is a meshing of Frank's diary and of Carmen's voice, Frank's awareness that not drinking was merely a negative resolution could be weighed against Carmen and Isabel's desire to leave home, which also constitutes a negative resolution instead of a plan of action. The difference is that Carmen and Isabel do not appear to be aware of this. The three characters' feelings toward home or the hometown are, however, quite similar. Frank writes that he grapples with the concept itself and tries to remember where he has mislaid his home or if he ever had one. "It certainly wasn't the house in Oregon," Frank decides (37). But Frank is one step ahead of Isabel, since "Paris hadn't been a home either, any more than a sauna bath with its boiling-freezing alternations can be considered a home" (37). It is Carmen who, for one fleeting instant, comes close to an authentic concept of home when she remembers that home for her was once to watch her mother coming along the corridor and her dad with his sayings and his doctor's satchel by the door. Unfortunately, as soon as Carmen grasps this truth she immediately lets it go and forgets. The result is that throughout the text, regardless of where the characters are from, there is a universal feeling that home just isn't good enough. While Santa Ana shrinks for Carmen and Isabel, the boys in Oregon tell themselves that, "A man's a fool to stay on the farm or waste his life away in a small town nowadays" (50). In other words, everyone is certain that things will turn out different if they manage to get away from home (67).

As to Paul's judgment of his unfulfilled aspirations as a writer, they are too heavy to be weighed against Carmen's weak, "I know Frank's feeling. Despite Paul and the children, I too feel that rudderlessness, that sense that I have lost something vital, that the horizon is closing in" (48). On the same note, Carmen also laments, "Carmen existed once: where did she go? Did she dissipate and vanish behind her masks and roles and labels? Whatever happened to Mother? Did husbands and children drain us both of our substance and leave only an empty shell?" (108). Blame is cast on home, as well as on the husbands and the children; never is there any self-questioning or even an effort to carry some of the burden of responsibility.

Carmen's internal dialogue is a closed circuit that questions, wonders, whines, feels nostalgic, lives and relives through other people's memories, and asks more questions, most of which do not even deserve an answer. In this sense, Carmen is indeed imprisoned or ensnared in a man's text and the ecofeminist message is delivered through this feeling and expression of imprisonment.

Carmen is a prisoner of Frank's text because her voice and her past are weaved in it. Carmen's mother is also a prisoner of this text because this is what is left of her truth. Furthermore, Isabel was also a prisoner of Frank's text because it could be said that Frank's text is all that is left of her and that it puts her in the realm of the living dead, of the dead who have not been forgotten. Isabel was also the prisoner, or at least felt like a prisoner in Santa Ana. Carmen felt like a prisoner of Santa Ana as well, and now that she is living in Washington she is still a prisoner. Carmen feels that her husband plans and controls everything although she does admit that he never argues about the abstract reproductions or the contemporary furniture she chooses, even if he would prefer heavy overstuffed chairs and massive mahogany tables. These reflections make Carmen come to the conclusion that her husband should have married someone else (66). The result, in any case, is that Washington turns out to be nothing more than a slightly bigger prison than Santa Ana.

Like Russian painted dolls, one prison inside the other, the mother and daughter are or have been prisoners of their house. Now that Isabel has managed to escape the prison of her house, through death, she turns herself over to her daughter, in a man's text. Prisoners of their gaze, their opinions, their mindset, their house, their home, their unfulfilled expectations, broken dreams, and of a text, these characters are prisoners of their nation as well.

Saporta Sternbach writes that this political dimension of the text is woven into three different stories: the volcanic eruption, the 1932 massacre, and the love affair between Frank and Isabel. All three of these stories contain the element of fire. "The trauma of the massacre is actualized in literary terms as the narrator attempts a resolution to the conflicts represented in her personal memory as well as in the collective memory of the country, both of which visit her like angry ghosts. This meeting point and playing field for all these issues erupts in the problematized mother-daughter relationship" (Boschetto-Sandoval 62–63).

By reading Frank's diary, Carmen discovers something about her mother and about her country. In other words, the reading of a masculine text allows her to discover her mother and her history. Sternbach comes to the conclusion that in this sense both Carmen's and Isabel's stories become the history of El Salvador. The novel, therefore, is a feminist novel because it suggests that women count enough for their stories to become confused with the history of their country. The novel also alludes to women's discontent, because Carmen is no happier in Washington than her mother was in Santa Ana. She regrets that her mother did not keep her in Santa Ana. As a matter of fact, every time her mother visited her in Washington and told her about how lucky she was to live there, Carmen felt a pang. "She [Isabel] was sure we would turn out differently just because we had gotten away from home" (67).

According to Sternbach, the novel is also feminist because it suggests that the way to the history of a country is through a family's documents. Almost always these documents are considered feminine objects because they are usually in women's safekeeping. "Why did she leave the diary for me to read? Why didn't she burn it and leave me with an unmixed image of her?" (57). Sternbach believes that the answer to Carmen's question is that Isabel and her story are trapped within Frank's story and that El Salvador's history is trapped within the collective memory of its people. In fact, Alegría attempts to unsilence this history particularly when it comes to the 1932 massacre of thirty thousand peasants in Izalco by members of the Salvadoran army in retaliation for an uprising led by the revolutionary Farabundo Martí. Frank's diary reveals two secrets: Isabel's secret and the 1932 massacre that a series of dictators had tried to erase from the country's history and memory.

The volcano contributes to this unearthing. "In Alegría's text volcanic metaphors inform her readers of another revolution being prepared: that of a woman who begins to take the reins to control her own freedom and destiny" (Boschetto-Sandoval 65).

Instead of victimizing woman, an ecofeminist reading of Alegría's message likens a woman to a volcanic eruption, this eruption suggesting a political and sexual liberation of women. At the same time, the landscape also changes, or at least the perceptions of it. What Frank expected to be an exotic, lush, tropical environment turned out to be a ring of fire, for Santa Ana is often portrayed as hell: it is where the volcano erupts, the peasants were massacred, all the secrets come out in the open, and it is the setting for this fragmented story, as fragmented as the story of two women, Carmen and Isabel, as fragmented as the history of El Salvador.

The response to the landscape is not only the response of the female protagonists, Isabel and Carmen, but a male protagonist's response as well. Frank Wolff is representative of the North American response to the Central American landscape. It is an ambivalent response because before his arrival in El Salvador, Frank was expecting a virginal landscape and, at the same time, wilderness to define his virility. But the plurality does not stop there. The application of Bakhtinian dialogics to a text such as *Ashes of Izalco* places an emphasis on the contradictory voices. The primal contradictory voices are the voices of the authors themselves, Alegría/Flakoll, the feminine and the masculine, two voices that soon become two other masculine vs. feminine voices, Frank/Carmen who, in turn, constantly allude to the silenced Frank/Isabel voices. These are simply the three primary groups of contradictory voices. There are, however, many more, mother and daughter, woman and nature, man and nature, nature/culture, and present and past, just to name a few. It is through these responses and this plurality of voices, sounds, and noises, that Alegría and Flakoll open the dialogue between past and present, and nature and culture.

Rereading

A reading of Alegría's text in light of ecofeminism calls for a definition of ecofeminism and an explanation of how it is to be understood in this context. Initially, ecofeminism was a movement that sought to establish a connection between women's oppression and the exploitation of nature and natural resources. The thesis of the French feminist Francoise d'Eaubonne was that the ecological crisis had two names: destruction of natural resources and overpopulation. "Le conflit des sexes se relie étroitement à l'écologique" (28). In other words, the ecofeminists saw a relationship between the domination of women and the domination of nature.

Karen Warren understands ecofeminism as a movement "committed to the elimination of male-gender power and privilege, or sexism" (3). Just as nature needed to be tamed and capitalized so that it yield crops and cease to be dangerous, likewise women needed to be domesticated and rendered dull, so that they obey, remain faithful, bear children, and tend to household chores without questioning their role. In other words, many ecofeminists considered both women and nature to be silenced, used subjects.

Petra Kelly affirmed that women suffered both from structural oppression and from individual men and that feminism's role was to alleviate their powerlessness (113). Obviously, such definitions of feminism and ecofeminism are far more militant than they are open or suggestive.

It is not necessary, however, to totally rid ecofeminism of its subversiveness. On the contrary, William Rueckert asks his readers to bear in mind that "ecology has been called, accurately, a subversive science because all these ecological visions are radical ones and attempt to subvert the continued-growth economy which dominates all emerging and most developed industrial states" (107–8). Rueckert then proceeds to invoke the first law of ecology: everything is connected to everything else. In other words, there does not necessarily need to be a bold dividing line between nature and culture.

But before delving deeper into that dichotomy, it would be most helpful to stop and attempt to define nature. What is nature? Frederick Turner replies that most of us begin by making a gesture toward a patch of green vegetation and saying that nature is what is out there as opposed to what is in here. However, as Turner soon points out, "It should be clear that this nature has very little in common with natural reality as it is illuminated for us by science. Nature, according to science, is as much in here as it is out there" (42). This statement, obviously, is reminiscent of the first law of ecology.

In this search for a proper definition of nature, Turner then affirms that it is of no help to fall back on saying that nature is something that has not been interfered with because "quantum theory shows that nothing can be observed or measured without being interfered with; if nature is what has not been interfered with, nature does not exist" (43).

Instead of being quiet and untouched, Turner points out that nature is violent, unbalanced, improvisatory, and dynamic (ibid.). Those are adjectives that can all be attributed to women and particularly to shrews.

Shrews need to be tamed because they go against the ideal of femininity that is linked to all that is quiet and untouched. But there seems to be a collective contradiction here. On the one hand, nature and femininity as ideals have to do with pastoral bliss and purity, while on the other side of the spectrum, nature is often opposed to culture, technology, and reason. It is often said and widely accepted that women are closer to nature and men are closer to reason. This is not simply an ecofeminist argument; it is a feminist one as well, and Richard Twine points out that the difference between the ecofeminist and the feminist view is that feminist theory only concentrates on what this means for women whereas ecofeminist theory concentrates on what this means for women and for nature.

In an effort to determine what this means for women and nature, Charlene Spretnak begins by defining body, nature, and place: "By 'body' I mean the unified bodymind; by 'nature' I mean not a scientifically theorized system or a cultural perceived looming threat, but our physical context, from which our bodies are not separate; by 'place' I mean the bioregion, the physical site of community and personal unfolding" (4).

Once again, Spretnak's definitions are reminiscent of the first law of ecology. Everything being connected to everything else is suggested with Spretnak's use of terms such as *unified*, *bodymind*, and *not separate*. This same law will apply to ecofeminism, a term that was first coined by Francoise d'Eaubonne in 1974, before a coherent ecofeminist theory even existed, since it was only at the end of the 1980s that ecofeminism finally became an academic discourse with Ariel Salleh and Val Plumwood, who gave it a global dimension and a presence in the United States, Canada, Europe, India, and Australia.

Regardless of this current global dimension, Richard Twine believes that it is problematic to refer to a singular ecofeminism because ecofeminism is not a homogeneous point of view. In fact, the only thing that all ecofeminisms have in common is this vision of the relationship between women and nature and that the two are connected.

As far as an ecofeminist approach to *Ashes of Izalco* goes, I propose that the *eco* of ecofeminism remain true to its etymon. It is the same as the *eco* in economy and in ecology and, obviously, it means *house*. The *eco* is this house in which women dwell. It is the place where their lives go by, where they learn to love or stop loving, to lead, to bear children, raise children, work, and nourish. Unfortunately, the house is also where Carmen hears herself "speaking on sticky sweet tones: the brave little heroine in a television household drama" (108).

Such a simple expression of regret makes it evident that it is not enough to leave home, much less to blame the Other, in this case, men and children and mothers. Karen Warren argues that the liberation of women cannot be achieved until "*all* women are liberated from the multiple oppressions that structure our gendered identities: women of color from racism, poor women from classism, lesbian women from heterosexism, young and older women from ageism, Jewish women from anti-Semitism, women of the South from Ethnocentrism" (4). Andy Smith adds white, economically privileged, heterosexual women to this list (21). What the list seems to take for granted—or implies—is that *all* women, poor women, Jewish women, Southern women, lesbians, and women of color suffer from some sort of oppression.

Unfortunately, the colors have run and the term *women of color* has faded into a comfortable stereotype. The two female protagonists in *Ashes of Izalco* would easily be labeled women of color, even Third World women because they come from El Salvador. The late Petra Kelly wrote that "Third World Women are oppressed both by national and international injustices and by family systems that give husbands, fathers and brothers absolute priority" (115–16). Now the question is, does Carmen's lament stem from this type of oppression, from this condition? Better yet, should Carmen and her mother be labeled Third World women?

All the elements are there. Both Isabel and Carmen are Salvadoran, and El Salvador is a tiny country in Central America that remained a colony of Spain until the 1820s only to become an oligarchy, ruled by an elite, landed gentry who owed their fortune to coffee monoculture. Obviously, both men and women formed part of the elite. Nonetheless, the family systems were there, and they did privilege the males who ruled as fascist generals until 1980. The dictator Maximiliano Hernández Martinez is a perfect specimen of Francoise d'Eaubonne's *Third World macho*.

It remains, however, difficult, if not impossible, to label Isabel and Carmen as Third World women. Petra Kelly affirms that "throughout the Third World, women are dispossessed, overlooked, and overworked" (116). Such is not the case for these two female protagonists. Let us start at the end. They were certainly not overworked, since there is never any mention of work in the novel. Isabel, the mother, spent her entire life in her house in Santa Ana, with all the keys to the house tied around her waist, managing the servants. "Mother didn't even go marketing; Cata took care of that. After breakfast you tell the cook what to prepare for lunch . . . then comes a long empty stretch" (16).

As to Carmen who left home for Washington, Carmen is "tied to the house—making beds, vacuuming, cooking, doing dishes—more than she ever was with servants to do all the work. Life is lonely in the States" (27). Isabel was a bored housewife in Santa Ana. Carmen is a bored housewife in Washington, D.C. Both women were bored indeed, but certainly not overworked unless the vacuuming, the cooking, and the other household chores were too much for Carmen.

Were they overlooked? It could very well be. Remembering her mother, Carmen had "the sensation of someone carrying a heavy burden except when she was away from home or hidden behind a book. That burden could only have been my father" (16). If the burden was her father, Carmen does not explain why. Perhaps it was because he never stopped to ask Isabel why she hid behind books and seemed to be carrying such a heavy burden, or perhaps he never even noticed that she was so miserable, busy as he was attending to patients and standing up for poor peasants.

On the other hand, perhaps it was the disdain that Isabel felt for Alfosno that made him such a burden. "For every minute you spent in the Louvre, you spent hours inspecting garters and silk stocking at the Moulin Rouge" (19). Isabel perpetually alludes to Alfonso's philandering, then turns around and has an affair with Frank under Alfonso's roof.

Alfonso, however, stands up for the poor peasants (28, 39, 74), whereas Isabel's reaction was, "I know it's awful, but have you ever imagined what a revolution would be like? Those people are filled with hatred" (41). Such a reaction makes if difficult equate the treatment of women, or at least of Isabel, with the treatment of nature and of the oppressed social classes. Instead of being overlooked, Isabel seems to be overlooking everything around her, from the husband, to her children, to her house, to her country. In fact, she seems to overlook everyone except Frank, the foreigner.

As to Carmen, she mentions that her father would have preferred for her to be the bad student, as opposed to her brother, and accuses her mother of preferring Alfredo to her (33). These could be instances of being overlooked, but instances that could certainly be overcome and do not warrant an unfulfilled life in Washington.

At the risk of becoming too judgmental, I will also add that these women were certainly not dispossessed, since they seemed to have everything, everything except love and a reason for living, something vital, because they felt no love and counted too much on negative resolutions such as leaving home.

Toward a Conclusion

If ecofeminism seeks to establish connections between the environment and women, it should avoid drawing parallels between the way women are treated and the way nature is treated and conclude that they are both mistreated simply because this is unfair for both women and nature. Instead of victimizing women and nature and of turning home into the place where women feel they are lesser beings, instead of calling for flight, vindication, and blame, for this only leads to degradation, be it personal or environmental, ecofeminism should call for a better understanding of home, a new consciousness that will allow the experience of home to expand and render the urge to flee needless. Liberation is not so much a breaking out of prison or a negative plan of action as it is expansion. Just as Cheryll Glotfelty suggests that ecocriticism remain suggestive and open, and so should ecofeminism (Glotfelty xxii).

As to the ecofeminist message in *Ashes of Izalco*, it does involve the connection between women and nature, but it should also demonstrate that not all women of color or Third World women are subordinated unless subordination can take on very different faces, and in this case even the so-called male dominators are subordinated. I would not call Isabel and Carmen subordinated women. They were not silenced, much less forced to do anything. On the contrary, the more I got to know them in this reading, the less subordinated they appeared. Instead of being oppressed, they often took on the roles of the oppressors. At this point in time, instead of putting the blame on male dominance or colonial oppression, comfortable stereotypes need to be questioned. Carmen as a Third World woman oppressed by men serves as a perfect example. Although she was raised in a small town in El Salvador, she had no difficulties questioning the role assigned to many women in her country. Very early on, Carmen decided that she would not marry in El Salvador or live there for the rest of her life because her hometown was not good enough for her. She deserved better. She refused to be dominated and domesticated like her mother and won that initial battle since she managed to leave without having to put up much of a fight. But after her mother's death, Carmen returns to Santa Ana and wonders what she would have becomes if she "had been forced to live here until the end" (16). *Forced? Here?* It is not even obvious that her mother had been forced, much less Carmen, consequently the use of this word is problematic.

As to *here*, there are some descriptions of *here* throughout the novel: Santa Ana with its long empty stretches of time, its volcano in the distance, hot earthquake weather, Santa Ana where nothing happens precisely because its inhabitants feel the weight of existence, of standing on the outside, convinced as they are that the center is elsewhere, to the north, perhaps in Washington, D.C. Everything has to be happening elsewhere, for Isabel's extreme individualism this elsewhere was Paris, and for her daughter's it was the United States. These convictions that stem from a colonial mentality are responsible for the ecological degradation of Central and South America, and in this particular case, El Salvador. Had it not been for the eruption of Izalco or the memory of this eruption, the landscape is mostly absent in this novel, just as it is absent from the memory of the people of El Salvador. In truth, there is no landscape, no space, only slow time, and this makes for a landscape and a home truly dispossessed, overlooked, and overworked.

Chapter 10

Pablo Neruda's Latin American Landscape

Nations, Economy, Nature

Beatriz Rivera-Barnes

In Pablo Neruda's *Oda a la Madera* (*Ode to Wood*) the future had the smell of trees falling, because fresh lumber meant the promise of a building.

> Mi pecho, mis sentidos
> se impregnaron
> en mi infancia
> de árboles que caían
> de grandes bosques llenos
> de construcción futura (*Obras Completas* 1035).

[My childhood heart and my senses were filled with falling trees, with great forests full of future buildings.] Now that there are no more great forests, simply endangered forests, the future has changed, and the utilitarian approach to nature is no longer as acceptable. There is a marked effort to become more environmentally conservative, regardless of the outcome, and whether or not there is any hope. So the poet was wrong, and nature is something other than a raw material out there, waiting to be written, consumed, experienced, or used.

But Neruda did not mind admitting that he had made mistakes, and what is of significance today is the immense role that nature played in his writing. Neruda's poetics can be approached as a lifelong effort to express the unsayable facet of the natural world. Many, many words were consumed in this attempt: from forests to oceans, from mountains to rivers, from beasts to vegetables. Just as important is Neruda's growing sense of environmental awareness, which began with *Canto General*, where the utilitarian attitude toward nature belonged to the times, and how this attitude evolved through the years, culminating in the ecological stances taken in many of the odes. In *Oda a la erosión* (*Ode to Erosion*), Neruda expresses environmental nostalgia when he writes, "Volví a mi tierra verde / y ya no estaba" (*Obras Completas* 1170). [I returned to my green land, and it was no longer there.] This same feeling of loss and of the impossibility of reversing the damages also transpires in *Oda al carro de la leña* (*Ode to the truck carrying lumber*) where Neruda questions unrestrained logging and presages the dire consequences of deforestation,

> Ay quién
> pudiera
> deterner
> el curso
> del río de la leña
> desandar el camino
> devolverlo a la selva (*Obras Completas* 1337).

["Oh, who could stop the flow of the river of lumber, un-walk the roads, give it back to the forest."]

The result is that although Neruda died in 1973, his textual residence on earth did not come to an abrupt end that year, nor did his depiction of the Latin American landscape. In other words, the ecological challenges that Latin America is facing in the twenty-first century were already contained in *Canto General*, which was published in 1950. Dedicated to all of Latin America, thus including parts of the United States, the historic narrative of *Canto General* spans several centuries and denounces the plundering and exploitation of Latin America's natural resources. The pillaging that began with the explorers and conquistadors in the fifteenth century and reached monumental proportions with the despots and multinational companies that ruled these countries from the nineteenth century on is at the root of present-day environmental degradation: pollution, deforestation, erosion, industrialization, toxicity, continued mindless exploitation of natural resources, and total lack of concern for the natural environment. Neruda's *Canto General*—that Enrico Mario Santí labels a "narrativización de la historia" (84) [a narrativizing of history]— presages all of the aforementioned ecological issues. In this effort,

Neruda collected innumerable volumes of books pertaining to the natural history of Latin America and thus came very close to expressing the importance of an environmental history. Among these books, Enrico Mario Santí lists *Compendio de historia de América* (1865) and *Historia General de Chile* (1884), both by Diego Barros Arana, as well as the anonymous *Las Aves de Chile* (1946; 68–69).

Certainly, the tone in *Canto General* is political, as well as radical and accusatory, at times rightfully more concerned with social injustice than with an endangered natural world, but given Latin America's natural resources nature *is* economy, nature *is* nation, and the political *is* ecological. Stuart McCook explains that to fully understand power in these agrarian societies, it is essential to understand nature (4). Subsequently, Neruda's conversion to communism in 1945 was ecological even if, as George Handley points out, "Neruda's understanding of environmental degradation was hampered by the hope inspired by socialist experiments with environmental engineering, feats that he hoped would prove capable of feeding the earth's poor" (180). Handley believes that later on in life, Neruda did become more cautious of his enthusiasm and more aware of the harm that was being done to the environment.

It was the natural environment of Latin America—its bounty and the commercial value of its bounty—that first attracted the European explorers and conquistadors, referred to as "carniceros" (butchers) by Neruda (*Canto* 145). Mindless of the Edenic quality of the place, these butchers "desolaron las islas" (devastated the islands).

> Y cuando el tiempo dio su vuelta de vals
> bailando en las palmeras
> el salon verde estaba vacío (ibid.).

[And when time stood up for its waltz, dancing in the palm trees, the green ballroom was empty.] The island of Cuba, which became Columbus's jewel, was tied on a rack, cut, raped, pillaged, burnt, and divided (146). Mexico's lowlands were stabbed and beaten, its jasmine trampled (149). The people of Guatemala were robbed of their natural science: "el temblor del río" (the tremor of the river), "la ciencia del polen" (the science of pollen), "las migraciones" (the migrations), "las leyes de la colmena" (the laws of the beehive), "el secreto del ave verde" (the secret of the green bird), "el idioma de las estrellas" (the language of the stars), and "los secretos del día y la noche /cogidos en las orillas / del desarollo terrenal!" (153). [The secrets of the day and of the night gathered along the shores of earthly creation.]

The conquistadors would soon be followed by the executioners and the oligarchies, the result being what Stuart McCook considers to be the largest environmental transformation of Latin America and what economic historians describe as the second conquest. At this point the natural world was seen in terms of economic production or export commodities. "They also saw the natural world in terms of state building, seeking to nationalize the natural world by producing national botanical inventories and ecological maps" (5).

"Los verdugos" (the executioners) and "Las oligarquías" (the oligarchies) are two subsections of Section 5, "La arena traicionada" (The betrayed arena/sand), of the encyclopedic *Canto General* that Hugo Méndez-Ramírez considers to be the linguistic equivalent of mural art (51). This is Neruda's gaze, this is his panoramic view of Latin America, country by country: a vertical and horizontal rendering of the landscape, the ruins of the indigenous past, two thousand meters worth of vegetation, beasts, birds, rivers, minerals, as well as the world's greediness and appetite for sugar, tropical hardwoods, precious metals, coffee to the last drop, and fruit to the last bunch of rotten fruit thrown in the garbage: "un rácimo de fruta muerta / derramada en el pudridero" (Canto 336).

Neruda sees that bunch of rotten fruit as something unnamed, a fallen number, "una cosa / sin nombre, un número caído" (ibid.). This lack of names and numbers is reminiscent of the poetic rendering of Latin America that begins with *Amor América* (1400), ninety-two years before the arrival of Columbus, when everything, including thunder, is still unnamed and prescientific, "sin nombre todavía" (*Canto* 105). *Amor América* is the first poem in the first section of *Canto*, titled *La lámpara en la tierra* (*Light on Earth*). This section evokes the *Fiat Lux* of Genesis (except that this time the light is earthly as opposed to heavenly) and unfolds in a prehistoric America that is all nature and no civilization, a nature before man, at least until Poem 4, the last poem of the first section.

In the beginning—before Poem 4, *Los Hombres*—there was a beloved, imagined, and unnamed America before America, "Tierra sin nombre, sin América" (ibid., 107). This is an America from before what Edmundo O'Gorman describes as the invention and naming of America. Obviously, Neruda was not present in this Adamic world, but rather than being a documentation of America's past, *Canto General* is memory as poetic creation and also, as Luis Sainz de Medrano writes, "la consideración de las cosas en el desarrollo de la destrucción" (99) [the taking into account of things in the unfolding of destruction]. In this unfolding, Neruda's poetic memory is a quasi-religious, animistic view of nature that Donald Worster describes as a conviction that "plants and animals act according to an indwelling, mysterious power that physics or chemistry cannot analyze" (17).

Consequently, in Neruda's *Canto General*, where there is a definite nostalgia for nature untouched by man, the intruders are the ones who cannot understand or analyze nature. On one end of the spectrum, there is a faith in all things green and a longing for a paradise lost where vegetation abounds, America the arboreal, a green uterus (ibid., 108–9). On the opposite end, and this is where the vision of nature becomes problematic, there is Neruda's text, the poet's many, many words, a product of culture that is often considered the enemy of the natural world. Handley explains that nature displaces language and that language, "in its recovery of the past or perhaps in its recovery *from* the loss of the past, resorts to *as if* constructions, to similes, metaphors" (61). To make matters more problematic, Neruda attempts to capture a prelinguistic experience in the Spanish language, a language that is—or was—the language of the intruder (at least until the intruder became the United States).

In reality, and even in nature, there is an impossibility of language in pure nature, in a region uninhabited by man. Greg Garrard points out a vision that suggests that nature is only authentic if we are absent from it has pernicious consequences: "The ideal wilderness space is wholly pure by virtue of its independence from humans, but the ideal wilderness narrative posits a human subject whose most authentic existence is located precisely there" (70–71). The result is that in spite of being in an unnamed and preverbal world, Neruda is capable of putting a name to everything, from trees, to crops, to beasts, to minerals, to every single resource that led to the exploitation of the Latin American landscape.

> Así fue devorada
> negada, sometida, arañada, robada,
> joven América, tu vida (*Canto* 319).

[Young America, this is how your life was devoured, negated, subjugated, torn to shreds, stolen.]

Trees and native plants are the first natural elements to be mentioned in the poem *Vegetaciones*, a poem dedicated to Latin American nature and its bounty. A total of ten native trees and plants are listed: *el jacarandá* (the jacaranda), *la araucaria* (the monkey puzzle tree), *la caoba* (the mahogany), *los alerces* (the redwoods), *el árbol trueno* (the thunder tree) *el árbol rojo* (the red tree) *el árbol de la espina* (the tree of thorns), *el árbol madre* (the mother tree), *el ceibo* (the silk-cotton tree), and *el caucho* (the rubber tree). Throughout *Canto General*, however, although there are many allusions to woodcutters, and even praise of the woodcutters as a symbol of simple working people who have remained close to nature, there are few references to deforestation in spite of the fact that, as Handley points out, Neruda saw the native hardwood forests of his youth being replaced by monocultural tree plantations. (157)

"Lo primero que vi fueron árboles" (What I first saw were trees), thus begins the poem titled *LA FRONTERA* (The frontier; 1904), the first poem of Section 4, *Yo soy* (Canto 595) [*I am*]. The date between parenthesis refers to the time that the poetic *I* in *Yo soy* is reminiscing, and not to the writing of the poem itself. Neruda was born in 1904, in an area of southern Chile known as La Araucanía or La Frontera (The Frontier). Handley points out that although this area is known for its natural beauty, its forests have been dramatically reduced over the last century. Native hardwoods such as the Chilean redwood may very well disappear within a generation (156–57).

In spite of the changes in the forest that Neruda witnessed, the poet does not overtly denounce the logging companies as he does the mining, oil, and fruit companies. There is a reference to the exploitation of rubber trees in *Los Abogados del Dólar* (*The Lawyers of the Dollar*),

> y miden tierra conquistada,
> estaño, petroleo, bananas,
> nitrato, cobre, manganeso,
> azúcar, hierro, caucho, tierra (324)

[and they (the lawyers) measure the conquered land, tin, oil, bananas, nitrate, copper, manganese, sugar, rubber, earth]. But there is no mention of the precarious situation of the Amazon rainforest in poems dedicated to Brazil or to other Amazon countries such as Columbia, Peru, Venezuela, and Ecuador. Deforestation does not appear to be one of Neruda's main concerns. Nonetheless, mining, oil extraction, and agricultural exploitation, which Neruda does denounce, have played a major role in present-day deforestation.

Richard Tucker points out that tropical hardwoods were a profitable export from the time of the first Spanish settlements. Initially, the hardwoods (Brazilwood, logwood) were logged mainly for dyes and since the size of the tree did not affect the extraction of dye, loggers took all the available trees. It was not until the seventeenth century that Europeans began to use mahogany in shipyards. Consequently, the loggers became interested only in the finest, tallest trees (186–87). "The best seed trees of mahogany were felled, and as the oxen dragged them to a nearby river for floating away, they damaged still more trees and tore the soil along the paths and riverbanks" (188). Tucker adds that it can take up to a hundred years for a mahogany tree to mature.

Logging has devastated just about every Latin American country, from Guatemala to the Caribbean islands, to Central Chile. At the time *The Diversity of Life* was published in 1999, Edward O. Wilson identified four hot spots in South America, areas of rain forest in danger of extinction: Columbia and western Ecuador, the Uplands of Western Amazonia, the Atlantic coast of Brazil, and Central Chile. Wilson writes that the forests of the Colombian Chocó have been invaded by timber companies since the early 1970s and that they are down to about three quarters of their original cover and still being destroyed at an accelerating rate (264). As to the Uplands of Western Amazonia, according to Wilson, about 65 percent of these forests have already been cleared or converted into palm-oil plantations. "The loss is projected to approach 90% by the year 2000" (ibid.).

Tucker writes that loggers attacked the forests in Cuba, Mexico, Guatemala, and Nicaragua "like commercial game hunters" (189). It is estimated that at the time of Columbus's arrival in Cuba, 60 to 75 percent of Cuba's land area was forested and that close to 80 percent of the island's forest cover was lost in the course of the next five centuries (Díaz-Briquets 140). Initially, Cuba's trees were felled to accommodate colonial needs, but soon the Europeans became aware of Cuba's fine woods and began to exploit the forest for lumber. The exploitation continued until the eighteenth century, which saw further deforestation when the forest was torched in order to open land for sugarcane. The result, according to Díaz-Briquets and Pérez-López, is that Cuba lost its forests incrementally between the late eighteenth and first quarter of the twentieth centuries. In 1959, only 14 percent of Cuba was still forested, but this increased by 30 percent over the next thirty years as a result of the reforestation policies of the Castro government (ibid., 146).

Cuba is just one example of many, and the only one that comes remotely close to the possibility of a happy ending. The American-Guatemalan Mahogany Company founded in 1907, for example, "cut over sixteen million board feet of mahogany in twenty-three years, whereas Casa Emery in Nicaragua was exporting in 1894 about one thousand mahogany and cedar logs monthly to Boston" (Díaz-Briquets 190).

Since many of the aforementioned facts and numbers were available in the 1940s and 1950s, it is interesting to note that Neruda did not stop to denounce logging in the monumental *Canto General* or the exploitation and logging of the monkey puzzle tree in *Oda a la Araucaria* (*Ode to the Monkey Puzzle Tree*). It could very well be that Neruda was not fully aware of deforestation at the time and was more concerned with denouncing those he considered to be the butchers and the executioners. In other words, Neruda was perhaps more concerned with the loss of human lives than with the loss of forests, and rightfully so.

It should also be taken into account that in the 1950s, the notion of scarcity was not as developed as in the twenty-first century; what mattered more was that Latin America had become a battlefield, the place where the United States and the Soviet Union were waging their war, thus pulling the Latin American nations either right or left. Consequently, for Neruda it was necessary to take sides, to commit to a political and economical ideology, and thus to defend humankind instead of the forest and its trees. In other words, the epochal urgency took precedence over the forests and the trees. At best, the forest and the trees served as metaphors, or as symbols for the human condition.

A vertical arrow, a tree reaches up and reaches down. An eternal promise, the tree is representative of knowledge as well as of the human life span, in the form of seasons. In *Alturas de Machu Picchu*, Neruda laments not having been able to love in every being a tree, carrying a small autumn on its back (the death of a thousand leaves), "No pude amar en cada ser un árbol / con su pequeño otoño a cuestas la muerte de mil hojas" (*Canto* 131).

Trees are sung in Section 4 of *Los Libertadores*. "Aquí viene el árbol, el árbol" (185). [Here comes the tree, the tree.] The tree of this unnamed poem represents the people, the fallen and unsung heroes, the poor, the tortured, and also "the prophetic and messianic call of the poet to engage in social revolution" (Méndez-Ramírez 134). Inhabited by the dead, the tree takes its sustenance from the dead and, in turn, fertilizes the earth. Neruda's tree is the tree of freedom as well.

> El árbol tierra, el árbol nube,
> el árbol pan, el árbol flecha,
> el árbol puño, el árbol fuego (186).

[The earth tree, the cloud tree, the bread tree, the arrow tree, the fist tree, the fire tree.] Neruda alludes to the tree coming close to drowning in the turbulent waters of the dark times, but finally managing to float and master these waters. In this sense, the tree is a symbol of power, never endangered. Instead of being a denunciatory poem, this is a poem of hope that calls for action: revolution, belief in the earth, in agriculture, and in uniting for a common, just cause.

In the poem SE UNEN LA TIERRA Y EL HOMBRE (*Man and Earth Unite*), the pre-Columbian ancestors were made of the substance of stones and trees (171). In the poem EL CORAZON MAGALLANICO (*The Magellanic Heart*; 1519), the poetic voice speaks for Magellan, the Portuguese navigator who sailed around the world and who finds himself in the middle of a dream, in the middle of the tree, wondering where he is from, where he is coming from, and what day it is (177). Magellan is accompanied by the endless night and the pine. Oftentimes, the tree and the mast on a ship are interchangeable as in "el árbol del mastil agachado" (180) [the bent tree of the mast].

Usually Neruda does not call trees by their specific names, but one poem, *Araucaria* (*Canto* 403), is dedicated solely to the monkey puzzle tree, and *la caoba*, (the mahogany), is mentioned in LA COLONIA CUBRE NUESTRAS TIERRAS (1) [*The Colony Hides our Land*], where he writes, "América, la copa de caoba / entonces fue un crepúsculo de llagas" (208). [America, the dome of mahogany thus became a sunset of open wounds.] Here Neruda could very well be alluding to the logging of mahogany and the open wound that their absence has left. The nation, however, is the child of woodcutters, of unbaptized children, of carpenters, "Patria, naciste de los leñadores, de hijos sin bautizar, de carpinteros" (216).

Just as the woodcutters represent the people, so do the farmers. Poem 11 of the first section of *Canto*, begins with the words, "Sube a nacer conmigo, hermano" (Come and be born with me, brother), and summons the farmer in this exhortation, "agricultor temblando en la semilla" (140) [farmer trembling in the seed"]. In fact, all of Latin America is a land of agriculture for Neruda, "tierra de agricultura con rocío" (378) [land of agriculture covered with dew].

Never does Neruda denounce agriculture. Méndez Ramírez even points out that, "At the outset, the ekphrastic association is not with the tree, but rather with the corn plant. In '*Vegetaciones*' when the corn stalk emerges, it becomes the vehicle of contribution and renewal" (134). By "ekphrastic association," Méndez-Ramírez is not referring so much to the description of something visual as to an experience that transcends language (34–35). (Literally, the term ekphrasis—from the Greek *ekphraisien*—means to speak out, but this speaking out goes beyond language, just as color and texture are borrowed from the visual arts.)

> Como una lanza terminada en fuego
> apareció el maíz, y su estatura
> se desgranó y nació de nuevo (*Canto* 108).

[Like a spear of fire, corn appeared, spread its seed and was regenerated.] Much like the tree, corn is a metaphor of cyclical renewal, and if it is tied to politics in several of Neruda's poems it is because it is a symbol of hope for the future of revolutionary struggle.

> México, huraña agricultura, amada
> tierra entre los oscuros repartida:
> de las espadas del maíz salieron
> al sol tus centurions sudorosos (261).

[Mexico, unfriendly agriculture, beloved land meted out to the dark people: from the spears of the corn your sweat covered centurions emerged.]

Only native crops are mentioned in the poem *Vegetaciones*: tobacco and maize. The botanist Ronald Petersen mentions that the Native Americans cultivated maize and were addicted to tobacco (78). In fact, corn and tobacco could be representative of the pre-Columbian world. Interestingly enough, Latin America was never exploited for corn. The Spaniards much preferred wheat and settled for corn when they had no other choice. Consequently, Neruda does not denounce farms, much less farmers who cut down trees to grow corn. What Neruda does denounce are the *encominedas* and *haciendas* that paved the way for the future oligarchies. "Hasta que toda la azul geografía / se dividió en haciendas y encomiendas" (*Canto* 209). [Until all the blue geography was divided into haciendas and *encomiendas*.] There are innumerable references to haciendas and constant allusions to haciendas being representative of a second demise of the Americas and of the subjugation of the native peoples.

> Cuando la libertad cambió de traje
> se transformó en hacienda:
> de las tierras recién sembradas
> salió una casta (*Canto* 310).

[When liberty changed clothes it became an hacienda: from the newly planted land came a caste.]

Not so coincidentally, it was in the *encomiendas* and in the haciendas that cultivated the imported crops that are largely responsible for

Latin America's present-day ecological, economical, and political devastation. They include sugarcane that Columbus brought along from the Canary Islands in 1493 and bananas that were also brought from the Canary Islands and introduced in 1516. Bananas and sugarcane are two intruders that have become representative of Latin America, much like tobacco and corn, that were present in the America before the America that Neruda convokes.

There is urgency and nostalgia in this invocation of pre-Columbian America with its ecosystems and crops that are forever lost. Here lies the unsayable that can never be said or named because there is no way of knowing what ecosystems and crops disappeared as a consequence of the discovery and of the conquest that Alfred Crosby believes to have produced the biggest biological revolution since the end of the Pleistocene era (66). Crosby adds that today an American botanist could find whole meadows in which he would be hard put to find a single species of plant that grew in pre-Columbian times (74): "In thousands and thousands of square miles of the Americas, the indigenous plants have been eliminated completely or restricted to uncultivated strips along the side of roads; and sugar, coffee, bananas, wheat, barley, and rye occupy the greater part of the land" (211). Crosby admits that this did have some positive results such as increase in food production, but negative results as well, such as the destruction of ecological stability. In 1950, at the time *Canto General* was published, Neruda believed that the future was in the positive results.

However, the haciendas could not produce the positive results because they paved the way for the foreign company, "la compañía extranjera" (*Canto* 324). These companies went wherever they smelled profit, "donde huele riqueza," from Puerto Limón to Ciudad Trujillo, from Caracas to Honduras (ibid., 325–26). As far as the exploitation of fruit goes, the most infamous of these companies is the United Fruit Company, which has now morphed into Chiquita and Dole. In Neruda's poem, when Jehovah sounded the trumpets and meted the world out to Coca-Cola, Ford Motors, Anaconda, and the United Fruit Company, the United Fruit Company received "la dulze cintura de América" (the sweet cincture of America) and named its lands Banana Republics (*Canto* 690). Instead of increasing food production, the United Fruit Company exploited the people of Central America and destroyed an irreplaceable ecosystem.

Entire books have been dedicated to the United Fruit Company whose saga began in 1870 when Captain Lorenzo Dow Baker discovered bananas in Jamaica and purchased 160 bunches, which he sold at a great profit in Jersey City eleven days later. Soon, Baker's Boston

Fruit Company was capitalizing on bananas from Jamaica, Cuba, and the Dominican Republic. By 1898, sixteen million bunches of bananas were being imported annually, but Cuba, Jamaica, and the Dominican Republic were producing all the bananas they could, so Baker had no choice but to expand his territory and merge with a Brooklyn-born entrepreneur named Minor Keith whose dream, according to Stephen Schlesinger and Stephen Kinzer, "had been to monopolize commerce in Central America by building and maintaining rail lines in areas where no other form of transportation was available" (66). Officially, the United Fruit Company was formed on March 30, 1899. It virtually owned Panama, Guatemala, Nicaragua, Honduras, and Costa Rica, and was largely, if not entirely, responsible for the 1954 Guatemalan coup.

> Entre las moscas sanguinarias
> la Frutera desembarca,
> arrasando el café y las frutas (*Canto* 336).

[Among the bloodthirsty flies, the Fruit Company disembarks, devastating the coffee and the fruit.] Neruda's message is urgent and epochal, and the result is that the poet is more concerned with the political than with the ecological destiny of these regions that are still enduring the consequences of mindless disproportional cultivation of bananas and other tropical fruit and will continue to endure these consequences well into the twenty-first century. Richard Tucker points out that the 1950s ushered in an era of intensified, chemical-based banana production. In other words, chemical spraying began in the 1950s and the toxic chemicals damaged the health of the workers and the environment (78). One example is Nemagon City in Managua, Nicaragua, where thousands of "affected" banana workers have taken over a downtown park. Living in makeshift huts made of sticks and black garbage bags, these workers and their families, who are suffering the consequences of exposure to the pesticide Nemagon that has long been banned in the United States but is still being used in Central America, are demanding compensation from Dole. Another example can be found in ecologically conscious Costa Rica, with its wide expanses of useless poisoned land that were once used for banana cultivation.

Those are only a few examples. Each Latin American country deserves careful consideration, a weighing of the pre-Columbian landscape, against the colonial landscape, against what was once the newly acquired national landscape, and finally against the landscape today, but that is not the purpose here. Much less ambitious, the objective is to demonstrate how in ecology, and in this case Latin American ecology, all things are connected. Native animals of the Americas, for example, have suffered much the same destiny as native crops. As Elinor Melville points out, the Europeans did not come alone to the New World, but brought along animals such as horses, pigs, chickens, sheep, goats, and cattle that would soon displace the native beasts.

"Era el crepúsculo de la iguana" (It was the sunset of the iguana): thus begins Neruda's poem *Algunas Bestias* (*Several Beasts*, *Canto* 109). In this poem, which immediately follows *Vegetaciones*, Neruda lists America's native beasts: iguanas, llamas, monkeys, butterflies, squirrels, pumas, jaguars, and anacondas. Then come the birds, VIENEN LOS PAJAROS (*Canto* 110–13). Some of the names of these birds can easily be translated into English: toucan, hummingbird, parrots, flamingo, quetzal, and condor. Some names, however, have no translation. Neruda's volumes of natural history are open, and he is writing as he leafs through these volumes: *el atajacaminos* (a native bird that eats butterflies), *la torcaza araucana*, *la loica del Sur*, *el chingolo*. This is a litany of birds whose habitats are endangered, a litany of birds that sing the history of Latin America from an ecological perspective.

Although, as Handley states, Neruda was not able to "reconcile his poetic impulse to foreground ecology *and* to decry human injustice" (218), Neruda does however express ecological understanding and does refer to the possibility of environmental degradation when he alludes to burning forests in the last poem of *Canto General*, *Termino Aquí* (*I End Here*).

> Este libro termina aquí. Ha nacido
> de la ira como una brasa, como los territorios
> de bosques incendiados, y deseo
> que continue como un árbol rojo (*Canto* 629).

[This book ends here. It was born from wrath like a wildfire, like burning forests, and I hope that it perseveres, like a flame tree.]

From the very beginning, blood irrigated what is now the Latin American soil, blood instead of water, culminating in the twentieth century, or one hundred years worth of America tied to the rack and pulled left and right. Nobody won, and the landscape lost. So now that both capitalism and communism are dead or dying, it is an appropriate time to revisit the Latin American landscape in its entirety and to reconsider an environmental future.

Neruda wrote much about nature. He often expressed how he loved nature and how nature played a great role in his writing. Neruda was not, however, a nature writer. In other words, he was not a protector of nature, he was not a conservationist, nor was he an ecologist. If nature was there, it was for utilitarian purposes, to feed and house the people, and also to inspire the poet. This is, or was, *América arboleda*, America the arboreal, the forest, the wild bramble, *zarza salvaje*, between the seas that balanced from pole to pole its green treasure, its denseness, "tesoro verde, tu espesura" (108). This is the America that Neruda tries to grasp, word after word, encyclopedia of natural history in hand, even if it takes a litany of the trees and plants as in *Botánica* (*Canto* 401–3), thus sounding the echo of the green core of America the arboreal, the unsayable, name after name after name. Perhaps it does not always take a writer with a green agenda to defend nature, simply one to point nature out, and to guide the reader. After all, environmental awareness may resemble Neruda's artichoke: it can be purchased, tossed in a bag next to a pair of shoes and a bottle of vinegar, then, served, and eaten, piece by piece until its green heart is discovered (*Obras Completas* 944–46).

Chapter 11

Love in the Time of Somoza

Gioconda Belli's Ambivalent Ecofeminism

Beatriz Rivera-Barnes

Untouchable Landscape

Initially, the idea of an untouchable landscape conjures romantic nature, forest primeval, a region uninhabited by man, and even the problematic idea of pure nature independent from humans. Such is not the case here, where the landscape may be untouchable but not untouched. The phrase is Gioconda Belli's. "Es el paisaje intocable" (70). [It is the untouchable landscape.] Untouchable, like volcanoes that cannot be moved, also like canyons, like the heavens, like the sun and the moon; that is all, for the rest has been cut and burnt and pillaged. This is Central America and the turbulent history that has shaped the description of its landscape.

"Delgada tierra como un látigo / calentada como un tormento" (Neruda 356). [Land as thin as a whip, as hot as torment.] The adjective *delgada* means thin, and since adjectives agree in gender with the noun they modify, thin is in the feminine. Thinness implies hunger, whereas the whip suggests servitude. Literally, *calentada* means heated, as when something is put on a stove, and it can also mean angered or aroused. This past participle—again, in the feminine—comes from the verb *calentar*, to heat up, to warm up, and also to hit, to strike, to annoy, to turn on, and to arouse sexually.

This same land as thin as a whip is "la dulce cintura de América" (the sweet waistline of America) in the poem titled "La United Fruit Co." (335; my translation). I chose sweet because *dulce* means sweet before it means anything else. But other translators of Neruda's poem have opted for delicate instead of sweet. The problem is that delicate does not suggest sweetness, which must come into account when referring to the isthmus, the shape of a handful of countries once known as *Tierra Firme del Istmo* and also christened *Castilla de Oro* by the Spanish conquerors. The isthmus is the waistline of *América*, as in *the Americas*, América with an acute accent on the *e*, not the U.S. land mass whose waistline is far from delicate.

In yet another poem by Neruda, the isthmus is "la cintura de nuestra geografía" (the waistline of our geography) and also "cintura de los sollozos" (356) [waistline of tears]. All these lines refer to the isthmus as if it were a (far from untouchable) woman; they feminize a handful of nations and codify them as bodies, while conveying a political message of the world's sweet tooth, agricultural exploitation, ecological devastation, and the fragility of an ecosystem.

I will be focusing on how the Nicaraguan landscape is portrayed in Gioconda Belli's novel, *La mujer habitada* (*The Inhabited Woman*), a fictional mirror version of her memoir, *El país bajo mi piel* (*The Country Under My Skin*). The purpose is not so much to identify women with nature, and much less to show that in Nicaragua women are treated or mistreated like nature is treated and mistreated. Woman is not necessarily a victim here, only a potential victim in that she is a daughter of history (D'Eaubonne, *Féminin et Philosophie* 21). Woman may be likened to the landscape and be as untouchable as the volcanoes that cannot be moved, but unlike volcanoes she is confronted with a choice, a weighing-in. There is either a delicate or a brutal balance regarding how to react when confronted with the reality of that sweet waistline and all its consequences: to accept, to protest, to resist, or give in to whatever is the most appropriate and opportune term for violence, be it armed struggle, terrorism, revolution, or war. In this sense, and by virtue of the choices to be made, woman, instead of embodying nature, transcends it.

A Double Telling

As far as publication dates are concerned, the fictional account, *La mujer habitada* (1988) precedes the memoir, *El país bajo mi piel* (2002). The fiction and the nonfiction can be read side by side and compared, or they can be read separately. A reader does not have to read both books; there is one that satisfies avid readers of autobiographies, and there is a novel for readers of fiction. The novel may also be read as an autobiographical novel, in search of clues, or keeping in mind that there can be more reality to fiction than to nonfiction, whereas the memoir may be read the way Columbus's journals, Cortés's letters, and Cabeza de Vaca's accounts are approached, without always trying to separate fact from fiction, because it is the texts that matter. Belli presents her readers with two different versions of a story, a double telling, a memoir and a novel. In a simple world, these could be labeled either true or false and there would be a thick, bold line separating the two. Unmindful of that divisive line, I am focusing on a fictional version of the truth simply because more ecological and feminist stances—in other words, ecofeminist stances—are taken in the novel than in the memoir.

Francoise D'Eaubonne writes that the destruction of natural resources is a result of the appropriation of fertile lands, just as overpopulation is the result of the appropriation of women's fecundity (*Ecologie/Féminisme* 28). In this sense, the women of Belli's novel seem to have escaped the constraints of their biology, for they are in full control of their sexuality and of their fertility. "Nos negamos a parir," says Itzá, Belli's woman warrior (116). [We refused to bear children.] This is evocative of Mary O'Brien's political control of reproduction (Mellors 90). Likewise, Lavinia chooses not to become pregnant because there was no place for a child in the midst of so much insecurity (115). Lavinia's is also a political choice.

Itzá is a voice from the past who fought the Spanish conquerors in vain, only to be pushed into "las tierras profundas, altas, y selváticas del norte, a las cuevas en las faldas de los volcanes" (116) [the farthest inland regions, the high forests of the north, to the caves on the edge of the volcanoes (142)]. In fact, Itzá is the past of Lavinia's present, and Lavinia (the main character), in turn, is Belli's fictional alter ego. In this novel, the past can be seen in the mirror of the present and vice versa, just as Itzá's reflection is in Lavinia's mirror, and Belli's is in Lavinia's or Itzá's.

These images momentarily caught in the mirror, images that establish a difference and an identity, transform the hot, dusty urban scene into a world of mirrors where the past constantly echoes the present. The first Spaniards do not belong to the distant past; they have not yet been fully assimilated so they remain right underneath the asphalt, trapped in the roots of trees along with the warrior woman whose tribe the Spaniards judged to be barbaric, bestial, and ignorant idolaters who worship images of stone and wood and clay (Gerbi 266). Much like a volcanic eruption, the past is always trying to find a fault and come to the surface. It is a silenced past, silenced like unbearable pain or trauma. A nation with a pattern of suffering, unable to escape this past, seems to be living it over and over again; it is a recurring nightmare.

Ambivalence

One way to put an end to the nightmare is to flee the nation. For a brief moment, while listening to the vivid descriptions of the torture of a member of the clandestine National Liberation Movement, Lavinia regrets not having stayed in Italy, but she immediately realizes that in Faguas (Managua) the challenges are different, "En Faguas, en cambio eran otros los retos. Se trataba de dominar la naturaleza volcanic, sísmica, opulenta, la lujuria de los árboles atravesando indómitos el asfalto" (12). [It was a question of taming the volcanic, seismic, opulent nature, the lust of the trees piercing the asphalt (14).] Just as the past and the present converge, so does the landscape and the political. In other words, if the landscape is volcanic, seismic, and opulent, so is the nation. And in spite of the ecological devastation—this novel takes place in a city with an urban crisis that is an ecological crisis—trees are still piercing the asphalt.

It is this opulent landscape that poses a challenge to Lavinia, but she is ambivalent in her response to nature. In spite of her love for this land, Lavinia uses the word *dominar*, to tame, when she is considering the natural world before her eyes. "Patriarchy seems to be everywhere," writes the feminist critic Mary Daly. "Even outer space and the future have been colonized" (1). The use of words such as dominate or tame reveals an inability to break away from a masculine alter ego, or a masculine self. "Nor does this colonization exist simply outside women's minds, securely fastened into institutions we can securely leave behind. Rather, it is also internalized, festering inside women's heads, even feminist heads" (ibid.).

The ecofeminist critic Vera Norwood points out that Hans Huth and Roderick Nash "document men's dominance in American natural history; Annette Kolodny and Richard Slorkin demonstrate that the myth of the masculine hero conquering virginal landscape is a primary source of male ambivalence" (323). It would appear that Lavinia is still inhabited by this male ambivalence since she feels the need to tame the natural environment; that is what she considers to be her challenge, a challenge that would not have existed had she remained in Italy.

But why does Lavinia feel a need to tame the natural environment? She herself, as seen through the eyes of the warrior woman, is a modern woman who lives alone, without a family or a master. "Actúa como un alto dignatario que solo se sirve a sí mismo" (17). [She behaves like a high dignitary who is only accountable to himself (21).] Lavinia herself felt she had a right to be something other than a bilingual secretary, to be an architect instead, to build houses, to live alone, and to be independent (9–10). But it is either her free spirit or her ambivalence when it comes to the natural environment that needs to tip the scale. Even her choice of career, architecture, directly impacts the environment, in other words, transforms it and subsequently tames it, as if Lavinia's European ancestors were expressing a desire for dominance through her, for they were quite adept at taking possession.

The opulent, volcanic nature, however, was never easily subjugated. Christopher Columbus was the first to describe it, and he did so in apocalyptic terms. From the Miskito Coast of Honduras, to cape *Gracias a Dios* in present-day Nicaragua, there is no marveling at the beauty of nature as in the journal of the First Voyage, only a battle for survival. Columbus writes that for sixty days the fleet sailed against headwinds and foul weather and only advanced sixty leagues. "En todo este tiempo no entré en Puerto ni pude, ni me dexó tormenta del cielo, agua y trombones y relámpagos de continuo, que parecía el fin del mundo" (280). [All this time I did not find a safe harbor, nor did the storm, the water and the lightning allow me to move forward, it seemed like the end of the world.]

Samuel Eliot Morison explains that the admiral named the low and ill-favored headland Cape *Gracias a Dios* (Thanks be to God) because it was at this point that the foul weather ended. Two days later, on September 16, 1501, the admiral named the present-day Matagalpa River *Río de los Desastres* (River of Disasters) because several of his men drowned at its mouth. There are no more attempts to name rivers and mountains after royalty or saints, or even to christen them with names evocative of their beauty; this is a landscape described in terms of struggle for survival, of horror, of ill-fate. Norwood explains these struggle-and-survival narratives in terms of ego-gratifying achievements that feed the "achievement-oriented male psyche, enabling men to return to civilization and improve their culture" (323). According to Pierre Samuel, this state of being in horror of nature, of seeing nature as an enemy that needs to be tamed, is at the root of the ecological crisis (D'Eaubonne, *Ecologie/Féminisme* 211).

However, the Central American jungle remained a hostile frontier, an unwanted place, until the nineteenth century when it became the sweet waistline of America. The original Spanish settlers never cared for the tropical lowlands. But in the nineteenth century and early twentieth century, the world discovered that it definitely had a sweet tooth and that there was profit to be made in the hot zone, profit to be made and profit to be defended. Soon enough, the sweet waistline of America became a waistline of tears, Neruda's "cintura de los sollozos" (356). Orion's belt became one made of tears instead of stars.

Since she was a child, Lavinia loved the greenness, the rebellious tropical vegetation that, unbeknownst to her, was already tamed by then. The voice that inhabits her, the voice of the woman warrior who in turn inhabits the orange tree outside Lavinia's window, remembers silent nights when she and her lover were crouched, ". . . en las entrañas selváticas de las montañas, escondiendonos para la enboscada. No se atrevían a seguirnos los españoles. Tenían miedo de nustros árboles y animals" (40). [The wild, innermost heart of the mountain, hiding in ambush. The Spaniards did not dare follow us. They feared our trees and animals (49).]

Magical Realisms

The point of departure of *The Inhabited Woman* may very well be an unnamed country where, "nadie sabe lo que no le conviene" (23) [no one knows what isn't convenient for them to know]. *Once upon a time in an unnamed country where no one knew* . . . Then again, the novel could begin on a warm January day in a city with a fictional name, Faguas. A taxi is going down dusty avenues toward the lake. Since there are volcanoes in the distance, the novel could begin with a gaze. The passenger in the taxi is admiring the beauty of the landscape and regretting that the lake had been transformed into a sewer. "Tan hermoso como imperdonable el hecho de que le hubieran asignado al lago function de cloaca" (11).

When D'Eaubonne points out that it is women who are directly confronted with urban and ecological crises, she conjures the memory of the 1970s German left-wing militant, Ulrike Meinhof, who went from being a mother and a respected journalist involved in the antibomb struggle to becoming cofounder of the far left Red Army Faction, a terrorist gang that participated in several bank robberies and bombings. When Meinhof began her life as a guerrilla in 1969, she made some radical decisions that cost her everything; she lost her freedom, and then her life. According to D'Eaubonne, Meinhof's stances were the result of a realization: the absence of armed struggle meant death, but staying alive meant being buried alive either in a prison, a new building, or a modern kitchen (*Ecologie/Féminisme* 186). Both Gioconda Belli and her fictional alter ego, Lavinia, are faced with that decision, not just to live or to die, but also to live to the death, or to live a life in death.

The first sign of the precarious future awaiting Lavinia is the lake that has been turned into a sewer. Since Lavinia is eager to reach the construction site indicated on her blueprints, the fact that the lake is polluted is noted in passing. The thought is almost casual, as if to say, "Too bad that such a beautiful lake has been turned into a sewer!" In this case, ecological degradation is merely a backdrop. Ecology is overshadowed by the urgency of the moment.

Ariel Salleh believes that ecological crisis displaces modernist political analyses such as liberalism, socialism, and feminism, thus forcing us to "reframe our history, to inscribe a new understanding of ourselves in relation to nature" (3). However, Salleh takes it for granted that the bourgeois and proletarian revolutions have already happened. Such is not the case in Nicaragua where the human crises, war, and the struggle for survival have left ecology in the darkest shadows. An excellent example is that within perhaps a quarter hour of having noticed the polluted lake, Lavinia will discover that she is starting her "practice" by designing a shopping center that will displace over five thousand poor people. Immediately, the polluted lake is forgotten; Lavinia is amazed that everyone is so utterly resigned (24).

Read with hindsight, in the present, the present being 2009, Lavinia's poor people uncannily announce *los afectados*, thousands of environmental refugees who have been living in an encampment in the center of Managua known as Nemagon City since 1996. These are banana or sugar farmers who were exposed to a pesticide known as Nemagon, which is "considered to be a risk factor for cancer, chronic kidney failure, acute respiratory disease, heart attacks, sterility, muscular atrophy, skin complaints and internal bleeding" (Adán Silva). *Los afectados* is such a discrete word, meaning the affected ones. They live in tents made of black garbage bags, and they are demanding "government response [to] their health needs and legal backing for their cause" (ibid.). Taxi drivers shrug when they are asked about *los afectados*; they have become part of the urban landscape, in the form of a bruise or a carcinoma, they have been there for so long.

When Lavinia returned to her air-conditioned office after having confronted her own poor people by the lake, one of her coworkers, Felipe, asks her jokingly, "Te echaron un balde de agua?" (23) [Did they throw a bucket of cold water on you?] Her reaction is, "¿Por qué no me dijiste?" [Why didn't you tell me?] After some further bantering, Felipe answers, "No tienen otra alternativa" (24). [They have no choice.] The word is resignation. And the novel could very well begin with a vivid portrait of resignation, or it could also begin the moment Lavinia feels attracted to her jaded coworker.

But it does not. It is time to give the beginning away. The novel begins with the very first sentence, "Al amanecer emergí" (7). [I emerged at dawn.] The first person singular in the opening phrase is coming from a tree outside Lavinia's bedroom window. Is this yet another example of magical realism? Perhaps it cannot be avoided since, as Mario Vargas Llosa points out, novels were not published in Spanish America until after the Wars of Independence, thus making Latin Americans victims of the revenge of the novel. "We still have great difficulty in our countries in differentiating between fiction and reality. We are traditionally accustomed to mix them in such a way that this is probably one of the reasons why we are so impractical and inept in political matters" (5). So the blame should be put on Columbus, on Pedrarias Davila, on Francisco Hernández de Córdoba, and on Pascual de Andagoya if Latin American "contemporary reality is still impregnated with the violence and marvel that those first texts of your literature—those novels disguised as history or historical books corrupted by fiction—told us about" (Vargas Llosa 15).

The Devil's Probable Accessibility through the Craters of Volcanoes

So there is a tree and a spirit inside the tree. This is an old orange tree trapped in a poor, dusty, hot city, "pobre, polvosa, y caliente" (11). The tree is surrounded by thick stone walls, "como las que nos hacían levantar los españoles" (8) (like the ones the Spaniards made us build). But not only is the orange tree that is inhabited by the spirit of a dead warrior woman encircled by Spanish-style walls, the tree itself is Spanish. "Fue de las pocas cosas buenas que trajeron los españoles" (35). [It was one of the few good things the Spaniards brought.] It seems that even the most innocent things are fraught with memory and meaning. There is no safety zone; the gaze cannot linger on anything that is not loaded from the inside like a volcano, and from the out, like a beast of burden.

Perhaps the spirit could have picked another tree, a native tree to inhabit; or perhaps there was no choice to be made. Perhaps it was the tree that the Spaniards brought who chose the warrior woman, forsaking all other spirits. Whatever the case may be, this tree is coming to life again with *her* own life. "Y este árbol vive de nuevo con mi vida" (17). The Spaniards may have brought death and destruction, but this tree that the Spaniards brought is being brought back to life with the spirit of Itzá. It is as if there were no burying the past, the Spaniards are ever present, dead or alive, even in the old orange tree that cannot be but representative of nature and of the feminine.

Just as the tree feels captive in the Spanish walls, Lavinia feels captive in a taxi listening to the news on the radio, a military doctor saying, "Al hermano del muerto—también acusado de conspirar—el alcalde lo había lanzado al volcán Tago. Un volcán en actividad, con lava rugiente en el cráter. En los atardeceres se veía roja desde el borde. Los españoles conquistadores habían creído que se trataba de oro fundido" (12). [The major had thrown the dead man's brother—also accused of conspiracy—into the Tago volcano. It was an active volcano, with roaring lava in the crater. At dusk the rim appeared red. The Spanish conquistadors had thought it was molten gold.] One moment Lavinia is listening to the news on the radio, and the next the Spanish conquistadors have returned. The man accused of conspiracy has been thrown into the very same volcano into whose crater the Spaniards once attempted a descent, convinced as they were that it was full of molten gold.

"A friar, they say, entered as far as the ledge half way down the mouth, and thence he looked down and saw a certain thing like metal, of the colour of fire, and he let down a link of an iron chain by rope, but when he drew it up he found nothing" (35). Such is the narrative of an officer of fortune named Pascual de Andagoya who accompanied the conquistador Pedrarias Davila to present-day Panama and Nicaragua in 1519 to 1520.

The constant echoing of the past and the present reverberates in the landscape. Pascual de Andagoya described Nicaragua as a land of abundance of good fruit, and of honey and wax and of volcanoes that smoke constantly. When de Andagoya stopped to describe the Massaya volcano, he could very well be describing it as it is today. "The mouth is round like that of a well, and half way down there is a ledge round the mouth; as when they make a well . . . At times the fire comes out with great fury, and sends forth many stones that look like great pieces of iron" (34–35). Rarely does a text from the sixteenth century describe a natural environment that still exists. Thus, de Andagoya is describing an untouchable landscape.

Another picturesque description of the crater of the Massaya volcano can be found in Gónzalo Fernández de Oviedo's *Historia general y natural de las Indias*, first published in 1535. Oviedo, convinced of the devil's probable accessibility through the craters of volcanoes, writes that there will not be a single Christian who will not repent his sins and recall the existence of hell after having stood at the rim (Gerbi 312). But the Spaniards were not the first to consider the Massaya as the devil's passageway. Oviedo recalled a Cacique depicting a witch who used to come up out of the well of the volcano to counsel the Indians, "just as the devil must be . . . a very old woman, naked . . . very old and wrinkled, and her teats hung down to her navel . . . and her teeth were long and sharp like a dog's" (Gerbi 313). Oviedo concludes that this witch must have been the devil in person and that one cannot deny that the Indians communicate with the devil (ibid.).

The coincidence of the past and the present is not only in the landscape, but it is also in Lavinia's traits. When the spirit in the tree stops to contemplate Lavinia, she describes her in terms of her Spanish and indigenous heritage. "Tienes rasgos parecidos a las mujeres de los invasores, pero tambien el andar de las mujeres de la tribu" (8). [She has traits that resemble those of the invaders women, but the gait of the women of my tribe.] Both the Spanish tree and the woman with Spanish traits are inhabited by the indigenous past, the time before 1519 when Pedrarias Davila sent Francisco Hernández de Córdoba in command of a force to conquer and settle Nicaragua. There is no erasing this past, just as there is no erasing the land that the Spaniards conquered or the landscape they described in terms of horror as well as profit.

Consequently, it should not come as a surprise that Lavinia used the word *dominar*, to tame, when she is contemplating the landscape before her eyes. Ecological feminists such as Karen Warren would immediately point to the connection that exists between the treatment of women and the treatment of nonhuman nature (3). Lavinia may be a woman, and a woman of color, but she cannot escape her cultural and social heritage, and the word *dominar* is part of her identity no matter how intensely she stands up for her rights and refuses to be subjugated herself. In other words, Lavinia is showing signs of being unable to shed the masculine, and this renders her masculine in her environmental thinking.

Another example of Lavinia being trapped in what Mary Daly would label "the patriarchal" is the fact that the toxic lake is only a passing thought. For Lavinia, this is not a feminist issue, she just happens to live in a city with a polluted lake, and this is a pity. She simply wonders what it would be like this morning if the city had not turned its back on the lake, but aesthetics had never mattered to the great generals. "Pero a los grandes generals nunca les había importado la estética" (11–12).

There is little protest and no resistance—no expression of shock, merely a quiet sigh of regret contained in a fleeting thought. In this instance, Lavinia does not muse on the fact that the environment never mattered to the great generals; it was beauty that they considered inconsequential. Unfortunately, there is an epistemological limitation to her thoughts. Just as the sun was once assumed to revolve around the earth, here environmental crisis seems to revolve around the generals. There is no question as to her own personal role; the issue is left to the generals. It is with this patriarchal bias that Lavinia speaks for nature.

Thus, ecological devastation becomes an evident truth, as normal as dictatorship, or as poor people being displaced to make way for a shopping center, or as banana workers dying of cancer because everyone wants their bananas to be yellow.

Love in the Time of Somoza

Although she is only twenty-three, Lavinia is beginning to show signs of existential ennui and resignation. She stops to remember a time when she thought things could be different. "Una época de efervescencia cuando ella tenía dieciocho años . . . Se encontró las calles cubiertas de afiches del partido de la oposición. La gente cantaba la cancón del candidate verde con verdadero entusiasmo . . . Una gran manifestación recorrió las calles demandando la renuncia de la familia gobernante, el retiro del candidato hijo del dictado" (18–19). [A time of effervescence when she was eighteen . . . She found the streets plastered with the posters of the opposition party. People sang the Green candidate's song with genuine enthusiasm . . . An enormous demonstration wound through the streets demanding the resignation of the ruling family, the withdrawal of the candidacy of the dictator's son (22–23).]

Obviously, the Somozas are the ruling family, and this is an autobiographical novel. Gioconda Belli was born in 1948, which means that she was eighteen in 1966, and twenty-three in 1971. The Somozas had been in power since 1933, and would remain in power until 1979 when they were overthrown by the left-wing FSLN (Sandinista National Liberation Front), usually known simply as the Sandinistas. Lavinia's Green candidate and his collaborators—in other words, Belli's FSLN—take refuge in a hotel and request the protection of the United States, a protection they will not get because in the eyes of the United States, the Greens of the novel or the Sandinistas of nonfiction are Communist subversives.

"The only thing we can do is resign ourselves," Lavinia's father comments (23). The few men surrounding Lavinia seem to be pushing her toward resignation. Felipe, her coworker, has a much similar reaction when it comes to the poor people being displaced in order to make way for a shopping center. At first, Lavinia does not quite understand what Felipe is about, nor does the reader. Felipe could very well have been put there to play a patriarchal role. "Solo quería aterrizarla," Felipe says to Lavinia (24). In other words, by suggesting that Lavinia go and visit the construction site, all Felipe wanted was to bring her down to earth. For this he uses the word *aterrizar* (to land), just as a pilot would land a vessel. Such an interchange is reminiscent of Mary Daly's chapter titled "Flying Fetuses" where she points out that Thomas Ford, an attorney for Robert Byrn, a pro-life professor of criminal law at Fordham University, once described the uterus as an astronaut in a human spaceship. "Since an astronaut is perceived as the captain of a vessel, there is a desire to see the fetus as controlling the woman" (Daly 58). Just as pilots lands airplanes, astronauts land spaceships, and in this case the fetus Felipe is simply attempting to *land* Lavinia who ends up spending the first month of work *aterrizando* (landing), "con la omnipresente cercanía de Felipe, quien asumió con gran gusto el rol de hacerla poner los pies sobre la tierra" (26) [while Felipe, with his ubiquitous presence, took on with gusto the mission of getting her feet firmly planted (32)].

Lavinia does not take Felipe's condescension poorly. On the contrary, she is all the more attracted to him. At this point, the reader wonders if this novel will turn into an office romance with a polluted lake, volcanoes, and tortured members of the Green Party in the background. One cannot help but conjure the United States where office romances are less about love and attraction than about potential lawsuits for sexual harassment. There are no such concerns for Lavinia or Felipe. One month into her new job, Lavinia flirtatiously asks Felipe—her superior—if he likes to dance. He says he does, but they do not make any plans; she simply lets him know where she will be. That very same evening they end up dancing together in a discotheque, with Felipe hugging her so tightly that she could barely breathe, it was almost painful. "El baile se estaba poniendo serio, pensó. Caían los diques. Se soltaban los frenos" (30). [This dance is getting serious, she thought. Barriers were crumbling. Brakes were being released (38).]

The next day, Itzá, the voice inside the orange tree, describes Felipe's and Lavinia's sexual encounter in Lavinia's apartment in terms of spells of love potions and warriors sizing each other up before a combat (33). This reminds Itzá of her own experiences with her lover, Yarincé. It would appear that both Lavinia and her alter ego, Itzá, are liberated women who have managed to escape biology for they are in control of their sexuality and of their fertility. But it could very well be that D'Eaubonne would qualify Felipe as a "Tiers monde macho" (Third World macho) when it comes to his relationship with Lavinia (*Ecologie/Féminisme* 61). Much like a warrior, Felipe is always busy, and his secret commitments force him to depart hastily the next morning. Much like a warrior's woman, Lavinia is left with a feeling of satisfied loneliness and a sensation that Saturday time is too slow for her liking (39).

Had Lavinia not consumed the orange juice—which can be equated to a love potion—a few days after her amorous encounter with Felipe, she could have been compared to Tristan's Yseut, and consequently would not have been responsible for her passion (42). But Lavinia is already under Felipe's spell by the time she consumes the juice from the tree that is inhabited by the warrior woman. This suggests that Lavinia did not go into the amorous relationship spellbound, but rather willingly, in full command of her senses. Passion, however, is by nature passive, and can easily take on the aspect of a magical potion. Lavinia goes into this love affair with confidence in herself. She is convinced she is in full control of the situation and does not even stop to question her passivity. Other women may be too romantic; Lavinia does not stop to see her own image in their mirror. Thinking she was merely giving her friend good advice, to beware of romanticism, Lavinia stated that love in the movies was just an illusion. Ironically, by telling her friend Sara that she was afraid of falling in love with Felipe before really knowing him, what she was in fact saying was that she was already in love, just like in the movies (37–38).

Why Are These Women Terrorists?

Soon after having consumed the orange juice from the inhabited tree, in this case a symbolic love or war potion, Lavinia will become inhabited and will very soon discover why Felipe is always so busy. He confesses that he is part of a militant faction intent on overthrowing the dictatorship. "Contra la violencia no queda más que la violencia," Felipe says (57). [Only violence can be used to combat violence.]

D'Eaubonne believes that no one has stopped to consider the origins of terrorism as an urban crisis that is a form of an ecological crisis. Consequently, D'Eaubonne explains that what she labels sensational headlines—such as "Pourquoi ces femmes sont-elles terroristes?" (Why are these women terrorists?)—do not take into account a new and surprising reality, "une adoption commune de la violence (ou plutôt de la contre-violence) par a la fois les femmes et la jeunesse poussés à bout par la déshumanisation du quotidien et de l'environment . . . et plus encore par la menace physique que cette meme civilization fait peser sur leur capital biologique" (*Ecologie/Féminisme* 186) [an adoption of violence, or rather counterviolence, by both women and young people pushed to the limit by the dehumanization of daily life and of the environment, and even more by the physical threat that this same civilization poses to their biological resources].

Initially, Lavinia refuses to become involved in Felipe's armed struggle. She does, nonetheless, very soon begin to "traspasar límites" (literally, trespass limits) and therefore to discover a person within her that she never knew existed or could exist (71). She is in awe of this person; perhaps just like Dr. Jekyll was in awe of Mr. Hyde, who was younger and dauntless. Jillian Becker uses the words "excitedly involved" to describe Ulrike Meinhof's initial involvement in the antibomb struggle. Becker then points out that, according to Monika Mitscherlich, a daughter of the psychologist Alexander Mitscherlich, Meinhof was more interested in organizing, arguing, and talking about politics than in reading or learning. Mitscherlich states that Meinhof was not really a socialist, did not understand Marxism, and perhaps had never even read Marx (130). Lavinia's situation is uncannily similar Meinhof's, especially when it comes to Felipe's cause. She does not stop to study the cause; she simply wavers on whether or not to join the cause and use violence against violence.

Had Lavinia not fallen in love with Felipe, perhaps she would not have opted to become a terrorist. Meinhof's husband, Klaus Rainer Rohl, was convinced that Meinhof's interest in politics began with her interest in him. Becker quotes Rohl, who claimed that Meinhof's love affair with communism and her love affair with him were the same thing (130). Then again, this could merely be patriarchal thought extended to the judgment of women terrorists. In other words, if they chose to become terrorists, it was because they loved men who were terrorists. Rohl, however, was no terrorist. He was merely a philandering editor. It was not until Meinhof left Hamburg and Rohl for West Berlin and for Baader that she became a terrorist (Kramer 201).

Either these women loved the wrong men, or they could not escape biology. For example, after the terrorist Gudrun Ensslin gave birth, it was rumored that she became more extreme in her political thought. Consequently, she was judged as being hysterical not just by fellow members of the Sozialistischer Deutscher Studentenbund (SDS), but also by Meinhof and Rohl, editors of the leftist student paper, *Konkret* (Becker 71–72). In this instance, had Gudrun not given birth, perhaps she would not have become hysterical, such a prisoner of her uterus, of her biology. The SDS accused her of making very emotional speeches, saying loudly, tearfully, "They'll kill us all—you know what kind of pigs we're up against— . . . They have weapons and we haven't. We must arm ourselves" (Becker 72). Eleven months after giving birth, motherhood felt like a trap to

Gudrun Ensslin. At this point, she appears to escape her biological destiny since she abandons her children shortly after she meets the terrorist Andreas Baader. Becker believes that Gudrun had been amply prepared for this sort of man, "not only by her boredom with Vesper and the child, or suddenly by her taste of violence, but by nature and by nurture" (73). In this sense, Gudrun's itinerary resembles a loop; she escapes biological determinism only to be catapulted back into nature and nurture.

Obviously, Lavinia does not adopt violence as extremely as Meinhof and Ensslin. She is more languid. She stops to consider the situation and decides that she does not want Felipe to be the center of her life, or for her to become a Penelope to Ulysses/Felipe (91). All this time, the warrior woman who inhabits the tree has been observing and judging. "Felipe emana el poder del coraje; ella nada en un mar de confusiones" (61). [The power of courage emanates from Felipe, while she swims in a sea of confusion.] In spite of being so patriarchal in her judgment, Itzá does, however, find Lavinia's fearfulness endearing, all the more so because she sees an untouchable landscape in the inner substance of Lavinia: "El hombre con sus obras puede . . . sembrar o cortar árboles, cambiar el curso de los ríos . . . pero no puede mover los volcanes, elevar las hondonadas, interferir en la cúpula del cielo . . . igual paisaje intocable tiene la sustancia de Lavinia" (70). [Man with his deed can change features . . . he can sow or cut down trees, change the course of rivers . . . But he cannot move volcanoes, lift up the canyons, interfere in the dome of the heavens . . . The same untouchable landscape is the inner substance of Lavinia (85).]

This could very well mean that man can change many things, he has the power to destroy and to alter, but he cannot move the unmovable, volcanoes and woman. Or it could mean that Itzá decides to do away with Lavinia's fearfulness because of her inner substance. So Itzá whispers in Lavinia's ear until Lavinia feels guilty. In this sense, guilt displaces fear, and guilt leads to the adoption of violence. Although Felipe urges Lavinia to become the shore to his river, Lavinia decides to become a member of Felipe's group and therefore to adopt violence (129). Be it understood, however, that Lavinia is never openly violent; she does not rob banks or murder innocent people, she is more of a nurse than a bloodthirsty subversive.

Why, indeed, are these women terrorists? What is the message? What is the ecofeminist message? This reader is receiving mixed messages. On the one hand there is an acceptance of female embodiment. It is obvious throughout the novel. The very idea of an *inhabited* woman evokes embodiment. Thus, Belli's ecofeminism concords with

Andrée Collard's assertion of the universal as an essential relationship between woman and nature (Mellor 77).

But the acceptance of embodiment is problematic because it threatens women's liberation. Lavinia, however, is in many ways liberated. Not only is she financially independent, but by deciding not to have a child in spite of her impulses she demonstrates reproductive autonomy. In Lavinia's world there is no place for a child, initially because of the prevailing dictatorship and finally because of her membership in a terrorist gang. In this sense Lavinia heeds Simone de Beauvoir whose only answer "is to escape, to abandon biology, to become a man" (Mellor 79).

Both Felipe and Yarince (Itzá's lover) urge their women not to become men: Felipe by constantly asking Lavinia to become the shore to his river, and Yarince by telling Itzá that war is no place for women. Even Itzá's mother reminds Itzá that her umbilical cord is buried underneath the ashes underneath the stove and that is where she belongs (106). Both Lavinia and Itzá, however, opt for war. "Yo sé usar el arco y la flecha, No soporto la placidez de los largos días," Itzá tells her mother before she sets out to join Yarince in combating the Spaniards (106). [I know how to use a bow and arrow. I cannot bear the quietness of the long days.] Again, these assertions ring concomitantly with those of feminists, such as Cecile Jackson, who warn women against embracing the body, motherhood, the comforts of home, and abandoning goals of freedom and autonomy because such conservatism can hardly claim empowerment (Mellors 73).

It would appear that by choosing war, both Lavinia and Yarince become empowered. They could be waging a war against a society built without them and against them (D'Eaubonne, *Ecologie/Féminisme* 186). They are, or they think they are, acting like men, doing the things that men do, dying for a cause, not simply standing next to a stove and bearing children. At this point the radical feminist D'Eaubonne asks why. "Pourquoi . . . les femmes préfèrent-elles s'assumer comme des males castrés (ou castrables dans l'order symbolique) plutôt que de revendiquer un ordre complémentaire à l'ordre phallique" (*Féminin et Philosophie* 21). [Why do these women prefer to identify with castrated males (or potentially castrated ones in the symbolic realm) instead of demanding a condition that complements the phallic order?] This question could very well be the answer to the sensational question, why are these women terrorists? But the question that is an answer does not end there. Why don't these women demand a reciprocative status "dans le vie réelle, et non dans l'imaginaire où on le leur concede souvent, ainsi que l'âme a l'esclave pharaonique?" (ibid.) [in real life and not in the realm of imagination where their demands are often met, just as a soul was granted to the pharaoh's slaves?]. D'Eaubonne explains that when slaves revolted in Egypt because immortal life was an elitist privilege, the priests did not hesitate to grant them immortal life. In this case, the voice from the past has the last word—Itzá's voice. Itzá, who was perhaps granted immortal life, has completed her cycle. Lavinia's body fertilizes the fields; she too has been granted immortal life. No one will possess this body of lakes and volcanoes. The men have become hummingbirds, they too have been granted immortal life. "Nadie que ama muere jamás" (342). [No one who loves dies.] Everyone has been granted immortal life!

But in the beginning there was a polluted lake, a landscape not only touched but sullied as well, a damaged environment that is mentioned in passing, therefore internalized, an internalized ecological crisis, dehumanization that ultimately leads to a repetition of violence and death. In the end, the voice from the past believes the characters in this tragedy were emancipated by love and violence. The red is wet and death becomes liberation. Is this a happy ending? Everyone is liberated, and everyone is dead. Freud would see the characters as organisms that have followed their own path to death. "What we are left with is the fact that the organism wishes to die only in its own fashion" (Freud 33).

So they died wanting to become one with the landscape, the nation. Now they fertilize the fields. Alas, the fruit left out to rot in the sun also fertilize the fields. I am referring to the unhappy ending of Neruda's "United Fruit Co." (336).

Chapter 12

The Landscape of the Consumer Society

Fernando Contreras Castro's *Unica mirando al mar*

Jerry Hoeg

The subject of this chapter, Costa Rican author Fernando Contreras Castro's novel *Unica mirando al mar* (*Unica Watching the Sea*; 1993), is emblematic of that country's, and by extension Central and, indeed, Latin America's struggle for ecological reform. The Costa Rican Ministry of Education has made the novel obligatory reading for all ninth graders, and it is regularly taught at Costa Rica's two public universities, the Universidad de Costa Rica and the Universidad Nacional (Calderón 173). In addition, it has been adapted for the stage and enjoyed success in various venues throughout the country, including the prestigious Teatro Mélico Salazar in the nation's capital, San José (Díaz 9; Hernández 2).

Another important factor is that the setting of the novel, Río Azul (Blue River), is an actual landfill in San José, Costa Rica. It first went into service in 1972, and since then has received 1,200 tons of garbage daily. When it first opened, it was billed as a sanitary landfill but quickly became an open-air garbage dump with neither controls nor treatment facilities. This unregulated dumping produced foraging grounds for various scavenger species, including vultures, rats, flies, dogs, and humans, all of which soon proliferated on the site and in the neighboring communities. Rainfall on the location dissolves a variety of contaminants and the chemical-rich concoction thus produced then infiltrates into the ground water, "inyectándose de manera intravenosa en el cuerpo de la tierra" (Contreras 49) [injecting itself intravenously into the body of the earth]. Additionally, contaminated runoff from the site is either improperly treated or not treated at all and allowed to flow into the local watershed and eventually to the sea. This problem is especially acute in the rainy season, with the additional problem that the rain causes the containment walls of the landfill to collapse, releasing the garbage onto the streets of the adjoining neighborhoods (Rojas Pérez 8). The odor from the landfill is released into the neighboring communities during all seasons, making these almost uninhabitable. In his research for the book, the author managed to visit only once, being driven off by the odor in subsequent attempts: "Pretendía ir más de una vez pero no me atreví, el olor es insoportable" (Contreras, qtd. in Villalobos 15). [I tried to go more than once but I couldn't bring myself to do it: the odor is unbearable.]

The offensive odor produced by the contents of Río Azul, which includes both the *buzos* and the garbage, is emblematic of the breakdown of society. Odor plays a role in all human societies, and these same societies expend much time and energy to control it, not the least of which involves supporting a billion-dollar perfume industry (Van Toller and Dodd). When the odor is out of control, the society is out of control. Humans are far more sensitive to our olfactory landscape than most of us realize. For example, women's sensitivity to odors is influenced by their menstrual cycle, peaking around ovulation (Doty et al.). Furthermore, odors play an important role in mother-offspring interaction. Babies recognize and react to their mother's odors (Chernoch and Porter), and mother's can recognize their own babies purely by odor (Porter et al.). Additionally, human mate choice is influenced by the diverse odors produced by different major histocompatibility complex (MHC) types (Penn and Potts). MHC genes control immunological self- and non-self recognition, and more diversity in MHC types translates to a more diverse, hence effective, immunological system, and also provides a mechanism for incest avoidance (Penn and Potts). Generally speaking, "'good' body odor tends to be weak, as ratings of intensity correlate negatively with ratings of pleasantness in our studies" (Wedekind 318). In the novel, the title character Unica goes to great lengths to save, and later use, the residual perfume she finds in discarded bottles. "Vaciaba los sobros de los perfumes en una sola botella . . . por la mañana se permfumaba siempre antes de salir a trabajar" (37). [She would dump the leftover perfumes in one big bottle . . . and perfume herself every morning before leaving for work.]

The novel is generally considered to be both a satire and a critique of wasteful consumer society and its negative environmental consequences (Díaz; Gamboa; Budd; Rojas Pérez; Hoeg). In this view, the unsanitary landfill, itself a product of overproduction and overconsumption, is a sign of the times, foreshadowing the eventual future of all of Costa Rica. Indeed, a major subplot of the novel revolves around the failed efforts to close Río Azul and open a new landfill in another location. This mirrors the events actually taking place in Costa Rica where, in spite of a Supreme Court ruling ordering the dump closed, it is still open due to the difficulty of finding a new location. All proposed alternatives have met ferocious opposition from the various threatened local communities, and so Río Azul slogs on.

The inhabitants of the garbage dump are known popularly as *buzos*, from the Spanish term for scuba diver for their scavenging actions on the landfill. They are seen as precursors of the future way of life of the inhabitants of the entire country unless changes are made to the disposable society: "todo el país se estaba convirtiendo en un basurero . . . todos, absolutamente todos, nos vemos obligados a bucear en las profundidades del humo de los escapes en busca de un poco de aire para respirar . . . en las profundidades de las aguas contaminadas en busca de algo de beber . . . a bucear entre los alimentos contaminados de agroquímicos y plagacidas en busca de algo fresco de comer . . . a bucear entre la basura que hablan los políticos en busca de una actitud sincera" (116). [The entire country was turning into a garbage dump . . . everyone, absolutely everyone, is obliged to dive into the contaminated air in search of fresh air to breath, into the depths of our contaminated waters in search of something clean to drink, to search among the foods contaminated with agrochemicals and pesticides to find something fresh to eat, and among the garbage politicians speak to find something sincere.]

In the novel, the *buzos* are considered already disposed of, useless items discarded onto the landfill along with the rest of the garbage. That the two central *buzo* characters, Unica Oconitrillo and Monboñobo Moñagallo, were previously a teacher and a library employee, respectively, indicates the precarious financial positions of all those who live paycheck to paycheck in modern consumer society. Ironically, although her name means "unique" in Spanish, Unica represents a sort of Latin American "every woman." According to the author, "Unica es un personaje que refleja el carácter arquetípico de la mujer latina: ser fuerte, estar decidida a luchar para seguir viviendo" (qtd. in Hernández 2). [Unica is the archetypical Latin America woman: strong, commited to struggle in order to carry on living.]

And struggle to carry on she does, forming a family from what is discarded onto the dump. Her adopted son, El Bacán, was abandoned on the dump as a baby and found and rescued/recycled by Unica. Moñagallo too was left for dead on the dump and subsequently rescued/recycled by Unica. Having lost his job as night watchman at the *Biblioteca General* (the public library; for denouncing the sale of library books to a toilet paper company), where he stayed awake every night for twenty years reading the classics, now homeless and unemployable, he attempts suicide—he calls it "identicide" (9)—by throwing himself into a garbage truck. This results not in death, but rather in the ignominious arrival of this symbol of humanistic erudition on both the literal and the figurative trash heap. In consumer society, anything but the latest model is considered disposable, and the landscape of the dump reflects this. In fact, Contreras does not focus on the landscape of the countryside, but rather on that of the city, and specifically on that part of the city that is most emblematic of the negative effects of the consumer society, Río Azul. The landscape of Río Azul is the "after" landscape of global production and consumption. We never see the "before" landscape of the consumer society, the good life of the continuously new and improved, only the aftermath.

Later in the novel the aforementioned ambassador of the liberal arts, Moñagallo, tries to organize and politicize the "masses" of the dump, "elucubrando fantasías de progreso" (44) [fantasizing about progress], with laughable (non)results. The other *buzos* correctly define his utopian faith in social constructivism as the fantasy of an old fool: "en fin, se estaba poniendo senil" (98) [in a nutshell, he was getting senile]. This failed effort at activism on the part of the marginalized is an important comment on the realities of modern Costa Rican society. Even the *buzos* themselves do not feel they have a makeable case when it comes to public assistance. When the police turn a water cannon on the protesting *buzos* at the Presidential Palace, they simply enjoy it: "Vio a todos los buzos tomar la cosa a la ligera y bailotear debajo del aguacero de artificio que se les estaba viniendo encima . . . La visita había sido todo un fracaso, pero solo Momboñombo Moñagallo estaba consciente de ello" (140–41). [He saw all the *buzos* taking it as a joke, dancing under the spray from the device . . . The visit had been a total failure, but only Momboñombo Moñagallo was aware of it.]

The essential problem for the *buzos* is an oversupply of unskilled workers in a free market economy. Unica herself was a "maestra agregada, es decir, de las que ejercieron sin título" (19) [an adjunct teacher, that is to say, a teacher without a university degree]. In a letter to the president of the republic regarding the proposed closing of Río Azul, Moñagallo, speaking on behalf of the *buzos*, writes, "El problema es que ¿que vamos a hacer nosotros? ¿de qué vamos a vivir cuando el basurero lo cierren? . . . el problema es que si existiera otra cosa que nosotros pudiéramos hacer para ganarnos el pan, pero mucha gente aquí no sabe ni leer ni escribir ni hacer otra cosa que rebuscarse una platilla con lo que se encuentran en el basurero" (119–20). [The problem is, What are we going to do? . . . The problem is, well, if there were something else we could do to earn a living, but, many people here don't even know how to read or wrote, or to do anything else except scavenge the dump.]

The fact that this satirical critique of Costa Rican society, and the government that mismanages it, has been institutionalized by the Ministry of Education begs the question of why the government should promote something so critical of itself. Minor Calderón Salas tackles this question by arguing that, in the final analysis, the novel is critical of the handling of the landfill, but not of social and family order and values writ large: "La novela es . . . transgresora . . . sin embargo, pienso que apoya ciertas instituciones sociales . . . la familia tradicional . . . ritos sociales . . . no "llama" a romper el orden social, la estructura vigente, etc." (184). [The novel is . . . transgressive . . . nevertheless, I think it supports certain social institutions . . . the traditional family . . . social rites . . . it doesn't call for a break with the social order, the current social structure, etc.] I believe this misses an important aspect of the novel. While Calderón Salas is certainly correct in pointing out that the novel does not call for a total break with the social order and does indeed appear to support certain values such as family and religion, the core answer as to its acceptability to the powers that be lies elsewhere. I will argue the novel confirms the uniquely human propensity for economic exchange. This is shared by all the parties in the novel, from the president of the republic down to the lowliest human scavenger on the dump. I believe the reason it is not, ultimately, subversive, is that, in the final analysis, it supports a market ideology of economic exchange and trade. Furthermore, the problems of the *buzos*, the environmental problems of Río Azul, and the political wranglings surrounding these issues are all fixable from within the system. The solution to all these problems is to be found through education, and so it is a small wonder that the Ministry of Education supports, indeed welcomes, this type of scrutiny. Nor is it surprising that the rest of the market forces in Costa Rica, especially in their political incarnations, support the Ministry of Education's choice of reading material for impressionable Costa Rican youth.

Education and prosperity go hand in hand in a free (market) society with opportunity for all. By humanizing the *buzos*, Contreras makes it easier for us to respect their culture and to support public education and the allocation of public funding for said education, for those who wish to avail themselves of it.

The very first page of the novel makes clear the economic motor that drives the *buzos*. The landfill is characterized as an ocean, and those scavenging it as divers, plunging below its surface to harvest valuable exchange goods: "Los buzos habían extraído varios cargamentos importantes de las profundidades de su mar muerto . . . se apresuraban a seleccionar sus presas para la venta en distintas reciladoras de latas, botellas y papel, o en las fundidoras de metales más pesados" (Contreras Castro 11). [The divers had extracted various important cargos from the depths of their dead sea . . . they hastened to pick over their catch for sale to various recyclers of cans, bottles, paper, or heavy metals.]

The continual work of the tractors as they spread out the endless flow of incoming garbage produced "una marea artificial" (12) [an artificial tide], which in turn set the rhythm of life on the "mar," or sea, of Río Azul. This natural flow, free of the clocks and schedules of industrialized society, evokes another era in human history, a time populated by an idyllic society free from the hustle and bustle of our modern era. It implies exchange is a mere *de novo* artifact of industrial civilization. But as Contreras points out, the majority of the *buzos*' cargo was destined for exchange to recyclers. Although in theory the dump could provide for all their essential needs without engaging in exchange, the *buzos* find it preferable to harvest exchangeable items as well as the bare necessities of everyday life. Even though they have the option of escaping from the world of trade and exchange by becoming self-sufficient on the dump, returning to the feed-as-you go mode of subsistence employed throughout much of our Australopithecine stage (two to five million years ago), and even now typical of most primates and grazing animals, they instinctively turn to an exchange-based economic model, even among themselves within the confines of Río Azul. As the Spanish philosopher José Ortega y Gassett pointed out some time ago, people want "no estar, sino bienestar" (328) [not simply to live, but to live well].

In human history there was also a turn to an exchange-based model, beginning about two million years ago. This model was the hunting-gathering-fishing hub, which involves division of labor, specialization in procurement, and food-sharing. Importantly, this also produces excess capital goods, be they food or materials. Stock piles of finished stone tools, raw materials from distant sources, and large amounts of animal remains, which when taken in concert imply both trade and specialized tool making, have been found together in East African sites dating back 1.5 to 2 million years. Additionally, genetic evidence shows humans worldwide comprise only one single species. At the present time, no subspecies exists, which demonstrates extensive human exchange patterns. As Haim Ofek summarizes, "It is clear, however, that under market exchange no subspecies can for any length of time maintain the genetic isolation required to sustain it apart from the rootstock of the species at large" (120). Paleolithic sites display evidence of mercantile exchange as well. A few examples include Mediterranean seashells appearing at Upper Paleolithic sites in central Europe, Black Sea amber found 700 kilometers away in central Russia, and distinctive flint stored 400 kilometers from quarry sites in eastern Europe (Linton; Klein; Schild). Even when prohibited, exchange continues clandestinely in human populations, as during the prohibition of alcohol in the United States, the prohibition of controlled substances during the current "war on drugs," and prohibitions on arms sales during the "war on terrorism." People caught breaking these embargos are sent to prisons, where a thriving black market exists (Redford).

As we saw earlier in the chapter on Andrés Bello, his call to abandon the evils of the cities and return to a simple, honest, agricultural way of life in the countryside was ironic in that the rise of cities is an artifact of agricultural production. Agriculture, it will be recalled, produces cities because of the need to exchange food and nonfood items. Similarly, in *Unica* there is a call for an alternative to the industrial development and runaway consumerism that produces the environmental devastation symbolized by Río Azul. Nevertheless, the recyclers who inhabit Río Azul participate in the same system of mercantile exchange that occasioned their sad circumstances in the first place. While in Bello's Silvas, and later in Gallegos's *Doña Bárbara*, we saw a call for a return to the countryside; in *Unica* we see no such distinction. Unica came from the countryside but makes no effort to return in order to solve her economic woes. The agricultural work force is also saturated, and available agricultural land area is shrinking. This is symbolized by the story told within the novel about Unica's garden. In her words, "Al principio, al puro puro principio, yo tenía un jardin aquí . . . Pero después la tierra como que se fue secando, muriendo, muriendo . . . el basurero todavía estaba lejos, pero fue creciendo . . . teníamos como Más espacio y más aire puro . . . Pero . . . la tierra se fue poniendo como arcillosa . . . las rosas no pegaron, se me murió una tortuga que tenía en el jardin . . . empezaron a llegar las cucarachas . . . las moscas"

(59–60). [At first, at the very, very beginning, I had a garden here . . . But the ground started drying out, dying, dying . . . the dump was still far away, but it kept growing . . . We used to have more space, more fresh air . . . But . . . the land turned to dust . . . the roses wouldn't grow, a turtle I had in the garden died . . . the cock roaches began to arrive . . . and the flies.] But in spite of the deteriorating situation, she does not leave, because the situation is the same throughout the small country: "Cualquier parte del país a donde huyera con su familia sería igual que estar en casa, porque al fin y al cabo, todo el país se estaba convirtiendo en un basurero" (116). [Whatever part of the country she chose to flee to with her family would wind up being the same as staying where they were now, because the whole country was turning into one big garbage dump.] Instead, she chooses to struggle on in Río Azul, fully enmeshed in the exchange economy, albeit at a subsistence level. It is only at the end of the novel when, having lost her adopted son El Bacán to the diseases endemic to the landfill, she seeks to escape to that other sea, the real one at Puntarenas on the Pacific coast. But even here, her sustenance is provided by her husband Moñagallo's participation in mercantile exchange. Shortly after their arrival, he "se iba a recoger cuanta cosa reciclable hallara por la playa . . . a bucear también por las calles y por el mercado . . . que vendía luego en un puestito . . . su mercancía" (156–57). [went out to collect whatever recyclable thing he could find on the beach . . . on the streets and at the market . . . merchandise he would later sell at a little stand he set up].

Prior to leaving, Unica had been a staunch advocate of family values within the *buzo* community. She had married Moñagallo in a ceremony presided over by the self-ordained *buzo* priest known as el Oso Carmuco, who had found priest's robes discarded on the landfill, donned them, and so become a "priest" himself. He now gave Mass and performed all the other priestly duties, albeit after his own fashion. Unica did her best to maintain other middle-class rites, including installing an antenna on the roof of her dumpside hovel: "En el techo de la casita había una antena de televisor que no cumplía fución, pero que Unica había puesto ahí para darle un toque de distinción" (31). [On the roof of the shack was a TV antenna that wasn't hooked up to anything, but that Unica had put there to give the place a touch of class.] Although I agree with Calderón Salas's assertion that the novel "apoya ciertas instituciones sociales . . . la familia tradicional . . . ritos sociales" (supports certain social institutions . . . the traditional family . . . social rites), it should be noted that it does so in a roundabout way. The novel actually undermines all these middleclass rituals when they take place on the landscape of consumer society. On Río Azul, the priest is not really a priest, the wedding is a parody, the shack has an antenna but no TV, and so on. Toward the end of the novel, Moñagallo makes this clear when he tells Unica, "Todo era falso. Te mentiste durante veinte años de tu vida . . . te trajiste todo para acá, la tradición familiar, las buenas costumbres, la maternidad . . . una vida basada en modelos aburguesados en medio del mierdero más ingrato del país" (149–51). [Everything was false . . . you lied to yourself for twenty years . . . you brought everything here . . . family traditions, customs, motherhood . . . a life based on bourgeois models in the middle of the biggest shithole in the country.]

The implication seems to be that these values cannot coexist with runaway consumer society. The alternative values Unica and Moñagallo construct in their new life in Puntarenas are those of alienated, withdrawn, and isolated individuals who cling only to each other because there is no one else to cling to. This is part of the utopian vision of the author who argues that pollution can be attacked through knowledge and environmental regulation, poverty through a more equitable distribution of resources, carcinogens by bans on food additives, and so on. But failing these alterations to our disposable society, our fundamental values will be undermined. At the same time, we have seen that the propensity for exchange is innate in the *buzos*. This portends a tragic end to any social engineering project that ignores human nature, unless society can control this nature sufficiently to create a new social order. So far, neither in the novel nor in life has the utopian vision produced a utopian landscape. To this day, Río Azul slogs on.

Works Cited

Adán Silva, José. "Nicaragua: Invisible Victims of Pesticide Protest Government Neglect." Aug. 2007. http://ispcnews.net/news.aso?idnews=38968.
Alegría, Claribel. *Ashes of Izalco*. Willimantic, CT: Curbstone, 1989.
———. *Cenizas de Izalco*. Barcelona: Seix Barral, 1966.
Alonso, Amado. *Poesía y estilo de Pablo Neruda*. Madrid: Gredos, 1997.
Alonso, Carlos J. *The Burden of Modernity: The Rhetoric of Cultural Discourse in Spanish America*. Oxford: Oxford UP, 1998.
Alvarez, Federico. *El Periodista Andrés Bello*. Caracas: La Casa de Bello, 1981.
Amory, Frederic. "Euclides da Cunha and Brazilian Positivism." *Luso-Brazilian Review* 36.1 (1999): 87–94.
———. "Historical Source and Bibliographic Context in the Interpretation of Euclides da Cunha's *Os Sertões*." *Journal of Latin American Studies* 28.3 (1996): 667–85.
Andagoya, Pascual de. *Narrative of the Proceedings of Pedrarias Davila*. Trans. and ed. Clements R. Markham. Facsimile. Elibron Classic Series, 2007. London: The Hakluyt Society, 1865.
Anderson Imbert, Enrique. *Historia de la literatura hispanoamericana*. Mexico: Fondo de Cultura, 1954.
Avellaneda, Gertrudis Gómez de. *Sab and Autobiography*. Austin: U of Texas P, 1993.
———. *Sab*. Ed. José Serverad. Madrid: Cátedra, 1997.
Ayala, Francisco J., and Camilo José Cela Conde. *La piedra que se volvió palabra: Las claves evolutivas de la humanidad*. Madrid: Alianza, 2006.
Balling, J. D., and J. H. Falk. "Development of Visual Preference for Natural Environments." *Environment and Behavior* 14.1 (1982): 5–28.
Barash, David, and J. E. Lipton. *Making Sense of Sex*. Washington, D.C.: Island, 1997.
Becker, Jillian. *Hitler's Children: The Story of the Baader-Meinhof Terrorist Gang*. New York: J. B. Lippincott, 1977.
Beer, Gillian. *Open Fields: Science in Cultural Encounters*. Oxford: Clarendon, 1996.
Belli, Gioconda. *El país bajo mi piel*. New York: Vintage Español, 2003.
———. *La Mujer Habitada*. Mexico, D.F.: Editorial Diana, 1989.
———. *The Inhabited Woman*. Trans. Kathleen March. Madison: U of Wisconsin P, 1994.

Bello, Andrés. *Obras completas.* 26 vols. Caracas: Fundación la Casa de Andrés Bello, 1981–1986.

———. *Selected Writings of Andrés Bello.* Trans. Frances M. Lopez-Morillas. Ed. Ivan Jaksic. New York: Oxford UP, 1997.

Bello, Fernando Vargas. *Andrés Bello, el Hombre.* Santiago, Chile: Editorial Andrés Bello, 1982.

Benitez-Rojo, Antonio. "Sugar and the Environment in Cuba." *Caribbean Literature and the Environment.* Ed. Elizabeth M De Loughney. Charlottesville: U of Virginia P, 2005. 1-22.

Bertol Domingues, Heloisa M., and Magali Romero de Sa. "The Introduction of Darwinism in Brazil." *The Reception of Darwinism in the Iberian World.* Ed. Thomas F. Glick, Rosaura Ruiz, and Miguel Angel Puig-Samper. Dordrecht: Kluwer, 2001. 65–81.

Bethell, Leslie, ed. *Latin America: Economy and Society, 1870-1930.* Cambridge: Cambridge UP, 1989.

Bhabha, Homi K. *The Location of Culture.* London: Routledge, 1994.

Blackburn, Alexander. *The Myth of the Picaro.* Chapel Hill: U of North Carolina P, 1979.

Borge, Tomás. *The Patient Impatience.* Willimantic, CT: Curbstone, 1989.

Boschetto-Sandoval, Sandra, Marcia Phillips McGowan, eds. *Claribel Alegría and Central American Literature.* Athens, OH: Ohio University Center for International Studies, 1994.

Bowles, Paul. *Without Stopping.* New York: Putnam, 1972.

Bravo-Villasante, Carmen. *Una vida romántica: la Avellaneda.* Madrid: Instituto de Cooperación Iberoamericana, 1986.

Bridgeman, Bruce. *Psychology and Evolution: The Origins of Mind.* London: Sage, 2003.

Brignole, Alberto J., and José María Delgado. *Vida y Obra de Horacio Quiroga.* Montevideo: Rodó, 1939.

Brown, Donald E. *Human Universals.* New York: McGraw-Hill, 1991.

Budd, Ruth. "Basura y tesoros en el relleno sanitario de Río Azul: Una nueva mirada a la 'Suiza de América Central.'" *Letras* 31 (1999): 121–30.

Budiansky, Stephen. *Nature's Keepers.* New York: Free Press, 1995.

Buell, Lawrence. *The Future of Environmental Criticism.* Cambridge: Harvard UP, 2001.

———. *Writing for an Endangered World: Literature, Culture, and the Environment in the U.S. and Beyond.* Cambridge: Harvard UP, 2001.

Bueno, Eva Paulino. "Three Theories, Three Writers, One Idea: Science and the Nation in the Brazilian Literature of Joaquim de Souzândrade, Euclides da Cunha, and Augusto dos Anjos." *Science, Literature, and Film in the Hispanic World.* Ed. Jerry Hoeg and Kevin S. Larsen. New York: Palgrave, 2006. 11–28.

Cabeza de Vaca, Alvar Núnez. *Naufragios.* Ed. Juan Francisco Maura. Madrid: Cátedra, 2005.

———. *The Narrative of Cabeza de Vaca*. Ed. Rolena Adorno and Patrick Charles Pautz. Lincoln: U of Nebraska P, 1999.
Caldera, Rafael. *Andrés Bello: Philosopher, Poet, Philologist, Educator, Legislator, Statesman*. Trans. John Street. London: George Allen & Unwin, 1977.
Calderón Salas, Minor. "Unica mirando al mar: entre la transgresión y la norma." *Letras* 35 (2003): 173–84.
Calvin, William H. *A Brain for all Seasons: Human Evolution and Abrupt Climate Change*. Chicago: U of Chicago P, 2002.
Caruth, Cathy. *Unclaimed Experience, Trauma, Narrative, and History*. Baltimore: Johns Hopkins UP, 1996.
Cavalli-Sforza, Luigi Luca. *Genes, Peoples, and Languages*. Trans. Mark Seielstad. New York: Farrar, 2000.
Chaunu, Pierre. *Conquête et Exploitation des Nouveaux Mondes*. Paris: Presses Universitaires de France, 1995.
Chernoch, J. M., and R. H. Porter. "Recognition of Maternal Axillary Odours by Infants." *Child Development* 56 (1985): 1593–98.
Clark, William R., and Michael Grunstein. *Are We Hardwired?: The Role of Genes in Human Behavior*. New York: Oxford UP, 2000.
Collichio, Terezinha A. F. *Miranda Azevedo e o Darwinismo no Brasil*. São Paulo: Editora da Universidade de São Paulo, 1988.
Colón, Cristóbal. *Los Cuatro Viajes. Testamento*. Ed. Consuelo Varela. Madrid: Alianza, 1982.
Columbus, Christopher. *Los Cuatro Viajes. Testamento*. Ed. Consuelo Varela. Madrid: Alianza, 1999.
Columbus, Christopher. *The Diario of Christopher Columbus's First Voyage to America 1492–1493*. Norman: U of Oklahoma P, 1989.
Contreras Castro, Fernando. *Unica Mirando al Mar*. 2nd ed. San José, Costa Rica: Farben, 1994.
Corballis, Michael C. "Phylogeny from Apes to Humans." *The Descent of Mind: Psychological Perspectives on Hominid Evolution*. Ed. Michael C. Corballis and Stephen E. G. Lea. Oxford: Oxford UP, 1999. 1–26.
Cortés, Hernan. *Letters from Mexico*. Trans. Anthony Padgen. New Haven, CT: Yale UP, 1986.
Costa Lima, Luiz. *Control of the Imaginary: Reason and Imagination in Modern Times*. Trans. Ronald W. Sousa. Minneapolis: U of Minnesota P, 1988.
Crosby, Alfred W. *The Columbian Exchange. Biological and Cultural Consequences of 1492*. Westport, CT: Praeger, 2003.
Cunha, Euclides da. *Rebellion in the Backlands (Os Sertões)*. Trans. Samuel Putnam. Chicago: U of Chicago P, 1944.
Cuomo, Chris. *Feminism and Ecological Communities*. London: Routledge, 1998.
Cussen, Antonio. *Bello and Bolívar: Poetry and Politics in the Spanish American Revolution*. Cambridge: Cambridge UP, 1992.
Daly, Martin, and Margo Wilson. *Homicide*. Hawthorne, NY: Aldine de Gruyter, 1988.

Daly, Mary. *Gyn/Ecology*. Boston: Beacon, 1978.
Dansgaard, W., et al. "Evidence for General Instability of Past Climate from a 250-kyr Ice-core Record." *Nature* 364 (1993): 218–20.
Darío, Rubén. *Songs of Life and Hope*. Trans. Will Derusha and Alberto Scereda. Durham, NC: Duke UP, 2004.
Davies, Catherine, ed. *Gertrudis Gómez de Avellaneda. Sab.* Manchester, UK: Manchester UP, 2001.
D'Eaubonne, Francoise. *Ecologie/Féminisme, Révolution ou Mutation?* Paris: Les Editions A. T. P., 1978.
———. *Féminin et Philosophie. (Une allergie historique)*. Paris: L'Harmattan, 1997.
De Fuentes, Patricia. *The Conquistadors*. New York: Orion, 1963.
De las Casas, Bartolomé. *Brevísima relación de la destrucción de las Indias*. Ed. Jean Paul Duviols. Buenos Aires: Stockcero, 2006.
De Loughney, Elizabeth M., Reneé K. Gosson, George B. Handley. *Caribbean Literature and the Environment*. Charlottesville: U of Virginia P, 2005.
Diamond, Jared. *Guns, Germs, and Steel: The Fates of Human Societies*. New York: Norton, 1997.
Díaz del Castillo, Bernal. *The True History of the Conquest of Mexico*. New York: Robert M. McBride & Company, 1927.
Díaz, Lidia. "Unica mirando al mar: una proliferación del sentido." *Káñina* 19.2 (1995): 9–14.
Díaz-Briquets, Sergio, and Jorge Pérez-López. *Conquering Nature: The Environmental Legacy of Socialism in Cuba*. Pittsburgh: U of Pittsburgh P, 2000.
Doty, R. I., et al. "Endocrine, Cardiovascular, and Psychological Correlates of Olfactory Sensitivity Changes During the Human Menstrual Cycle." *Journal of Comparative Physiology and Psychology* 95 (1981): 45–60.
Dunn, Oliver, and James E. Kelley, Jr. *The Diario of Christopher Columbus's First Voyage to America 1492–1493*. Norman: U of Oklahoma P, 1989.
Duran Luzio, Juan. "Alexander von Humboldt y Andrés Bello; Etapas hacia una relación textual." *Escritura* 12.23–24 (1987): 139–52.
Eidt, Robert C. *Frontier Settlement in Northeast Argentina*. Madison: U of Wisconsin P, 1971.
French, Jennifer L. *Nature, Neo-Colonialism, and the Spanish American Regional Writers*. Hanover, NH: Dartmouth College P, 2005.
Fernandes, Raúl C. "Euclides e a literatura: Comentarios sobre a 'moldadura' de *Os Sertões*." *Luso-Brazilian Review* 43.2 (2006): 45–62.
Fernández de Lizardi, José Joaquín. *El Periquillo Sarniento I*. Madrid: Editora Nacional, 1976.
———. *El Periquillo Sarniento II*. Madrid: Editora Nacional, 1976.
———. *The Mangy Parrot*. Ed. David Frye. Indianapolis: Hackett, 2005.
Foley, R. "The Adaptive Legacy of Human Evolution: A Search for the Environment of Evolutionary Adaptedness." *Evolutionary Anthropology* 4 (1996): 194–203.

Framer, David. "Ulrike Meinhof: An Emancipated terrorist?" *European Women on the Left*. Ed. Jane Slaughter and Robert Kern. Westport, CT: Greenwood, 1981. 193–219.
Freud, Sigmund. *Beyond the Pleasure Principle*. New York: Norton, 1961.
———. *The Uncanny*. New York: Penguin, 2003.
Fuson, Robert H. *Juan Ponce de León and the Spanish Discovery of Puerto Rico and Florida*. Blacksburg, VA: McDonald & Woodward, 2000.
Gaard, Greta. *Ecofeminism. Women, Animals, Nature*. Philadelphia: Temple UP, 1993.
Gallegos, Rómulo. *Doña Bárbara*. New York: Crofts, 1942.
———. *Una posición en la vida*. Mexico City: Ediciones Humanismo, 1954.
Gamboa, Marjorie. "A propósito de *Unica mirando al mar*." *Imágenes* 6 (1999): 111–14.
Gandolfi, Arthur E., Anna Sachka Gandolfi, and David P. Barrash. *Economics as an Evolutionary Science: From Utility to Fitness*. New Brunswick, NJ: Transaction, 2002.
Garrard, Greg. *Ecocriticism*. London: Routledge, 2004.
Gerbi, Antonello. *Nature in the New World*. Trans. Jeremy Moyle. Pittsburgh: U of Pittsburgh P, 1985.
Gifford, Terry. *Pastoral*. London: Routledge, 1999.
Girard, René. *Violence and the Sacred*. Trans. Patrick Gregory. Baltimore: Johns Hopkins UP, 1977.
Glotfelty, Cheryll, and Harold Fromm, eds. *The Ecocriticism Reader*. Athens: U of Georgia P, 1996.
Glotfelty, Cheryll. "Literary Studies in an Age of Environmental Crisis." *The Ecocriticism Reader*. Ed. Cheryll Glotfelty and Harold Fromm. Athens: U of Georgia P, 1996. xv–xxviii.
González Echevarría, Roberto. *Myth and Archive; A Theory of Latin American Narrative*. Cambridge: Cambridge UP, 1990.
Gordon, A. L. "Circulation of the Caribbean Sea." *Journal of Geophysical Research* 72 (1967): 6207–23.
Grases, Pedro. *Doce Estudios Sobre Andrés Bello*. Buenos Aires: Nova, 1950.
———. *Tiempo de Bello en Londres y otros ensayos*. Caracas: Ministerio de Educación, 1962.
Grove, Richard H. *Green Imperialism, Colonial Expansion, Tropical Island Edens and the Origins of Environmentalism 1600–1860*. Cambridge: Cambridge UP, 1995.
Gutiérrez Girardot, Rafael. "Para una interpretación de la 'Silvas' de Andrés Bello: Un esbozo." *Romanica Europaea et Americana; Festschrift fur Harri Meier*. Bonn, Germany: Bouvier, 1980. 232–34.
Handley, George B. *New World Poetics*. Athens: U of Georgia P, 2007.
Harter, Hugh. *Gertrudis Gómez de Avellaneda*. Boston: Twayne, 1981.
Hernández, Edin. "*Unica*: La forteleza de la desesperación." *Signos: Semanario cultural* 36 (1994): 1–2.
Hoeg, Jerry. "The Discourse of Science in Fernando Contreras Castro's *Unica mirando al mar*." *Revista de Estudios Canadienses* 20.3 (1996): 491–504.

Hoffmeister, John Edward. *Land from the Sea, The Geologic Story of South Florida.* Coral Gables: U of Miami P, 1974.
Holden, Constance. "The Violence of the Lambs." *Science* 289 (2000): 580–81.
Jaksic, Ivan. *Andrés Bello: Scholarship and Nation-Building in Nineteenth-Century Latin America.* Cambridge: Cambridge UP, 2001.
Jane, Cecil, trans. and ed. *The Voyages of Christopher Columbus.* New York: Argonaut, 1970.
Jitrik, Noe. *Horacio Quiroga. Una obra de experiencia y riesgo.* Montevideo: Arca, 1967.
Johnson, Ernest A., Jr. "The Meaning of Civilization and Barbarie in *Doña Bárbara.*" *Hispania* 39.4 (1956): 456–61.
Jones, R. O. *Historia de la literatura española, 2. Siglo de Oro: Prosa y Poesía.* Barcelona: Editorial Ariel, 1998.
Kaessmann, Henrik, Victor Weibe, and Savante Pääbo. "Extensive Nuclear DNA Sequence Diversity Among Chimpanzees." *Science* 286 (1999): 1159–62.
Kaplan, S. "The Role of Nature in the Urban Context." *Behavior and the Natural Environment.* Ed. J. Altman and J. F. Wohlwill. New York: Plenum, 1983. 127–61.
Kelly, Petra. "Women and Power." *Ecofeminism. Women, Culture, Nature.* Ed. Karen J. Warren. Bloomington: Indiana UP, 1997. 112–19.
King, John. *On Moderrn Latin American Fiction.* New York: Farrar, 1987.
Kirkpatrick, Susan. *Las Románticas, Women Writers and Subjectivity.* Liverpool: Liverpool UP, 1989.
Klein, R. G. *Man and Culture in the Late Pleistocene: A Case Study.* San Francisco: Chandler, 1969.
Kohler, T. A., and C. R. Van West. "The Calculus of Self-Interest in the Development of Cooperation; Sociopolitical development and Risk Among the Norther Anaszai." *Evolving Complexity and Environmental Risk in the Prehistoric Southwest.* Ed. J. A. Tainter and B. B. Tainter. Reading, MA: Addison-Wesley, 1996. 169–96.
Leon-Portilla, Miguel, ed. *The Broken Spears. The Aztec Account of the Conqust of Mexico.* Boston: Beacon, 1962.
Levinson, Stephen C., and Pierre Jaisson, eds. *Evolution and Culture.* Cambridge: MIT P, 2006.
Levy, Kurt. "*Doña Bárbara*: The Human Dimension." *The International Fiction Review* 7 (1980): 118–22.
Linden, David J. *The Accidental Mind: How Brain Evolution Has Given Us Love, Memory, Dreams, and God.* Cambridge: Harvard UP, 2007.
Linton, R. *The Tree of Culture.* New York: Alfred Knopf, 1956.
Liscano, Juan. *Rómulo Gallegos y su tiempo.* Caracas: Monte Avila, 1980.
Lopez Cid, Maria Rosa. "O aperfeiçoamento do homen por meio da seleção: Miranda Azevedo e a divulgação do darwinismo, no Brasil, na década de 1870." Diss. Casa Oswaldo Cruz/Fio Cruz, Rio de Janeiro, Brazil, 2004.

López de Gómara, Francisco. *Cortés. The Life of the Conqueror by his Secretary.* Trans. Lesley Bird Simpson. Berkeley: U of California P, 1964.
Luis, William. *Literary Bondage.* Austin: U of Texas P, 1990.
Manes, Christopher. "Nature and Silence." *The Ecocriticism Reader.* Ed. Cheryll Glotfelty and Harold Fromm. Athens: U of Georgia P, 1996. 15–30.
Mann, Charles C. *1491 New Revelations of the Americas before Columbus.* New York: Vintage, 2005.
Martinez Estrada, Ezequiel. *El hermano Quiroga.* Montevideo: Instituto Nacional de Investigaciones y Archivos Literarios, 1957.
Marx, Karl. *Economic and Philosophic Manuscripts of 1844.* New York: Prometheus, 1988.
McClelland, I. L. *The Origins of the Romantic Movement in Spain.* Liverpool: Liverpool UP, 1975.
McCook, Stuart. *States of Nature: Science, Agriculture and Environment in the Spanish Caribbean, 1760-1940.* Austin: U of Texas P, 2002.
McKibben, Bill. *The End of Nature.* New York: Random, 1989.
Meeker, Joseph W. *The Comedy of Survival.* Tucson: U of Arizona P, 1997.
Mellors, Mary. *Feminism & Ecology.* New York: New York UP, 1997.
Melville, Elinor K. *A Plague of Sheep.* Cambridge: Cambridge UP, 1997.
Méndez-Ramírz, Hugo. *Neruda's Ekphrastic Experience.* Lewisburg, PA: Bucknell UP, 1999.
Meza Márquez, Consuelo. Personal Interview. 13 July 2006.
Mies, Maria, and Shiva Vandana. *Ecofeminism.* London: Zed Books, 1993.
Mignolo, Walter. "Cartas, crónicas y relaciones del descubrimiento y la conquista." *Historia de la Literatura Hispanoamericana.* Vol.I.Madrid: Cátedra, 1998.
Miranda Azevedo, Agusto Cesar de. "Darwinismo: Seu passado, seu presente, seu futuro". *Conferências Populares da Frequesia da Glória.* Numbers 1–10. Rio de Janeiro: J. Villenueve S. C., 1876.
Mock, Douglas W., and Geoffrey A. Parker. *The Evolution of Sibling Rivalry.* Oxford: Oxford UP, 1997.
Mock, Douglas W. *More than Kin and less than Kind: The Evolution of Family Conflict.* Cambridge: Harvard UP, 2004.
Morison, Samuel Eliot. *Admiral of the Ocean Sea—A Life of Christopher Columbus.* Boston: Little, 1942.
Murphy, Dallas. *To Follow the Water.* New York: Perseus Books, 2007.
Neruda, Pablo. *Canto General.* Ed. Enrico Mario Santí. Madrid: Cátedra, 1997.
———. *Canto general.* Madrid: Cátedra, 1950.
———. *Obras Completas.* Buenos Aires: Losada, 1962.
Norwood, Vera L. "Heroines of Nature, Four Women Respond to the American landscape." *The Ecocriticism Reader.* Ed. Cheryll Glotfelty and Harold Fromm. Athens: The U of Georgia P, 1996. 323–50.

Ofek, Haim. *Second Nature: Economic Origins of Human Evolution.* Cambridge: Cambridge UP, 2001.
Ordaz, Ramón. *El pícaro en la literatura iberoamericana.* Mexico City: Universidad Nacional Autónoma de México, 2000.
Orians, Gordon, and Judith Heerwagen. "Evolved Responses to Landscapes." *The Adapted Mind.* Ed. Jerome H. Barkow, Leda Cosmides, and John Tooby. New York: Oxford UP, 1992. 555–79.
Ortega y Gasset, José. "El mito del hombre allende de la técnica." *Obras completas.* Madrid: Revista de Occidente, 1947. 317–75.
Padgen, Anthony, ed. *Hernán Cortés. Letters from Mexico.* New Haven, CT: Yale UP, 1986.
Pastor, Beatriz. *Discursos narratives de la conquista: mitificación y emergencia.* Hanover, NH: Ediciones del Norte, 1988.
Pavlocic, Milija N., and Roger M. Walker. "Roman Forensic Procedure in the *Cort* Scene in the *Poema de Mío Cid.*" *Bulletin of Hispanic Studies* 60.2 (1983): 95–107.
Penn, Dustin, and Wayne Potts. "How do Major Histocompatibility Genes Influence Odour and Mating Preferences?" *Advances in Immunology* 69 (1998): 411–36.
Pérez Martin, Norma. *Testimonios autobiográficos de Horacio Quiroga.* Buenos Aires, Corregidor, 1997.
Petersen, Ronald H. *New World Botany: Columbus to Darwin.* Konigstein, Germany: A. R. G. Gantner Verlag K. G., 2001.
Phillips, Dana. *The Truth of Ecology.* Oxford: Oxford UP, 2003.
Pinker, Steven. *The Blank Slate: The Modern Denial of Human Nature.* New York: Penguin, 2002.
Pino Iturrieta, Elias. "Aproximaciones a los límites del período contemporáneo en Venezuela." *Actualidades* 1 (1976): 37–43.
Plotkin, Henry. *Evolutionary Thought in Psychology: A Brief History.* Oxford: Blackwell, 2004.
Plumwood, Val. *Feminism and the Mastery of Nature.* London: Routledge, 1993.
Poirot, Louis. *Pablo Neruda: Absence and Presence.* New York: Norton, 1990.
Popol Vuh. Tran. Dennis Tedlock. New York: Simon and Schuster, 1985.
Porter, R. H., J. M. Chernoch, and F. J. McLaughlin. "Maternal Recognition of Neonates Through Olfactory Cues." *Psychology and Behaviour* 30 (1983): 151–54.
Pratt, Mary Louise. *Imperial Eyes: Travel Writing and Transculturation.* New York: Rutledge, 1992.
Quiroga, Horacio. *Cuentos de la selva.* México D.F.: Losada, 1999.
———. *Cuentos de amor de locura y de muerte.* New York: Penguin, 1997.
———. *Los desterrados. El regreso de Anaconda.* Buenos Aites: Losada, 1994.
Redford, R. A. "The Economic Organization of a POW Camp." *Economica* 12: 48 (1945): 189–201.

Repton, Harry. *The Art of Landscape Gardening.* Boston: Houghton-Mifflin, 1907.
Reséndez, Andrés. *A Land So Strange: The Epic Journey of Cabeza de Vaca.* New York: Perseus Books, 2007.
Revista Envío. "Victims of Nemagon Hit the Road." 29 Jan. 2008. http://www.envio.org.ni.
Revkin, Andrew. *The Burning Season.* Washington: Island, 2004.
Rivera-Barnes, Beatriz. "To Discover, an Intransitive Verb: Christopher Columbus's First Encounter with the American Landscape." *Ometeca* 12 (2008): 43–58.
Rodriguez Monegal, Emir. *El desterrado. Vida y obra de Horacio Quiroga.* Buenos Aires: Losada, 1968.
Rojas Pérez, Walter. *Flujo y reflujo en Río Azul: Análisis ecocrítico de* Unica mirando al mar. San José, Costa Rica: Porvenir, 2006.
Royle, Nicholas. *The Uncanny.* New York: Routledge, 2003.
Rueckhert, William. "Literature and Ecology: An Experiment in Ecocriticism" *The Ecocriticism Reader* Ed. Cheryll Glotfelty and Harold Fromm. Athens: U of Georgia P, 1996. 105–23.
Ruíz Ramón, Gerardo. "Basura de Río Azul no irá a La Carpio." *Diario Extra* 5 June 2006.
———. "Imposible cerrar Río Azul en 6 meses." *Diario Extra* 30 May 2006.
Rutherford, John. *Breve historia del pícaro preliterario.* Vigo, Spain: Universidad de Vigo, 2001.
Sainz de Medrano, Luis, ed. *El Periqiuillo Sarniento.* Madrid: Editora Nacional, 1976.
———. *Pablo Neruda: Cinco Ensayos.* Rome: Bulzoni, 1996.
Salleh, Ariel. *Ecofeminism as Politics: Nature, Marx, and the Postmodern.* London: Zed Books, 1997.
Schild, R. "Terminal Paleolithic of the North European Plain: A Review of Lost Chances, Potential and Hopes." *Advances in World Archeology* 3 (1984): 193–274.
Schlesinger, Stephen, and Stephen Kinzer. *Bitter Fruit.* New York: Doubleday, 1982.
Schneider, Paul. *Brutal Journey, Cabeza de Vaca and the First Epic Crossing of North America.* New York: Henry Holt and Company, 2007.
Scott, Nina M., ed. *Sab and Autobiography.* Austin: U of Texas P, 1993.
Serres, Michel *Parasite.* Minneapolis: U of Minnesota P, 2007.
Shaw, Donald L. *Gallegos: Doña Bárbara.* London: Grant and Cutler, 1971.
———. *El Siglo XIX.* Barcelona: Ariel, 1972.
Shiva, Vandana, and Maria Mies. *Ecofeminism.* London: Zed Books, 1993.
Singer, Peter. *The Expanding Circle: Ethics and Sociobiology.* New York: Farrar, 1981.
Slaughter, Jane, and Robert Kern, eds. *European Women on the Left.* Westport, CT: Greenwood, 1981.

Smith, Andy. "Ecofeminism through an Anticolonial Framework." *Ecofeminism. Women, Culture, Nature.* Ed. Karen J. Warren. Bloomington: Indiana UP, 1997. 21–37.
Spretnak, Charlene. *The Resurgence of the Real.* London: Routledge, 1999.
Tedlok, Dennis, trans. *Popol Vuh.* New York: Simon and Schuster, 1985.
Todorov, Tzvetan. *La Conquête de l'Amérique—La question de l'autre.* Paris: Seuil, 1982.
Trivers, Robert. *Social Evolution.* Menlo Park: Benjamin/Cummings, 1985.
Tucker, Richard P. *Insatiable Appetite.* New York: Rowman and Littlefield, 2007.
Turner, Frederick. "Cultivating the American Garden." *The Ecocriticism Reader.* Ed. Cheryll Glotfelty and Harold Fromm. Athens: U of Georgia P, 1996.
Twine, Richard. "Ecofeminisms in Process". 12 Jan. 2009. http://www.ecofem.org/journal.
Ubieto, Antonio, et al., eds. *Introducción a la Historia de España.* Barcelona: Teide, 1984.
Van Toller, S., and G. H. Dodd, eds. *Perfumery: The Psychology and Biology of Fragrance.* London: Chapman and Hall, 1991.
Vargas Llosa, Mario. "Latin America: Fiction and Reality." *On Modern Latin American Fiction.* Ed. John King. New York: Farrar, 1987. 1-17
Vila, Marco Aurelio. Lo geográfico en *Doña Bárbara.* Caracas: Ministerio de Relaciones Exteriores, 1986.
Villa, Marco Antonio. *Canudos: O povo da terra.* São Paulo: Atica, 1995.
Villalobos, M. L. Carlos. "*Unica mirando al mar* de Fernando Contreras." *Tertulia: Taller de literatura de San Ramón, Costa Rica* 2.3 (1994): 15–16.
Virgil [Publius Vergilius Maro]. *Georgics.* 12 Jan. 2009. http://classics.mit.edu/Virgil/georgics.html.
Visca, Arturo Sergio, ed. *Cartas inéditas de Horacio Quiroga.* Montevideo: Instituto Nacional de Investigaciones, 1959.
Vogel, Joseph Henry, and Camilo Gomides. "Ecological Debt and the Existence Value of Biodiversity: The Evidence begins with the *Diario of Columbus' First Voyage to America, 1492–1493.*" *Ometeca* 9.1 (2005): 206–19.
Vogeley, Nancy. *Lizardi and the Birth of the Novel in Spanish America.* Tallahassee: UP of Florida, 2001.
von Th‚nen, Johann Heinrich. *Isolated State.* 1826. Trans. C. M. Wartenberg. Ed. P. Hall. Oxford: Pergamon, 1966.
Waizbort, Ricardo. Letter to the author. 25 Aug. 2008.
Wall, Derek, ed. *Green History: A Reader in Environmental Literature, Philosophy and Politics.* New York: Routledge, 1996.
Warren, Karen J., ed. *Ecofeminism. Women, Culture, Nature.* Bloomington: Indiana UP, 1997.
Wasserman, Renata R. Mauter. "Mario Vargas Llosa, Euclides da Cunha, and the Strategy of Intertextuality." *PMLA* 108.3 (1993): 460–73.

Wedekind, Clau. "Body Odours and Body Odour Preferences in Humans." *Oxford Handbook of Evolutionary Psychology*. Ed. R. I. M. Dunbar and Louise Barrett. Oxford: Oxford UP, 2007. 315–20.

Wilson, Edward O. *The Diversity of Life*. New York: Norton, 1999.

Winterhalder, Bruce. "Risk and Decision-Making." *The Oxford Handbook of Evolutionary Psychology*. Ed. Robin Dunbar and Louise Barret. Oxford: Oxford UP, 2007. 433–45.

Worster, Daniel. *The Wealth of Nature*. New York: Oxford UP, 1993.

———. *Nature's Economy*. Cambridge: Cambridge UP, 1994.

Zaderenko, Irene. "El Procedimiento Judicial de Riepto entre obles y la Fecha de Composición de la *Historia Roderici* y el *Poema del Mío Cid.*" *Revista de Filología Española* 88 (1998): 183–94.

Index

Adorno, Rolena, 33, 35, 37
Aggazis, Louis, 89
Alegría, Claribel, 1, 6, 131–37, 139–43
Alemán, Mateo, 41
Alvarez, Federico, 56
Álzaga, Florinda, 70–71, 74
Amory, Frederic, 85–87
Andagoya, Pascual de, 166–67
 "Despedida a la Señora Da D. G. C. de V," 73–74
 Sab, 68–82
Anderson Imbert, Enrique, 12
Association for the Study of Literature and the Environment, 2
Atwood, Margaret, 108
Avellaneda, Gertrudis Gómez de, 1, 5–6
Ayala, Francisco J., 90
Aztecs, 28, 40, 45, 49–50

Baader, Andreas, 172
Baker, Lorenzo Dow, 155–56
Balling, J. D., 119
Barash, David, 129
Barros Arana, Diego, 147
Bates, Henry, 86
Becker, Jillian, 172–73
Belli, Gioconda, 6, 159–73
Bello, Andrés, 1–2, 5, 183
 early life and education of, 53–54
 founder of University of Chile, 56

 leaves Venezuela for London, 56
 "Ode to Tropical Agriculture," 57–66
 tutor to Bolívar, 55
Bello, Bartolomé, 53
Bello, Fernando Vargas, 55
Benítez-Rojo, Antonio, 73, 82
Benjamin Constant (Botelho de Magalhaes), 85
Bertol Domingues, Heloisa M., 86
biophobia, 4, 38
Blackburn, Alexander, 40–41
Boas, Franz, 87
Bolívar, Simón, 55–56
Bonpland, Aimé, 2, 55
Borges, Jorge Luis, 111
Boschetto-Sandoval, Sandra, 136–37
Bowles, Paul, 103
Bridgeman, Bruce, 118–19
Broca, Paul, 86
Budd, Ruth, 179
Buell, Lawrence, 2, 47, 50–51, 101–8, 111, 114
Bueno, Eva Paulino, 98

Cabeza de Vaca, Alvar Núñez, 4, 25–38, 104, 161
Cabot, Sebastien, 104
Caldera, Rafael, 66
Calderón Salas, Minor, 177, 181, 184
Carlos IV, 56

Carpentier, Alejo, 54
Castro, Fidel, 151
Cavalli-Sforza, Luigi Luca, 62, 90, 118
Cervantes, Miguel de, 43
Chang Rodriguez, Raquel, 52
Charles V, 26, 41, 104
Chernoch, J. M., 178
Clark, William, 99
Collard, Andrée, 174
Columbus, Christopher, 3–4, 28–36, 73, 82
  Journal of the First Voyage, 3, 9–24, 27–28, 67, 161, 163
Comte, Auguste, 85–86, 95
Condillac, Etienne Bonnot de, 55
conquistador, 25–28, 40–43, 105, 146–48, 150, 167
Conselheiro, Antônio (Antônio Vicente Mendes Maciel), 83, 85, 92, 95
consumerism, 2, 177–85
Contreras Castro, Fernando, 2, 177–85
Corballis, Michael C., 92
Córdoba, Francisco Hernández de, 166, 168
Correns, Carl, 90
Cortés, Hernán, 4, 28–31, 34, 161
  on *Mesyco* province, 44–45
  Moctezuma and, 46, 48–50
  as *pícaro*, 39–52
Costa Lima, Luiz, 85–87
Crosby, Alfred, 155
Cunha, Euclides da, 1–2
  Os Sertões (*Rebellion in the Backlands*), 83–98
  positivism and, 85–86
Cussen, Antonio, 57, 59, 63–64

da Cuneo, Michele, 28, 68
Daly, Martin, 129
Daly, Mary, 162, 168, 170
Dansgaard, W., 62
Darwin, Charles, 2, 85–94

Davila, Pedrarias, 166–68
D'Eaubonne, Francoise, 137, 139–40, 160–61, 163–64, 170–71, 174–75
de Vries, Hugo, 90
Diamond, Jared, 61
Díaz, Lidia, 177, 179
Díaz-Briquets, Sergio, 151
Díaz del Castillo, Bernal, 52
Dickens, Charles, 47, 51
Dodd, G. H., 178
Doty, R. I., 178
Dunn, Oliver, 9, 11, 13–22, 24, 67
Duran Luzio, Juan, 55

ecocriticism, 1–4, 7, 39, 102, 115, 142
ecofeminism, 6, 79, 133, 135, 137–39, 142, 161–62, 173–74
Eidt, Robert C., 103, 105, 107
Elder, John, 2
Ensslin, Gudrun, 172–73
environmental studies, 2

Falk, J. H., 119
Ferdinand of Aragon, 13
Ferdinand VII, 56
Flakoll, Darwin, 1, 6, 131–37, 139–43
French, Jennifer, 105, 114
Freud, Sigmund, 78–81, 175
Fuson, Robert, 33

Gallegos, Rómulo, 5, 66, 117–29, 183
Galton, Francis, 87
Gamboa, Marjorie, 179
Garrard, Greg, 115, 149
Gerbi, Antonello, 10, 14, 22–24, 67–69, 161, 167–68
Gifford, Terry, 114
Girard, René, 128
Glotfelty, Cheryll Burgess, 2, 102, 112, 142

Gomides, Camilo, 13, 15–16, 23–24
Gordon, A. L., 30
Gowdy, Barbara, 114
Grases, Pedro, 55
Grunstein, Michael, 99
Gutiérrez Girardot, Rafael, 54, 57

Hadly, George, 89
Haeckel, Earnst, 86
Handley, George, 147–50, 157
Harter, Hugh, 71, 75, 81
Heerwagen, Judith, 119
Hegel, Georg Wilhelm Friedrich, 90–91
Hernández, Edin, 177, 179
Hernández Martinez, Maximiliano, 140
Herrera y Tordesillas, Antonio de, 33
Hoeg, Jerry, 179
Hoffmann, E. T. A., 78
Hoffmeister, John, 35
Holden, Constance, 123
Homberger, Eric, 47
Humboldt, Alexander von, 2, 55–56
hurakan (hurricanes), 25–38

Interdisciplinary Studies in Literature and the Environment, 2
Irisarri, Antonio José de, 55
Isabella of Castile, 9, 13, 17
Issac, Jorge, 54

Jaisson, Pierre, 99
Jaksic, Ivan, 54–56, 59
Jentsch, E., 78
João VI, Dom, 84
Johnson, Ernest, 122
Joyce, James, 101

Kaessmann, Henrik, 90
Kaplan, S., 119
Keith, Minor, 156

Kelley, James, 9, 11, 13–22, 24, 67
Kelly, Petra, 138, 140
Kinzer, Stephen, 156
Kipling, Rudyard, 110–11
Kirkpatrick, Susan, 72, 76–77
Klein, R. G., 183
Kohler, T. A., 61

Las Casas, Bartolomé de, 10–11, 13, 19–24, 28
Leon-Portilla, Muguel, 45
Levinson, Stephen C., 99
Levy, Kurt, 125
Linden, David, 99
Linton, R., 183
Lipton, J. E., 129
Liscano, Juan, 118
Lizardi, José Joaquín Fernández de, 4, 39–43, 46–51
Locke, John, 55, 66
logging, 3, 102, 113, 146, 150–53
Lope de Vega, Félix, 55
López de Gómara, Francisco, 52
López Méndez, Luís, 56
Lopez-Morillas, Frances M., 57
Lucretius, 57
Lugones, Leopoldo, 103–4
Lyell, Charles, 88

Magalhaes, Benjamin Constant Botelho de, 85
Manes, Christopher, 45, 114
Mann, Charles, 42
Martí, Farabundo, 136
Martí, José, 67
McCook, Stuart, 147–48
McKibben, Bill, 50
Meeker, Joseph, 40, 52
Meinhof, Ulrike, 164, 172–73
Mellors, Mary, 161, 174
Melville, Elinor, 157
Melville, Herman, 47
Mendel, Gregor, 89, 94
Méndez-Ramírez, Hugo, 148, 152–53

Mendoza, Pedro de, 104
Menéndez Pidal, Ramón, 40, 54
Meza Márquez, Consuelo, 134
Mignolo, Walter, 12, 16
Miranda Azevedo Collichio, Agusto Cesar de, 86
Miruelo (Narvaez's pilot), 29, 31–33
Mock, Douglas W., 122
Moctezuma, 46, 48–50
Morison, Samuel Eliot, 11–20, 31–32, 163
Müller, Fritz, 86
Muir, John, 115
Murphy, Dallas, 30, 32

Napoleon Bonaparte, 56, 70
Narvaez, Pánfilo de, 25–38
natives, naturalization of, 36–37
natural sciences, 2, 51, 55
Neruda, Pablo, 6–7, 54, 79–82, 145–58, 159–60, 163, 175
Norwood, Vera, 162–63

Ofek, Haim, 61, 183
O'Gorman, Edmundo, 148
Orians, Gordon, 119
Orr, David, 2
Ortega y Gassett, José, 182
Oviedo, Gónzalo Fernández de, 22–23, 68, 167–68

Pääbo, Savante, 90
Palm, E. B., 17
parasites, 15, 39–40, 46–49, 52
Parker, Geoffrey A., 122
Pastor, Beatriz, 4, 13, 16–17, 20, 22, 26, 38
pastoral, 12, 52, 61, 69, 114–15
Pautz, Patrick Charles, 33, 35, 37
Pedro I, Dom, 84
Pedro II, Dom, 84–85
Peixoto, Afrânio, 95–96
Penn, Dustin, 178
Pérez-López, Jorge, 151

Pérez Martin, Norma, 103
Petersen, Ronald, 19–20, 23, 73, 154
pícaro, use of the term, 39–41
Pinker, Steven, 119–20
Pino Iturrieta, Elias, 118
Pliny, 9, 22
Plotkin, Henry, 119
Plumwood, Val, 139
Polo, Marco, 9, 14, 21–22
Ponce de Leon, Juan, 30, 33
Porter, R. H., 178
positivism, 85–86, 94–95
Potts, Wayne, 178

Quatrefages de Breau, Jean Louis Armand de, 86
Quevedo, 41, 43
Quiroga, Horacio, 2–3, 101–16

Redford, R. A., 183
Repton, Harry, 119
Reséndez, Andrés, 27, 32–36
Rivera, José Eustacio, 54
Rodriguez Monegal, Emir, 101–11, 116
Rohl, Klaus Rainer, 172
Rojas, Fernando de, 40
Rojas Pérez, Walter, 178–79
Rosas, Juan Manuel de, 84
Rueckert, William, 34, 108, 138
Rutherford, John, 40

Sainz de Medrano, Luis, 41, 148
Salleh, Ariel, 139, 165
Santí, Enrico Mario, 146–47
Sarmiento, Domingo F., 118
Schild, R., 183
Schlesinger, Stephen, 156
Schneider, Paul, 30–31, 37–38
Scillacio, Nicolò, 69, 71
Scott, Nina, 74, 77, 79–81
Serres, Michel, 46, 52
Servera, José, 75
Shaw, Donald L., 118, 120, 124

Singer, Peter, 119
Smith, Andy, 79–80, 140
Solano Lopez, Francisco, 84
Spencer, Herbert, 86–87
Spretnak, Charlene, 139
Sternbach, Saporta, 134, 136

Third World women, 133, 140–42
Thoreau, Henry David, 115
Thünen, Johann Heinrich von, 60–61
Todorov, Tzvetan, 11, 23, 49–50
Trivers, Robert, 129
Tucker, Richard, 73, 150–51, 156
Turner, Frederick, 138
Twine, Richard, 139

Ubieto, Antonio, 56

Van Toller, S., 178
Van West, C. R., 61, 87, 166

Vargas Llosa, Mario, 83
Velasquez, Juan, 35, 41, 43
Vespucci, Amerigo, 68
Vila, Marco Aurelio, 117, 121, 128
Villalobos, M. L., Carlos, 178
Virgil, 5, 47, 54, 57–58, 63
Visca, Arturo Sergio, 111–12
Vogel, Joseph, 13, 15–16, 22–24
Vogeley, Nancy, 48

Wallace, Alfred Russel, 86
Warren, Karen, 138, 140, 168
Wasserman, Renata, 87
water, drinking, 10, 38, 44–46, 177–79
Wedekind, Clau, 178
Weibe, Victor, 90
Wilson, Edward O., 52, 151
Wilson, Margo, 129
Winterhalder, Bruce, 61
Worster, Donald, 44, 149